GIRL TO COUNTRY:

A Memoir

AMY RIGBY

SOUTHERN DOMESTIC

First paperback edition September 2025

All lyrics quoted © Amy Rigby, except
"Keep It To Yourself" © Bill DeMain & Amy Rigby

ISBN 979-8-9998207-0-9 (paperback)
ISBN 979-8-9998207-3-0 (ebook)

www.amyrigby.com

For my Dad—we got there in the end

Perhaps it will turn out that you are called to be an artist.
Then take that destiny upon yourself and bear it,
its burden and its greatness,
Without ever asking what recompense might come from outside.
--Rainer Maria Rilke

PROLOGUE

Sunday morning worship was in full swing at Nashville's Green Hills YWCA. A band was set up along one wall: bass, drums, several guitar players, electric and acoustic; piano, organ, and a couple of singers. Everyone was dressed for church, though some of the musicians looked like they had yet to recover from Saturday night. They sang and played a high-energy "Jesus Is Just Alright With Me." All but the very hungover smiled beatifically.

It was 1994, the year Kurt Cobain killed himself and Michael Jackson married Lisa Marie Presley. A few months later, O.J. Simpson would be arrested for murder.

I was thirty-five, which in the music circles I ran in or aspired to felt uncomfortably close to being over the hill. After years of playing in bands and working temp jobs, combined with raising a six-year-old and trying to keep my marriage to another musician together at New York City prices, the thought that maybe a move to Nashville was a solid plan for the future was becoming more insistent.

The friends I stayed with, Liz and Stella Swope, mother and daughter both of the south – long resident in Nashville but with ties to New York's no wave music scene (Liz and her brother Bobby had been in bands with Lydia Lunch) – invited me along to Sunday service as a sort of sociological excursion. Liz and Stella shared my love of good old-fashioned trash and treasure, thrift stores, and flea markets, and had introduced me to some of the best five dollar plate lunches around town.

"It's called Church of the Scientific Mind," said Stella, about the service. "They have pretty good snacks afterwards."

Church sounded like it could be interesting, or at least amusing. Maybe even helpful? I didn't know what I believed anymore.

I'd set off by car from Brooklyn on a chilly afternoon, stopping for the night in a motel west of Staunton, Virginia before rolling into Tennessee on I-40 West. Another five hours to Nashville; Tennessee is a long state.

By the time I reached Music City, I was exhausted but amped up on the country radio I'd been listening to since sunrise: Faith Hill, Mark Chestnutt, Alan Jackson. None of it exactly my kind of music, except maybe "Blame It On Your Heart" sung by Patty Loveless—the ache in her voice reminded me a little of Angel Dean, who'd been the singer in my old country band, Last Roundup. But I was willing to find the good qualities in the latest commercial stuff. I felt ready to take on the town or at least begin to tackle my typed-out list of song publishing folks, names I'd collected from music biz friends in New York.

Why not start with the most intimidating option first? I had an 11 AM appointment at Reba McIntire's company, Starstruck. Reba was another artist, like Patty Loveless, whose sassiness and smart song choices spoke to me as a songwriter. There was an edginess and willingness to take chances from these women that hinted I might have a place in the world they operated in. That's why I'd sent a cassette of a few of my songs to Cliff Williamson, the director of A&R at Reba's company. He'd left an enthusiastic message on my answering machine, telling me to look him up next time I made it to town.

Now, here I was.

Starstruck was tucked away in Oak Hill on the other side of the interstate from Music Row; Nashville's Tin Pan Alley centered around Sixteenth and Seventeenth Avenues. That small neighborhood of cozy houses was where most of the publishing and record companies lived; songwriters traipsed from building to building hoping to get a song covered by one of the artists played on country radio. I had an appointment scheduled there later that day to visit BMI, my performing rights organization. PROs were tasked with keeping track of any time a song was played on the air—in my case usually a college radio or noncommercial station. I imagined a song I'd written playing, a little bell ringing, and a small amount of money tumbling into a piggy bank somewhere, to be disbursed via quarterly check. Not enough to pay rent, but with enough plays in the right places—commercial radio earned more, music in TV and movies even more—it could add up to something resembling a living. Which explains why I'd driven here in a ratty Pontiac wagon, with a bagful of song demos and my acoustic guitar.

BMI had recently broken ground on a fancy new building that would set the tone for Music City in the future. In a short while, Reba's Starstruck would follow suit with sleek offices nearby (that would be torn down in the mid-2010s). Songs are built to last a long, long time but the vagaries of the music business guarantee that nobody ever knows for sure what's coming next. Could I maybe be part of whatever that was?

For now, back over in Oak Hill, Starstruck's digs were disarmingly humble. An attractive assistant welcomed me into the reception area. The women down south took grooming to a whole different level from the women I knew up north. I instantly felt like a hobo in comparison, with my scraggly hair, shiny complexion, and office casual shirt bought off the clearance rack at Daffy's Fifth Avenue.

Cliff Williamson welcomed me into his office. He was dressed in jeans and a shirt with the sleeves rolled up, casually exuding power. "How do y'all like Nashville?" he asked.

I started to answer truthfully that I'd only just arrived after driving for two days, but quickly adjusted to bland pleasantries, mumbling something about the lovely spring weather. Nashville was already working its reverse magic on me, making me even more self-conscious than usual, incapable of relaxing and being myself. Cliff looked at me expectantly. "Let's hear what you've got."

I handed him a three-song cassette. I'd duped a few copies back in Brooklyn on our double-cassette player. "Don't Break The Heart" was the first track. A chiming guitar figure and sing-along chorus with reflective verses, the song was one of the first I'd performed solo and had a way of grabbing people. Cliff nodded along, respectfully allowing chorus, verse, chorus to go by—he'd gotten the idea—then fast-forwarded to the next track, "Twenty Questions." This was the song that had prompted his call to me, and he sat up straight, hanging on till the very end, and nodded his appreciation. The third song, "Just Someone I Had In Mind," had a classic country vibe; you could hear any good female singer floating and belting her way through. I pictured a thought bubble over Cliff's head: "Solid country song. Too bad it isn't still 1965."

He punched the stop button and ejected the cassette. "You're a good writer," he said. "You've got something different from the same old stuff everybody's doing around here. There is almost definitely a place for you in this town."

I leaned forward eagerly, nodding.

"But it takes being in Nashville," he continued. "Writing with other writers, meeting the artists, producers, and musicians." He paused. "Have you ever thought about moving here?"

I would hear "Move here" at the heart of every conversation as I made my way around town. In most cases, I wouldn't mention that I was trying to get my own record out—*Diary Of A Mod Housewife*, a concept album I thought filled a void; music for people who lived everyday lives but had grown up believing in the magic and transcendence promised by rock music. An early version of the album existed solely on a cassette, looking for a record label home. My embryonic solo artist career seemed beside the point when what I was hoping for was Reba, the Judds, Trisha Yearwood, or Patty Loveless to record my songs. If I worked hard enough, I felt I had what it took to be a female Tom T. Hall, Bobby Braddock, or Kostas. They were the creme de la creme of songwriters who'd written part of the canon of classic country hits, never following fashion, always pushing the envelope. If I achieved something like that in Nashville, maybe I could make a living doing what I loved to do and wouldn't feel so guilty and selfish pursuing music when I had a child to raise.

I'd heard that in Nashville, you had to choose to enter through one of two doors: this one said "Artist" and that one said "Writer." Take me as either or both, I wanted to say. Just take me!

Cliff was waiting for an answer. Would I consider moving to Nashville? He looked at his watch.

"I'm definitely thinking about it," I said. He shook my hand and showed me out of his office, telling me to keep in touch.

There were very few high-rises in Nashville in 1994, and only one I remember near Music Row. That's where Hazel Smith lived. I knew Hazel's work as a country music journalist. I felt her devotion to authentic songwriting ring true as a chuckwagon dinner bell whenever I caught up with her column in *Country Music* magazine. She was so much more: publicist, songwriter, radio host—the Grande Dame of Music City. Bluegrass king Bill Monroe's longtime lover, she'd coined the term "outlaw country" for Waylon Jennings and Willie Nelson.

Taking the elevator up to meet Hazel, I realized I'd never been in an elevator in Nashville before. Maybe I was coming up in the world? I'd traveled to this southern city a few times with Last Roundup, to play gigs and record an album that was never released. I'd fallen in love with the town's country music mystique and down-home restaurants, and driving the streets felt an even greater connection to songs I already loved: Hank Williams' "Lovesick Blues," Loretta Lynn's "Fist City," Kris Kristofferson's "Help Me Make It Through The Night." My husband Will had wooed me with a cassette of George Jones and Tammy Wynette's duet "Golden Ring," written not by the married, then divorced, then remarried and re-divorced couple but by songwriters Bobby Braddock and Rafe Van Hoy. I lapped up every detail I could find about country songs and the people who made them, feeling sure if I'd been born a few decades earlier, I could have written at least a few of those hits myself.

When Hazel Smith greeted me at the door of her apartment/office, I felt like I was meeting one of the Gabor sisters, if they'd been from Kentucky instead of Budapest—she was that expansive and dazzling. I remember smoked glass and white carpet; she may have been wearing a caftan.

Hazel sat down regally behind her desk and popped my cassette into a player.

"Martha and Chet looove you," she drawled. Chet Flippo, author of *Your Cheatin' Heart*, the definitive Hank Williams biography, had moved from New York to Tennessee as country music editor of *Billboard* magazine a few years before. His wife, Martha Hume, was a brilliant writer in her own right—I'd discovered her through her country music compendium, *You're So Cold I'm Turning Blue*. They'd hosted Last Roundup in their Knoxville home in 1987, and my all-girl trio, the Shams, more recently. Now, they were living just outside Nashville and, eager to open some doors in that town for me, had sent me Hazel's way.

Hazel loved that I had a daughter Hazel of my own. The old-fashioned name was mostly relegated to tombstones and memories of redoubtable church sistren in those days. She laughed when I told her Bill Monroe had blessed my pregnant belly when Last Roundup opened for him and his Bluegrass Boys in 1988. She grabbed a lip gloss wand from a drawer and swiped her generous mouth. "Tell me a little about yourself," she said.

I gave her the condensed version: born in the Pittsburgh suburbs, only sister to four brothers; Irish-American dad, Italian-American mom. Catholic school. Big rock music fan. Moved to New York City to attend art school in 1976, just as punk and CBGB exploded for a small segment of the population and took me with it. I told her I'd met Chet and Martha through noted music photographer Stephanie Chernikowski, who I'd met through my husband Will Rigby, drummer for the North Carolina-bred/New York-based band, the dB's.

I said I was a lifelong reader who found my voice writing songs. I learned to play acoustic guitar and formed bands with friends for fun; I played clubs and made recordings, hoping for fame and fortune or at least a life in music. Now, having a child made it all more urgent to make a living, create something that matters. Making work that matters mattered so much that I'd dumped my bands and was struggling with my marriage as I searched for a label to release my first solo album.

"I'm no Johnny or June come lately!" I felt it was important that she understand how much I loved country music, how I'd fallen in love with songwriting when I'd discovered old LPs by Hank Williams, Merle Haggard, and George Jones, as well as more obscure but essential artists like Skeeter Davis and the Louvin Brothers. Maybe I muddied the clear country waters with pop, folk, and rock reprobates like Bob Dylan, Loudon Wainwright, Lou Reed, the Roches, and Gram Parsons. Still, a good song was a good song, and that's why I was there in Nashville. I thought I knew how to write songs as well as anyone, and this was where songwriters came to prove themselves.

"I just want to earn a living!" I wanted to shout. "But I also want to be AN ARTIST —to create work no one else has even thought of doing. In addition, I'd like L-O-V-E and/or S-E-X, to live in a decent home, and to raise a happy child to adulthood. All while looking cool. That isn't too much to ask, is it? IS IT?"

Hazel pressed PLAY, and as she listened to my cassette, I silently willed, "Please think I'm good, please think I'm good." I was always looking for someone to confirm what I felt deep down to be true. Except on the days when I thought the opposite.

"Whoever mixed these tracks is not your friend," Hazel said. I started to apologize, but she held up a hand. "Your voice is buried! They won't like that around here. We want to hear the lyrics, especially good ones ..." I held my breath. "... like yours."

Over the next week, I had appointments with a few more publishing people and met up with musicians, writers, and producer contacts. Some would become lifelong friends, others I'd cross paths with once or twice or never see again. For a small town, Nashville had as many layers as a Brenda Lee crinoline.

The town had changed since Last Roundup attempted to make a record there ten years earlier. The homey old Country Music Hall of Fame and Museum that had reminded me of a cartoon barn was on its way out—a vast new complex more fitting for the mega-industry country had become was under construction. Many of the old-timers we'd encountered backstage at the Grand Ole Opry then—Roy Acuff, Minnie Pearl— were gone. Hank Williams' house, which had been moved from Franklin Road to the foot of Music Row in hopes of turning it into a museum, was now an abandoned, weed-bedecked eyesore.

A number of New York musicians had taken the leap and left the Big Apple behind: Tim Carroll, Buddy Miller, and Greg Trooper were a few of the names I knew from venue ads and in critics' picks in *The Village Voice*. Others I knew as friends of friends were Yo La Tengo's engineer Roger Moutenot and his wife Barbara, and Katy K, the clothing designer. I was glad to have at least one friend from Last Roundup days: Lonesome Bob, who I'd shared many bills with back when he played drums (including a `69 Rambler hubcap) with the Ben Vaughn Combo.

And there was a West Coast contingent, too. I'd met Duane Jarvis, a cool guitar player and songwriter when he'd come through New York with Lucinda Williams' band. He was part of the Los Angeles diaspora that relocated after the massive Northridge earthquake of earlier that year. DJ, as he was known by his friends, which included pretty much everyone who'd ever met him, had recently come through New York promoting his own album, and we'd shared a bill or two.

DJ asked me to play a few songs during his set at a downtown Nashville coffeehouse, and getting up there all alone in Music City, without the safety and camaraderie of a band, was terrifying. In New York, I'd begun to get at least a little bit comfortable playing solo, but it was home turf and a place where an odd idea carried as much, or even more, weight than a technically correct performance that trod old ground. In Nashville, it occurred to me you'd better have your shit together, no matter how original the goods you were peddling.

Buoyed by a good response at DJ's gig, I decided to sign up for the Monday night open mic at the Bluebird Cafe. I'd seen a fictionalized version of this songwriter's mecca in the Peter Bogdanovich film, *The Thing Called Love*, starring River Phoenix as a songwriting hopeful. I stood outside the club with my guitar in a case, among a few dozen other hopefuls with their guitars in cases, waiting to put my name on the sign-up sheet. Men and women in denim shirts or sports team jackets, ball caps, and a few cowboy hats. I wore my usual low-slung boot-cut jeans and black V-neck sweater with Asics sneakers—trying to say, "Hey, I'm New York; we wear black" but not be off-putting.

I'd been recording and playing gigs with bands for over a decade. I'd performed at Town Hall opening for the Indigo Girls, the Ritz for Los Lobos, and toured with Urge Overkill. But that had all been within the context of a scene, as part of an outfit. Why was I putting myself back in the novice category?

I wanted to find out if I could come across with nothing but my voice, guitar, and a song. I had to know if I could really speak to people—any people, not just ones who were predisposed to listen and like what I was doing. The Bluebird felt like the songwriters' O.K. Corral—in a strip mall.

My number was somewhere around fourteen. I spent the nerve-wracking hour before my turn listening to a succession of decent singers and players perch on a stool with their acoustic guitars or boldly stand and face the crowd, mainly made up of the rest of us about to subject ourselves to each other's scrutiny. There were a lot of love songs, and quite a few performers thanked the Lord for giving them the chance to play at the Bluebird. It was shocking how beyond proficient everyone was.

Everyone got the chance to play two songs. When my turn came, I stood up and nervously launched into "Don't Break The Heart," thinking it a solid choice, with its strong melody and heartfelt lyrics anyone could relate to. Not many of my songs led with a singalong chorus like "Don't Break The Heart" does.

The applause was warm and enthusiastic. I relaxed. I could do this. I put a capo on my Guild and got the G seventh groove of "Twenty Questions" going, then sang like I was talking to the room: "Well, it's nothing, he told me / 'Don't worry your pretty head' / Then he stumbled out of his cowboy boots / And fell across the bed," and I knew I had them. By the time I got to questions seventeen, eighteen and nineteen ("Do you love me? Do you still love me? Did you ever love me?") and finished with "When are you gonna get a real job? That's twenty questions," the place went crazy. Men, women—even Amy Kurland, the owner—everyone mentally high-fived me. It was thrilling.

Other performers came rushing over to congratulate me, ask who I was, did I do any co-writing? A male/female pair who seemed harmless enough invited me to an In the Round across town that night and I said, "Why not?" I'd heard about these performances, where four songwriters sat in a circle of chairs and took turns playing songs and telling stories. I was high from my triumph at the open mic, with fantasies of Reba or Trisha Yearwood calling my number back in Brooklyn: "Hey, I just happened to be at the Bluebird the other night and *that song you sang? I want to record it!*" Nashville had this element of unreality reinforced by the high ratio of genuine talent and success: billboards loomed over the interstate celebrating #1 singles and album releases. It could all make a person believe in miracles.

The round the couple had invited me to took place in the West End Holiday Inn lounge. I found the lack of irony refreshing. None of the songwriters referred jokingly to the tacky setting, the fake Tiffany lamps, potted ferns, or convention-goers trooping in and out of the bar to scoop up free popcorn from the machine in the corner. They just spoke sincerely about this co-writer, and that cut, or a possible hold on a song.

I sat with my new Bluebird friends, terrified I'd be called up to play a song, at the same time wishing I could show this anonymous barroom what I had. I appreciated the Nashville ethos where you only acknowledged success—never failure, fear or uncertainty. It was the opposite of the modest New York world I ran in, where cool mattered most. I wondered if I could ever be so upbeat and positive, so unflappable and sure. I ended the evening applauding sincerely for the writers in the round and said goodbye to the Bluebird couple, thinking maybe we'd meet up again. I tucked their business cards in my wallet and made a mental note to print up some cards.

Later that week, I was invited to a more exclusive songwriters round in a private home. With a well-thumbed atlas next to me on the passenger seat of the family station wagon, I spent an hour going in circles up and down Nashville's long roads that radiated, "like spokes of a wheel" as the locals told me, from downtown out into the countryside surrounding the city. I finally gave up and stopped at a gas station on White Bridge to ask for help.

"Knob Road," the guy behind the counter said. "You must be going to the round up there—you a songwriter?"

I shrugged, wondering if it would distinguish me more if I said, "No."

"Tell 'em Jimmy says, 'Hey,'" he said. "I might try to get up there when I get off work."

Following Jimmy's instructions, I found Knob Road and parked, then climbed what felt like the side of a mountain to reach the house. I heard music coming from the big open living room. Someone let me in, then shushed me—there were four women seated on straight-backed chairs in the center of a crowd. They held Martins and Gibsons and Guilds in their laps—no Takamines or Alvarez guitars like at Bluebird audition night. This was serious.

"Now this one," said a pretty brunette in a denim work shirt as she strummed a few chords, "just got cut." The woman with a blonde perm to her immediate right let out a joyous whoop and started applauding, and the rest of the room joined in. Everyone waited to find out—who? I held my breath with the rest of the crowd. Was it Reba? Garth? Trisha?

The answer came. "Nana Mouskouri just recorded this song." I started to laugh, expecting the rest of the room to join me. It was a joke, surely? Not that there was anything wrong with the bespectacled Greek singer. She'd sold many, many records the world over. But wasn't it just a little bit funny?

Nobody else thought so, and for a brief second I understood a little bit how Nashville worked. There was no cool or uncool when it came to making a living with music. A cut was a cut. When you sat down with your guitar and channeled your pain and joy into words and chords and melody, a safe bet, middle of the road singer wasn't exactly what you were aiming for. Maybe it wouldn't buy much artistic kudos or indie cred, but you could buy a house with the publishing royalties from a song on a big-selling album.

As they went around the circle a few times, there were Wynonna cuts and Trisha Yearwood holds, as well as proven hits people recognized as soon as the opening chord was played. The women all sang and strummed like the pros they were. I thought it all felt a little self-congratulatory, at the same time wondering how, if ever, I could be in that circle.

I opened my eyes and realized I'd nodded off on my folding chair in the Green Hills YMCA. The musical portion of the Science of the Mind service wound down with a flurry of acoustic guitar strums. Then they were on to what really mattered, the reason we were all there (at least those of us who weren't just looking for an easy laugh and some snacks): to bring good into our lives.

The next day, I'd drive back to New York and my real life: temping at Sony or CBS, taking my daughter to PS 116 in Manhattan via subway from Brooklyn, and gigs here and there. Thrift store clothes, alternate side parking. Beer bottles piled up in the hallway of our rundown Williamsburg apartment building, across the street from the ice cream truck depot. Would anyone ever put my record out? Was I kidding myself thinking I was good enough to be an artist? Maybe the Writer's Door — Reba and Starstruck — was the answer.

Several speakers stood up and talked about visualization: how if we IDENTIFIED what we needed in our lives and BELIEVED, it would come to us. Then, through the power of VISUALIZATION and BELIEF, it would happen. Then they told us to write what we wanted for ourselves on a slip of paper, find a person in the room to give the paper to, and they would work on things for us.

I couldn't stop myself. I wrote my desire on a piece of paper, folded it up and handed it to a powerful-looking lady in a flowered dress and strappy sandals. She unfolded the paper and smiled a feral, lipsticked

smile as she read what I'd written:
I WANT TO MOVE HERE.

Chapter One

New York City was home, and anywhere else I went I felt like an outsider. But maybe that sense of not fitting in fueled me as an artist. I was ready for a change.

I was tired of playing the alternate-side-of-the-street parking game. Keeping an eye on street sweeping days and times, and moving your car from one side of the street to the other was a part-time occupation in New York City, if you dared to require the convenience of a vehicle.

I was also tired of being broke. My marriage was over. Will Rigby and I tried our best to be good co-parents, driving our daughter Hazel's mattress across Williamsburg once or twice a week, from the old Grand Street apartment I'd held onto to Will's new place in the Italian section just on the other side of the Brooklyn Queens Expressway. Breaking up costs money, and we didn't have any. My dad had given us $1000 to buy the small station wagon we dubbed Gray Ghost, so I kept it—our only asset.

In 1996, my first solo album *Diary Of A Mod Housewife* had done phenomenally well for an unknown artist's debut on an independent label that no one had ever heard of. The record earned rave reviews in almost every publication in the land, except maybe *Car and Driver*. *Spin* magazine called me Songwriter of the Year, and my album placed eighth in the Village Voice's Pazz and Jop Poll, with votes cast by hundreds of music critics across the country. It sat below Beck and the Fugees, but above Pulp and Patti Smith. These things hardly registered at the time. I was coming to terms with my marital breakup and trying to keep my head above water financially while I toured, buying plane tickets, renting vehicles and paying musicians to back me.

Gradually, my unexpected ride for glory had slowed to a crawl. It began to sink in towards the end of 1997 that my album had done all it was going to do when the label, Koch Records, pulled the budget for the music video I'd planned. At the time, I didn't imagine Mod House-wife would become a permanent fixture in anyone's record collection like *Marquee Moon* or *Goodbye Yellow Brick Road*. Pop music was built to be disposable—I felt like I was in the dumper.

Before I went solo, my bands had all been underground, if that's the right word for respected, even loved, by a small audience. Last Roundup played small clubs and support slots for five years before the Rounder label released our first and only album. The ensuing coast-to-coast U.S. tour took two months and was eye-opening: it proved how big the U.S. was, and how few of its inhabitants had ever heard of us. Broke and de-jected by the time it was all over, I'd imagined maybe getting pregnant was the answer.

And maybe it had been. Becoming a mom fueled me as an artist. But my next group, the Shams, also struggled under the radar, appealing to other artists and promoters and attracting opening slots, but spending most nights post-gig dissecting what exactly it was we were doing wrong; wondering what it would take to break out of our tiny little cult status?

I'd labored in obscurity for a long time, but I'd done it without know-ing how good it felt to connect with a bigger number of people. Now I knew that feeling, and what came with it: more offers of gigs supporting bigger artists, interview requests, radio airplay. For a brief moment I'd connected. Once you've known that feeling, it's something you'll chase forever.

It was clear I needed to come up with new work. Here's where the dreaded sophomore slump— second album second-guessing–- began. It wasn't a lack of material—I was a leaky faucet spewing lyrics and tunes while I took the subway to or from office temp jobs or drove to gigs. I even wrote songs in the night while I slept—in the morning I woke up with words and melodies and rushed to write them down, whispering snippets into my Sony cassette recorder before the day started and I had to move the car, pack Hazel's school lunch, or make myself presentable for a midtown office.

I'd been happy working with guitarist Elliot Easton on *Mod House-wife*, and I'd liked recording in L.A. It made sense to go back out west again to work on a follow-up. But given that sales had failed to reach the hoped-for numbers (20,000 copies sold instead of the projected mini-mum of 100,000), I figured there must be something wrong. As an artist you don't want to blame yourself. You need to believe in your vision.

But I decided my vision must be blurry and that maybe what just a year or two ago had felt like a winning team — me in Los Angeles with Elliot, engineer Mark Linett, drummer Don Heffington— was the wrong approach.

During Hazel's spring break, March 1997, I drove the two of us down to Nashville to make demos with Jay Joyce. My daughter and I stayed with Duane Jarvis and his wife Denise in what back then felt like a very far-flung neighborhood — the Inglewood section of East Nashville. Musicians that owned a house? It was a modest '50s-era jewel box, but I marveled how such a thing was even possible. In New York City, home ownership seemed unthinkable. Duane wrote songs, made records, and toured, just like me. And he had his own *driveway.*

I went to Nashville more frequently, to write songs and try other people's lives on for size. I visited as often as I could manage the time and expense of traveling away from my daughter, temp jobs, and playing solo shows up north. I located New York friends who'd settled in and found their place in this much smaller but competitive town. Katy K, a downtown designer whose party dresses made the scene at Pyramid bar and Danceteria dance club, ran a vintage and Western clothing store in a midcentury storefront on rundown but promising 12th Avenue South (that a mile further out turned into good old Granny White Pike— there was some poetry in Nashville's maddening road system). Katy made extra cash renting out a studio apartment in the basement of her pretty Tudor-style house off of Belmont Boulevard. She'd smartened the space up with ranch and country touches, Hatch Show Print posters, and '50s furniture.

My stays there gave me a feel for what life could be like in Nashville. It was easy to forget while I played gigs and ran around town seeing other artists tear it up with a rocking band, or show off their songcraft in the round with other songwriters, that back home I was a nearly full-time mom. Hazel's dad Will had started playing drums with Steve Earle and they toured constantly.

I played a short set at local alternative country radio personality Billy Block's weekly live broadcast from the Sutler, a bar next to a bowling alley just down the street from the near-derelict Biltmore Motel, where Last Roundup had stayed over ten years before. I remembered how in love Will and I had been, booking in to the Don Gibson room where some say the classic country songwriter wrote "Oh Lonesome Me." It was hard to remember a time before Hazel, or being married, when even the idea of being in a band was still new and not something I'd outgrown. I wondered what had happened to the photos of Don Gibson that looked on as Will and I rocked our motel room bed.

Now we were like business associates, practicing distance and detachment. And like we'd changed, Nashville was changing, as the twentieth century drew to a close. Lower Broadway hosted a Hard Rock and a Gibson Cafe, flashy chain restaurant/venues that overshadowed the downhome charm of Ernest Tubb's Record Store and Tootsie's Orchid Lounge. Justin Tubb, Ernest's son, who'd welcomed Last Roundup from the stage of the Opryland store back in 1984—assuring us his dad, the Texas Troubadour, was listening from his hospital bed— had died recently. So had Grandpa Jones, Tammy Wynette, Roger Miller, and Bill Monroe. The ghosts of country music were getting younger. They weren't just the distant ones I'd only encountered through records and books— artists like Hank Williams and Lefty Frizzell—but stars who'd recently walked these same streets. They might be slipping into the mists of myth and legend or cruel obscurity, but I'd heard and seen them in person.

I wondered if anyone beyond a few keepers of the flame for that authentic country music—people like Jack Emerson and Andy McLenon, who recorded Last Roundup for their Praxis label, Jim Sherraden of Hatch Show Print, and writers like Robert K. Oermann, Chet Flippo or Michael McCall—even cared about the past anymore?

But Emmylou Harris had rallied locals to save the Ryman Auditorium from demolition in the early 1990s. Clearly there were other believers, and some even had faith there was money to be made in preserving and celebrating the past. There was positive energy around Music City, and I felt its pull. I'd spent the last decade and a half listening, studying and learning —practicing the art of songwriting. It helped me find a focus as an artist: plainspoken honesty; the poetry of the everyday.

Was that enough to justify planning a move there?

It felt like enough.

Chapter Two

I began to feel a little at home in Nashville, staying in Katy's apartment or with friends like the Swopes, or Duane and Denise. Sometimes I relied on the kindness of strangers.

Tommy Whitlock was a music business success. He'd grown up in Springfield, Missouri and was friends with Lou Whitney and Jim Wunderle, raggedy roots legends who'd been so important in the recording of my band Last Roundup's album, *Twister*, at Column One studio in Springfield, and continued to be supportive presences in my life. Wunderle gave me Tommy's number and said to give him a call next time I made a trip to Nashville. The two of them still played together in a band called Dog People when Tommy made it back to Springfield.

Tommy was out on the road when I arrived at his house, but he'd left instructions to make myself at home. He lived near Radnor Lake, a beautiful nature spot I'd discovered was perfect for early morning walks, if I could quell my feelings of inadequacy every time I passed an impeccably-groomed woman on the trail at seven A.M. I knew of a few people who lived along Granny White Pike, but Tommy was the first I'd known who lived *that* far out. Was he...rich? From music?

I let myself into his lovely ranch house, with a home studio sophisticated beyond anything I'd seen in other musician friends' houses. But the most stunning thing was the Oscar on Tommy's coffee table.

An Oscar. For Best Original Song, 1986. Tommy co-wrote "Take My Breath Away" with Giorgio Moroder, recorded by the group Berlin for the hit film, *Top Gun*. Legend had it he used his Ozark wit and auto mechanic skills to connect with hitmaker Moroder, offering to fix his Ferrari if he'd listen to a demo tape. I'd met another Dog People alumnus in Nashville, Supe Grande. Supe played with Ozark Mountain Daredevils, as musicians from Springfield were inclined to do, but he lived the type of musician lifestyle I was used to: homey, casual; a little rough around the edges. I wondered if Tommy Whitlock was still nice in that Springfield way, or if big success had changed him. But then, wasn't he letting me, a complete stranger, put my feet up next to his golden statuette?

Alone in Tommy's house, I worked on songs at the glass-topped dining table, imagining what it would be like if this was my house, with my Oscar in the living room. Trying on self-confidence like a suit of clothes was easier in Nashville than in New York, where calling bullshit was almost a full-time occupation.

When Tommy arrived home, I played him one of the songs I'd written. He was Springfield-nice, so encouraging he offered to help me record a demo in his studio with the full treatment: drums, guitars, bass all at our disposal, and he was good on all of them, and on the production end too. The four-track demos I made at home on a Tascam Portastudio were pretty stark stuff compared to the full-blown production we came up with. On a high, after hours crafting a backdrop for my heartfelt song (that sounded a bit like a John Lennon *Mind Games* reject), Tommy suggested we get it to a Christian music publisher in town.

Did I say "hell, no"? Hell, no. Communicating through song was my goal. I did feel a little queasy trying to pass myself off as righteous or remotely religious, but not queasy enough to stop me. Nashville already had a way of making me tractable like that. A giddy feeling of possibility overtook me as soon as I saw the spires of the Batman building from the interstate. New York City may have been Gotham, but Music City was the Bat Cave, a mythical lair visible only to insiders. If you could penetrate the stone surround, it seemed like a whole world of wonder awaited. You just had to believe enough to leave your city slicker cynicism at the outskirts, somewhere near the large, hideous statue of confederate general Nathan Bedford Forrest riding a horse alongside Interstate 65. The statue is long gone, but I'm sure Nashville still has a way of attracting ambitious believers willing to turn a blind eye to the unsavory parts.

It made sense to explore making a record there. The musicians I'd played gigs with for years back in New York— and made my first attempts at touring with, most of them friends—felt too familiar; too connected to my old identity as Will's wife, the plucky temp. But my attempt to record with Jay Joyce was fraught. Like pretty much every musician I encountered in Nashville, he was personable and easygoing. He did stellar work, had been successful with Patty Griffin's album *Flaming Red*, and would go on to produce records for huge-selling country artists like Eric Church and Miranda Lambert. In 1997/98, his harder, visceral sound worked perfectly with Patty Griffin's big voice, but after two songs I felt it was the wrong approach for me. My insecurities said Jay disliked my voice and saw it only as useful as a vehicle for effects and studio wizardry. I kept thinking the tracks we worked on sounded like music you'd hear playing from a stereo in a living room in a porno movie. That darker undercurrent may have intrigued me years later, but at the time I reacted strongly against the approach. Maybe I was better off sticking with my original formula: raw, real-life lyrics over catchy, rocking music. Approachable. Familiar-sounding. Elliot, Mark, Don; Los Angeles.

I'd spent enough time in L.A. to decide I didn't have the ego or confidence to live there; it was simultaneously too sprawling and too insular. The thought of finding a place to live and a school for Hazel, while trying to book gigs and navigate the industry side of town, intimidated me. But I returned there in the spring of 1998 to record my second solo album. Elliot Easton and I chose a dozen songs and worked at Mark Linett's studio in Glendale, where we'd pulled together all the tracks for *Mod Housewife* two years before. Elliot played bass and overdubbed guitars. I played guitar; Don Heffington was back on drums and percussion, and keyboard player Tom Canning joined us on a number of songs. Recording the basic tracks was alternately blissful and hilarious— the songs came to life with Elliot full of ideas and everyone else bouncing suggestions. Nothing felt too wacky.

Some of the vocals slipped out easily: "Summer Of My Wasted Youth" and "Invisible." But recording the harder-edged songs was torment. I wanted to be a rock vocalist—felt like a strutting rock belter in my soul— but when I stood at the microphone, all that came out were my feelings. They weren't elevated or made majestic by lung power or bravado and technique. Try as I may, I was usually just...a person, singing my songs.

"All I Want" felt so raw, I considered leaving it off the album entirely. Don the drummer said, "Are you kidding? It needs to be the first track." I looked up to Don. He was sideman royalty, having played in Emmylou Harris' Hot Band and on Dylan's epic "Brownsville Girl." I conceded he must know what he was talking about. The realness of my vocals with the plaintive lyrics left me feeling exposed and that's scary. Making records is not a game for the timid, or maybe it is if you just like getting your ass kicked sometimes.

With the album mixed, I took the red-eye back to New York. LAX felt hushed as a wake, everyone glued to airport bar TVs watching the disappointing *Seinfeld* series finale. Crossing that space from L.A. to New York, it was possible to forget which was the real place and which was the show biz one. Nashville sat right there between the two.

Middlescence came out in September 1998. Many of the elements that lined up so perfectly with *Mod Housewife* went askew for the second album, making the magic of my debut feel that much more like catching lightning in a bottle. How often does that happen? There'd been staff changes at Koch Records. My first and biggest supporter, Nick Hill, was no longer working there. Neither was Barry Feldman, the A&R guy and label manager who'd had the idea to introduce me to Elliot Easton, a boyhood friend of his brother. Like a recipe gone awry, everything was shifting around: salt swapped out for sugar, margarine instead of butter. The only thing was to try and make the best of what ingredients were left.

Publicity, radio play, and touring. If any of these elements happened in a vacuum — gig in a town with no press or radio; radio play or album review somewhere I had no possibility of doing a show— it was almost as if it didn't happen at all. I played disparate gigs opening for bigger artists here and there: John Hiatt, Billy Bragg; Iris DeMent. At my sole Lilith Fair appearance, in my hometown of Pittsburgh, I played my set on a small stage just as the gates were opening. Joining Emmylou Harris and Natalie Merchant with Sarah McLachlan for the finale, I looked out at thousands of smiling faces, mostly female, shimmering in the humidity, feeling the sisterhood but also the distance between myself and the star performers. They would go on to another amphitheater the following day, and I had a gig at a cozy bar in Columbus, Ohio. Would I ever be good enough to merit a tour bus?

All the gigs helped strengthen my performing skills but didn't add up to much in terms of momentum. *Spin* magazine ran a feature, with writer Kim France accurately describing me and Hazel's charming bohemian existence in dowdy '90s Williamsburg, and the temp jobs I still worked. But the photo shoot to illustrate the article was a high fashion spread, with a room in a massive loft on the edge of Chinatown full of red gowns for me to choose from, each one worth more than I made in a month of word processing at CBS. The photo shoot team ordered lunch from a fancy Thai place on their expense account while a hairstylist fluffed my bangs and the team debated whether or not I should show my forehead. I begged them to soften the look that threatened to present me as the first Queen Elizabeth, the one with the ruffled collar. I felt outnumbered, and wished I had a person to tell me who I was supposed to be. In the end they compromised, one with bangs and one forehead forward. What I remember most fondly is that lunch, and my glee at being able to order whatever I wanted off the menu, a fantasy come true in my penny-pinching, single mom life.

I struggled to keep hold of all the elements and make the right decisions while juggling everything else. When the label said they'd be spending big bucks on a massive poster—striking photos by George duBose, double-sided with red artwork on one side and blue on the other, and four times bigger than your average gig poster—I thought, oh great, they must really believe in me and want to spread the word! A cooler head might've realized that the poster was way too large for any club to hang in a window or vestibule, because then there would be no room for anybody else's poster. Years later I'd see it in dressing rooms, safe from the eyes of the public it was intended for, and think wow, that Amy Rigby must've really been something, to merit such a poster. I wonder what ever happened to her?

One night in Boulder, Colorado, the Gavin convention— the U.S.'s non-commercial radio confab—was in town, and Koch Records set up a few things for me to do. I played one show at a pizza place in front of a wall plastered with those behemoth blue and red posters, while the big names performed at the Boulder Theater across the street. Pizza customers came and went, picking up their orders at the counter just next to my bass player. I wished I could crawl through a hole in the stage —if only there'd been a stage. I had yet to learn to cherish the highs and laugh at the lows. All I could think was, "I've been at this for a good fifteen years already and surely my dues have been paid."

Yes, I had put in plenty of time by 1998, but the meter is always resetting, and it isn't just the destination but the road you take to get there. Hadn't I scored that great western wear blazer from Kenny Rogers' short-lived fashion label at a thrift shop somewhere en route? And weren't we staying in relative luxury at the Broker Inn, Hunter S. Thompson's favorite Boulder watering hole? I crossed town from the gig back to my hotel, bare-legged in a black satin mini-skirt and gingham mules, carrying my acoustic guitar in a hard case. The town was full of students in shorts, ball caps, and drug rugs, and I felt old and out of place: "I'm a throwback. Like a corny old traveling salesman."

Later that weekend, I watched Billy Jo Shaver, then John Kay, play solo sets in the hotel bar. These men were in their late fifties, had overcome all kinds of hardship to create hits – Billy Joe the songwriter of classics like "I'm Just An Old Chunk Of Coal," Kay as lead singer of Steppenwolf ("Born To Be Wild'). They were still plying their wares, but had left proximity to a pizza oven behind. Would I ever accept and be okay with it—the way the hustle never ends?

Being a mom added an extra challenge to the hard reality of touring. I needed to get back to New York every week or two, and even without that, it was always a puzzle routing a string of dates in a country the size of America. But how to exist as an artist without touring and the adjacent radio station visits, write-ups in local press, stops at local record stores, and, as they became a major and plentiful outlet for music in the '90s, large bookstores like Borders and Barnes & Noble?

In 1998, the music business still existed as a big hand reaching down from the sky with money to bestow even on mortals like me. I had a record deal. Koch was already finding video game production and licensing more profitable than putting out something so subjective as original music, but they'd contracted me to make three albums, each with a modest budget to pay for a studio, producer, engineer, and any musicians I might hire. In return, I'd signed away my rights to the music, for eternity. If the records sold a lot, I'd make money. It was life as Monopoly board, with the label as the guy with the mustache and moneybags. Did anyone really know what that guy's job was? Or what he was called?

I imagined the answers to some/most/all of life's questions lay outside of New York City. As the twentieth century gave way to the twenty-first, I felt sure the answers lay in Nashville.

In Nashville, I would be appreciated for my songwriting talent and financially rewarded for my devotion to songcraft, country music, and barbecue. In Nashville, I'd find the successful side of myself that I couldn't get to in New York, where I'd come first as an art student and remained a struggling artist. The struggle seemed built into my New York, and to break free, I'd start fresh in a town that must be the place where they invented the term "mailbox money" — royalty checks delivered by the postman that meant you were getting paid to sit home and do what you did best.

Parenthood was an important excuse for all kinds of compromise. Songs written and demoed in between temp jobs, play dates, and subway rides. Brief rehearsals for gigs. I rarely had a chance to see other musicians play, unless they were doing it outdoors, in daylight, for free. Or down on the subway platform. Williamsburg now had a hipster coffee shop and a few artist/performance spaces like Galapagos and Teddy's, but I planned my own gigs around my and Will's co-parenting schedule.

Since he'd started playing drums for Steve Earle, he spent lots of time touring. The big difference, besides the fact that he was a dad and I was a mom—his music work *paid*. Mine generally just sent me further into debt.

In New York City, our middle school search was on, a kind of Death Race 2000 affair that felt like it would determine the entire course of Hazel's future. If you hadn't started figuring it all out when the kid was still in diapers, you were probably too late. Lab School, Math magnet, the Writer's School —the middle school (grades 6-8) game was only a warm-up for the big show: getting your kid into one of the top public high schools like Stuyvesant, Bronx Science, or the FAME school. Hazel was such a good student, it felt like she could go anywhere. But how was I going to let my tiny nine-or-ten-year-old ride the subway alone? We'd fought the good fight, but I was running out of steam with this aspect of city life.

Hazel and I had a cheap apartment large enough to share with a roommate, or a babysitter in exchange for childcare. Hazel even talked me into taking on a kitten, James. He was huge, white with a black Elvis quiff marking on his head. He also sported opposable thumbs. I didn't know anything about cats and didn't realize that his size or thumbs were unusual until visitors remarked on them.

It seemed he was quite a special cat, but I wasn't convinced. "If it doesn't work out, we can always give him away," I said, not having grown up in a pet household.

Hazel draped James in a gold lamé fabric square tied around his furry throat like a cape. He strutted and shimmered, parading back and forth in front of the hallway mirror. "He's with us 'til he dies," she said. She was the wise, grounding force in my life. Wasn't that too much responsibility for a kid? I think, looking back now. I often relied on that cool wit she possessed, even at the age of nine.

"1998's gonna be our year!" I said. No matter the paltry number of copies my second album was selling. I felt sure it was only a matter of time before Hazel, James the cat, and I lived in comfort with brand-new clothes, furniture that hadn't come off the street, and a car newer than ten or fifteen years old. "When a big Nashville star cuts one of my songs, we're going to Peter Luger to celebrate." We drove by the expensive steak house every day, exiting the Williamsburg Bridge towards dumpy Bedford Avenue, dodging Town Cars and yellow cabs that deposited overcoated businessmen and well-heeled couples at the entrance. "Luger steak in '98, it's gonna happen!" I said.

Hazel looked up from her Game Boy. "Sorry, Mom—did you say something?

Chapter Three

Maybe, I thought—newly single and free from the weight of my romantic history—I could even find somebody.

Love.

I wanted it.

My whole life I'd been a mass of hormones and hope, a lightning rod for romance or, barring that, some sex. It's what I lived for. My girlhood diary entries (*"Jeff broke up with me today. He still likes me as a friend. What did I do wrong...Sonny talked to me. He's cute - I think I like him."*) weren't so different from my journals of the late '90s, where I alternated between pep talks about making money and reaching a bigger audience and laments over men I either desperately wanted to be with or hoped to distance myself from. Two entries from my journal in 1998: *"I feel so cheated and hurt but I won't call, I'll just take it like a man;"* *"I find his lack of motivation pretty irritating. And his footwear! Still, I get so lonely sometimes..."*

The upside of the obsessions, the crushes, the thrill of the chase and the agony of disappointment was that I never ran out of things to write about. Like my second-grade kiss with Bobby Barnhart, where all the girls in my class wanted to know, "How did it FEEL?" I was still doing research for the whole class. Didn't everyone go through romantic turmoil? And if their lives were now too stable or streamlined for that kind of madness, didn't they at least want to remember how it felt?

There was the drummer from Toledo I considered marrying before my divorce was even final—I was that happy to enjoy sex again free from the weight of negotiation.

And the mandolin player with a frame just built for western shirts: I fell fast and hot, reason obscured by desire while my family and friends shook their heads ("Here she goes *again*") and my patient daughter looked on with huge eyes and proffered a Simpsons quote, something about not being able to make friends with salad.

Then there was Sam. Sam was a secret I kept to myself.

Sam was the embodiment of everything that was always just out of reach. Music biz hotshot, West Coast sybarite; his nonchalance a welcome relief from East Coast guilt and angst. There was something reptilian about him, like a lizard forged of sterling silver and fashioned into a belt buckle or bolo tie. He owned a few houses, didn't sweat about money or...anything. He was talented, funny, and repelled drama.

Being married had for better and then worse kept my raging libido in check. How many missteps can I blame on hormones? It all felt tied together: ambition, emotion, and estrogen seesawing with testosterone to create a tsunami I was always fighting through to stay the course. I envied Sam his detachment.

If I couldn't *be* him, I only wished I could have him.

"Fuck you, Sam," I thought. "Why won't you just love me, so we can both be happy forever? Or at least for now."

I sat in a songwriters' circle at the Bluebird in Nashville. Five years since I'd stood up on Monday audition night, just to see if I could. Now, I felt, if not exactly part of a scene, at least encouraged to participate. The critical success of my first two solo albums may not have led to the hoped-for sales figures, but at least it earned me credibility with other artists and writers.

Bill Lloyd had invited me to join this round. His career was a cool intersection of his good-natured Kentucky roots, Nashville songcraft and pop idiosyncrasy. That mix led to success with duo Foster & Lloyd, back in the '80s when Nashville rediscovered authentic simplicity, harmony, and the guitar sounds of the '50s.

To my right was Bob Neuwirth, who most folks remember for his withering commentary in D.A. Pennebaker's Dylan documentary, *Don't Look Back*. I'd started learning more about him as a poet, artist, and songwriter as he'd become my labelmate on Koch. It was just beginning to dawn on me in my late thirties how many lives any artist has to create for themselves in order to stick around for a while.

Don Henry sat across from me. He co-wrote "Where've You Been," a massive hit for Kathy Mattea, along with many songs recorded by other artists. I didn't yet know his most creative and devastating songs were the ones he sang himself.

I'd decided to move to Nashville, and possessed the confidence of the neophyte. "Of course I can do it." I'd accepted Bill's invitation to a songwriters' round in Nashville blithely, seeing it as a great opportunity to play a few songs for a rapt audience and meet some of the artists I hoped to one day call peers.

It was only sitting there, on the spot where actual real legends – who'd done this for a living for decades – sat every night, that my head began to spin. "Oh shit, what have I gotten myself into? There's no way I'm as good as these people. What made me think I was anywhere near ready to put myself under this kind of scrutiny? Oh, dear God..."

But the round was starting as Bill eased into one of his Foster & Lloyd hits. A murmur of satisfaction rippled through the crowd. A recognizable hit pulled us all up with it. Oh, I wanted that feeling so bad!

The appreciation was deep and loud for Bill, and for Bob Neuwirth too. As soon as Neuwirth opened his mouth, you knew you were in the presence of a traveler, a wizard. He was a man of substance who took none of it too seriously.

Don Henry was next. His songs had a balance of humor and pathos that brought wry smiles and then reduced the audience to tears. It occurred to me that sitting there listening to the other artists in the round was a kind of performance in itself. I found myself overcome by the emotion of Don's song, "Beautiful Fool," about Martin Luther King Jr, and had to grip my guitar and focus my gaze inside the sound hole, to stay in the moment and keep myself from blubbering in public.

When it was my turn, I played "Magicians," a song I'd shown Bill on my last visit to town. He'd loved it and helped me record a simple demo. I'd felt, as the words and melody spun out of me, that I was making some kind of breakthrough with my writing. I'd created songs about marriage with all the hope and disappointment of the Catholic girl inside of me, but was venturing into darker, almost shameful waters. If marriage wasn't necessarily forever and fairy tales weren't real, a person could really get into trouble.

Magicians

You say there's nothing in the future for us
This lust is just a passing thing
You tell me late at night while lying in bed
That we're not really happening
You tell me this is nothing real

That we can touch but we can't feel
Let's leave reality out of this shall we
No need to mention it it's always here
Give the cold hard facts back to the mathematicians
We're magicians, we make reality disappear

We're really something when we take off our clothes
I wish that we could stay this way
It's not a healthy way to live, I suppose
At least that's what I was raised to say
You tell me life is just unfair
But I can hear that anywhere
Let's leave reality out of this shall we
No need to mention it it's always here
Stick the rhetoric with those old slick politicians
We're magicians, we make reality disappear

Suspend belief - it's a must to
My fantasy - I don't trust you
But I won't hold it against you
As long as you hold me against you

I felt the attention and focus of everyone in the room that night at the Bluebird. (Thank God I didn't learn until after the show that one of my teenage music crushes, Peter Frampton, was in the audience.) Nobody had heard this song before except Bill. But the notes and words and chords I put together captured a complicated set of feelings: lust, love, resignation, and that magic ingredient called hope, and the nods of recognition and applause when I finished told me other people felt it too.

"Man," Neuwirth said when I finished. "If you're ever on a stage someplace and you're not sure what you're doing there, just play that song."

He said it with such gravitas I believed him. A song can wield the kind of power to fend off foes, turn naysayers into believers. An undeniable song was a forcefield, a magic cloak, Excalibur pulled out of the stone to slay men and dragons. It was enough to get me to the next place: Nashville. Was it enough to make everything else—somewhere to live, a way to make money, school for my daughter; the challenges of daily life—fall into place?

I was about to find out.

Chapter Four

Hazel and I left New York for Nashville the day after John F. Kennedy Jr. died: July 17, 1999. The whole city was in mourning. TV and the daily papers showed images of all the notes and bouquets left in tribute outside the building in lower Manhattan where JFK Jr and his wife Caroline lived. In only a matter of hours, the flowers reached halfway to the first-floor fire escape.

I'd been saying farewell to friends in Time Cafe on Lafayette Street, upstairs from the cozy club Fez that had been a big part of my progress as a solo performer, when my brother Riley came in from the outside world—the main place news broke back in those days—and shared what he'd heard about a small plane going down off the coast of Connecticut. I'd just reprised my version of Monkee Mike Nesmith's song, "Some of Shelly's Blues," for a Loser's Lounge Greatest Hits show. I'd bequeathed my apartment to Joe McGinty, who ran these downtown tributes to the giants of pop music. I can't say I was subletting, because there never really was a lease.

Something about the low-ceilinged room and intimate seating at Fez felt like home. I'd played shows there where I was learning to lead a band, and a few where I braved things solo. Others like the one this last night, where I'd pick another artist's song I thought I could bring something to. I wasn't comfortable simply standing up there behind a microphone. I wanted to be part of the band, playing my rhythm guitar to dictate the feel of the song. The guitar felt as much a part of me as my voice, connected to breathing. Some performers bring humor, others sheer lung power and prowess. I rock—you probably wouldn't expect it, looking at me, but I do.

At Fez, or Mercury Lounge— a rock club around the corner on Hous

ton Street near Katz's Deli—or the Bottom Line, where co-owner Alan
Pepper put me on as support for bigger artists or in the round sharing
songs, I'd gained confidence. It had taken me so many years to build —
can I call it a career?—in New York. I'd kept myself busy the past year:
touring, co-writing, a love affair, all at a manic pace to smooth over my
doubts and fears about moving away.

The news of the plane JFK Jr piloted going down added a tinge of
sadness and finality to my farewell to this city I came to as a teenage art
student and was leaving two decades later an artist and a mother. John
John moved in a rarefied world that hardly ever touched *my* NYC, but
he somehow felt like an extra brother I'd known vaguely my entire life.

The next morning in Williamsburg, my actual brothers, Michael and Riley, carried boxes to the U-Haul my oldest brother John had driven up
from his home in Virginia. Friends and former bandmates Sue and Angela traipsed up and down the two crooked flights of our Grand Street
walkup with armloads of clothes and linens to pile high in the back of my
car. Amanda, another friend and bandmate of many years, breezed in at
the last minute holding a large iced coffee. It was the hottest day of that
record-breaking summer of 1999.

Michael was dressed impeccably as always in '50s earth tone gabar-
dines, wing tip shoes, and a felt hat. He still lived in the same East Village
apartment our band Last Roundup rehearsed in back through the '80s,
though he'd long ago done away with the egg cartons on the walls.

Riley was a hip, mustachioed musician living just up Bedford Avenue in Greenpoint, the bedroom of his railroad apartment housing a
busy recording studio.

Sue still spoke with that soft Georgia drawl; still painted fancy apart-
ments and played in a downtown band called Run On.

Angela lived in the East Village apartment her sister Hilary helped
warehouse back in the early '80s, just after Tier 3, the downtown club
we'd all had a hand in, closed down. She was that rarity, a New Yorker
born and bred who, in her espadrilles and light cotton dress, seemed
almost European after years of living in Barcelona.

And Amanda was chic as always, tall and languid in white loafers
and one of her menswear-inspired shirts. As a clothing designer she was
a New York success – staying independent and true to her vision while
making a living at her art. She pushed her baby daughter in a stroller.

We'd all stood together onstage in dingy East Village clubs through
our twenties, unsure but full of youthful chutzpah. We were full-grown

adults now, but in my mind we were still those twenty-somethings. New York has a way of holding you in the forcefield of your early years, cast in amber with the ones who'd been there with you. How could I leave that familiarity behind?

"If you need a change, why don't you just move to the Upper West Side?" asked Michael. He'd followed me to the city and *he* would never leave. We all talked about JFK Jr's demise as the end of an era. When I came back, *if* I ever came back— I had, after all, hedged my bets by simply loaning my apartment to Joe, just in case things didn't work out down south—the city would have changed further.

I drove up Grand Street one last time, windows rolled down, smelling coffee and sweet rolls from the Dominican bakery on the corner of Bedford. The Kool Man ice cream truck version of "Send In The Clowns" sounded especially mournful. Maybe it was playing for John John, but I liked to believe I'd counted for something in New York City too. If not, what had all the struggle—the dreams and heartaches and moving my car from one side of the street to the other every single weekday except Wednesdays, holidays, and snow days—been for? I crossed the dirty, down-to-a-single-lane Williamsburg Bridge with my daughter and all our earthly goods. We'd usually belt "New York, New York" any time we arrived back home. What did you sing when you were saying goodbye?

"Ma'am, are you anywhere near Exit 6, just past Bowling Green?"

Hazel and I sat on the shoulder of I-65 South in our 1985 Pontiac Safari wagon. Trucks and cars whizzed past. I was thankful they sent a breeze our way—the car's air conditioner had bitten the dust a long time ago. James the cat quivered in a box in the footwell of the back seat. I held my first-ever cellphone, an object as large and heavy as a brick, away from my ear and looked ahead. Could it be? Was it possible Exit 6 was just a hundred yards in front of us?

Much of this part of my adult life can be catalogued in vehicles broken down by the side of the road or trundling into service stations providence had kindly placed just within reach. I wasn't entirely lacking in luck. My daughter was often on hand to bear witness. We'd already suffered one breakdown on the journey, when the U-Haul driven by my older brother John sputtered and died a block away from our childhood home just south of Pittsburgh. Why had I insisted we take the route via Pennsylvania, West Virginia, Ohio, and Kentucky instead of the shorter Virginia one? Did I have some primal need to sleep in my parents' house in the middle of this, the most significant move of my life?

When I'd left Pittsburgh for art school in New York City, I'd never confronted what it meant to leave home. I hadn't thought of myself as brave, or a risk-taker—I just knew I needed to go to New York. Now, at forty, after over two decades in the city, I was making a deliberate move. New York felt like it would always be the center of my universe, but it was also my college town. It's where I learned to play music. I'd gotten married there, and would soon finalize my divorce. Sometimes you need a fresh start, to test yourself and chase new dreams. For me, that meant Nashville.

My dad and brothers John and Patrick helped me move my entire life from one U-Haul truck to another in full view of the neighborhood where I'd ridden my bike, babysat neighbor kids, and chased boys. Ten-year-old Hazel stood sentry, helping to ferry across the occasional box of Barbies or Simpsons figurines.

John had traveled the world via naval aircraft carrier, and had long ago left military life behind. Still, he lived a few blocks from the site of one of the bloodiest Union defeats of the Civil War, in Fredericksburg, Virginia where he taught high school. He was still my rock music-loving older brother, tender-hearted beneath the brawn and bluster. "Irishman Available for stories, songs, and fighting," read a plaque on his front porch. He stood or sat first row at any gig I played within a seventy-mile radius of Fredericksburg or DC. This was the third time he'd helped me move.

Younger brother Patrick had returned to Pittsburgh after a peripatetic UPI stringer's life in Kentucky, Florida, and the wilds of West Virginia. He worked for the local daily paper, the *Post-Gazette*, and had married a lovely hometown girl, Karen. We called Pat "the normal one," but he simply kept the family touch of eccentricity well hidden.

At the rear of the U-Haul, Hazel shouted out that a chair leg had fallen off, and I wondered how all our furniture was so busted and grimy. Those charming pieces scavenged from New York City sidewalks looked more like the trash pickings they were in the hazy light of a Pittsburgh summer evening.

Back in my parents' house, my mother sat helplessly at the kitchen table, her hands around a coffee mug, red-lipsticked mouth in a perpetual part smile/part grimace that broke my heart. I asked her if she remembered the pale green-and-cream-colored enamel-topped table from the antique and crafts shop she'd started and run successfully until being badly head-injured in a car accident eleven years earlier. "You're a nice young lady," she said. It was her go-to phrase that meant she wasn't sure what was going on, but deep down felt proud of me. Or that's how I read it.

Maybe I should have involved myself in my mom's rehabilitation after her accident, but that seemed like my dad's job. I'd put my energy into raising my daughter and making something of myself. Spending the night in the house where I grew up, surrounded by the country antiques and baskets and plants my mother had a real talent for collecting and displaying, I felt the loss of her creative energy and spark all over again.

I couldn't help but feel guilt for not having been there when she needed me. We'd had a rocky relationship since I'd hit adolescence, but nobody else believed in me like she did. I'd lost the support of my mom just when I became a mother myself. I don't think a person ever gets over something like that. But you keep going.

With John driving the replacement U-Haul and Hazel and me in the Safari, crammed with bedding plus James, we left my parents' house early the next morning. I-70 West through a small corner of West Virginia; around Columbus, Ohio then south through Cincinnati on I-71 to I-65. Summer highway repairs slowed things down and we checked into a motel outside Bowling Green, just one hour north of Nashville. I couldn't face arriving for our new life in the middle of the night. James kept us all awake rambling around the motel room with John in one bed, Hazel and me in the other. Why hadn't I sprung for a cat carrier? I was always trying to save a buck. Moving was hard, harder still on a shoestring.

"Ma'am, we're just off that exit ramp," the mechanic told me. I took a second to find the cellphone's END button, having only used it once or twice before, and put the car back into drive, rolling lopsidedly along the shoulder. A mile back, the tread of one of the Pontiac's retreaded tires detached and wrapped itself around an axle with an almighty bang—thank God I hadn't lost control of the steering wheel. People who live in New York City aren't always as savvy as they like to think they are about practical matters. I knew where you could buy the chewiest bagels, and how to save three dollars by taking the Willis Avenue Bridge instead of the Triboro, but I had no idea when I bought retreads how dangerous they could be on a long, hot highway trip.

The Pontiac rolled unevenly around the bend and along a tree-lined road to a small cinderblock garage. I pulled up to the building and a couple of mechanics watched as Hazel and I got out and walked into the office to talk to the boss. I was over the hill as far as the music biz was concerned, but I was wearing a stars-and-stripes miniskirt circa 1976

Bicentennial, my legs bare and suntanned. With our New York license plates, the skirt felt like a Union flag —hello boys, we're Yankees; we're not from around here.

Maybe the guys felt sorry for us. Hazel held our quivering cat in a cardboard box. The heat and stress must have been getting to him. Our lives sat piled up in the back of a fifteen-year-old car. All I could think was, "Please let James be okay." I began to understand how people care about their pets in a way they can't feel concern for themselves.

The mechanic replaced our two front tires, and I tried not to gasp at the price of the new ones. It was a hundred degrees with one hundred percent humidity at ten in the morning, and we had sixty more miles to Nashville.

Chapter Five

I pulled up to our new place on Nevada Avenue to find that my brother John, lacking a front door key, had unloaded the contents of the U-Haul onto the front lawn for the whole neighborhood to see. Only there was nobody around. Not one soul. I immediately saw how life moved at a slower pace outside of New York City, where a piece of furniture set down for one second might not be there the next.

Friends had characterized Sylvan Park as a transitional neighborhood. I'd lived in the transitional East Village of Manhattan and then transitional Williamsburg Brooklyn, so considered myself well-versed in moving into a part of town recently discovered by artist types who might not have considered the neighborhood a possibility if things hadn't grown too expensive in other parts of town. It seemed there was always another city area just over there, even a little less desirable, and the gentrification train rolled on. I didn't feel like gentry and only moved to these kind of neighborhoods because they were cheap, so I didn't know where we even fit on the train. Maybe we were the cowcatcher?

Sylvan Park was full of quaint bungalows and graceful old trees on streets named for the states and a few local historical figures we'd never heard of. The neighborhood was bordered by noisy Charlotte Avenue—a low-rent conduit from downtown to the western suburbs, filled with fast food restaurants, car repair shops, and thrift stores. Charlotte cut through black to white to black to white neighborhoods, so by Nashville standards was integrated.

I'd rented the house sight unseen. Singer/songwriter John Sieger and his graphic designer wife Linsey did their time in Nashville and had just returned to their home town of Milwaukee, passing their rental on to us. The Craftsman cottage was the type of house I'd pass when I was on tour and wish was my own: 1920s red brick, wood trim painted silvery green looking out on a small front yard, crowned by a cozy front porch.

And, like a mirage through the steaming, shimmering pollen, I saw it: my own driveway. I nearly fell to my knees.

The backyard looked promising, if the weather ever cooled off. And from just beyond Charlotte Avenue, you could hear the low hum of I-40, the interstate running east to west nearly across the whole United States. I remembered stopping at the McDonald's just around the corner years ago, when Hazel was a toddler and Will and I were still married. We'd been driving back from a wedding in Memphis. Will, Hazel and I had taken our burgers, fries, and chicken tenders to a little park that felt to me like it was on the edge of civilization. I'd been to Nashville before, to play gigs and record, so this wasn't my first time through. But I'd suddenly felt alien in a way that being a musician insulates you from. When you're there to do a job, you're automatically a part of things. As a mere passerby, all I could think was: so this is America. Even the distance from swings to slide to merry-go-round felt overwhelmingly wide.

Back then, we'd been a complete family unit, three of us against the world. Now, with this move, it was just me and Hazel. I wondered how I'd handle whatever might befall a mother and her child in the wilderness outside New York City.

Tennessee wasn't exactly a foreign country. It was mid-south, only two states—Kentucky and West Virginia— away from my birthplace of Pittsburgh. But for day-to-day living—not just a colorful place to make music, score folksy thrift shop finds, and gorge on delicious southern cooking—we were in unknown territory. The Native Americans called Nashville "Land of the Ill Wind," the city's bowl-shaped topography making it a pollen trap; a series of depressions and gentle rises crisscrossed by highways that passed through places people came here to get away from: Clarksville, Lewisburg ... Paducah. "Depressions and gentle rises" — I hoped that wasn't a description of the life I was about to begin in that town.

After we moved the contents of the truck and car into our new home, I waited in a broiling parking lot for John to drop off the U-Haul. Then the Pontiac's battery died. John crossed the parking lot again, into a nearby AutoZone for a new battery. He pried the old one out and replaced it in the brutal afternoon heat, then hightailed it out of Nashville forever. This move had tested his laidback filial loyalty to the limit.

I took a cool bath in the elegant bathroom of our house. The place had been beautifully renovated by the landlord, a music biz lawyer. I luxuriated in the glow of the antique stained glass window and tried not to do sums in my head, wondering how I'd make the rent every month. Wasn't this the stuff I should've figured out before piling our lives into the back of a truck? Like most big decisions, if you think things all the way through and weigh the decisions too much, you'll never change anything.

Everyone had raved about the benefits of a place like Nashville for a kid, but I felt guilty for taking Hazel away from New York, where she'd gotten into Lab, one of the best middle schools in the city. I soon learned there were no available spots at the private University School, where every music-related person I knew sent their kids. The tuition was as high as some colleges, but apparently there was loads of financial aid available.

I'd left it all too late. Up north, the day after Labor Day was sacred as the first day of school. Down south, school started up in August. Were they insane? People said it had something to do with farming. School would begin in two weeks, and the only available option was the zoned middle school with a name that sounded like someone's idea of a joke: Head Magnet.

Head was an underfunded public school situated in a marginal neighborhood made up of truck depots, warehouses, and fast-food places. It was a shabbily-built sixties structure, with some of the classes held in trailers. (Referring to them as "portables" didn't make the back of the place look any less like a trailer park.) I wasn't sure how Head qualified as a magnet school—that late twentieth century desegregation model incorporating academic merit—but it was the best we could do.

During the first week, Hazel came home with a permission slip asking me, her parent, to choose whether or not my child was allowed to be disciplined via physical punishment. I got the sense they wanted me to say yes, but I checked a hearty NO! and wondered if I'd made a terrible mistake moving us here.

I didn't want my daughter spanked or beaten by a teacher, or anyone. What made me think I could make it professionally in this town? And at what cost to my daughter? I'd thought living in the city (meaning, always, New York City) was hard on a kid, but I began to see all the advantages we'd given up: decent schools, if you put in the time and effort to find them; a whole world of cultural enrichment, and easily accessible public transportation. Family and friends. What had I done?

Still, we enjoyed the novelty of Sonic Drive-In, where the servers came to your car on roller skates, or Mrs. Winner's Chicken dinners with biscuits and gravy. The massive Target superstore was a revelation after the cramped and understocked Manhattan Astor Place K Mart. For all my artistic ideals and aspirations, maybe I just wanted to live a middle-class life, with easy parking and a cute shower curtain.

August 1999. The sun bounced off the Batman building, the eerily dramatic BellSouth skyscraper that loomed over downtown Nashville. Ten minutes before eight in the morning and already the sidewalk was steaming. Why oh why hadn't I listened when the temp agency told me to take the shuttle to this week's assignment?

I'd scoffed at the shuttle suggestion. Nashville's downtown was only ten blocks long and a few blocks wide. "I'm a New Yorker!" I said. "I love to walk. I *live* to walk!" Apparently, I was the only one in the entire town who felt that way, I noted as I stuck to the shady side of the street. A grimy-looking cowboy poked his head out of a doorway, then settled back against the entrance of a vacant storefront. I saw or maybe just imagined a battered acoustic guitar leaned up beside a bedroll and duffel bag. "You too?" I thought. He looked about my age with a lot of wear and tear, and I imagined he'd been kicking up and down Music Row and lower Broadway for a decade or two, trying to catch a break, playing his songs for anyone who'd listen. Isn't that what I'd come here to do?

I wondered if he had any kids to raise; a partner he left behind somewhere. Was there anyplace he could go back to, and if not, when had the moment passed when he could still return?

I'd parked my car at a distant lot, hoping to save a few dollars. Life in Nashville continued to prove more expensive than New York, which shocked and terrified me. The starting pay was eight dollars an hour: I'd been making at least double that in Manhattan. I realized a week or two after arriving with barely the means to open a bank account that instead of working on music as I'd hoped to do, I needed to get some income flowing fast. With Hazel situated at Head, I'd signed up with a random employment agency, thinking my years of experience at top media companies like CBS and Sony qualified me for something decent.

Decent is relative.

In the August heat, my black blouse stuck to my back and the waistband of my black secretary skirt was soaked with sweat as I crossed Broadway and headed up a hill to the real estate property management company I'd been assigned to. Nashville felt like a ghost town. Where was everybody?

In their cars. Always in their cars. When people in Nashville weren't in their automobiles, driving the endless main arteries that clogged with traffic from seven to nine AM and then again from three PM to five, they magically materialized in stores and restaurants. Hiking trails were the only outdoor places you ever saw a person on foot.

Since arriving in Sylvan Park, Hazel and I often stood at the front window of our cute rental house, watching for a person, a car—a dog, a coyote; anything!—to go past. After years of feeling one with the flow of life in New York, we'd begun to repel civilization by our very existence.

And as for New York, it occurred to me during my first weeks in Nashville that outside of Manhattan, Brooklyn, Queens, the Bronx and Staten Island, people didn't actually care about The Greatest City In The World. They didn't think about it at all.

Some of them even detested the very idea of the place. I felt this most acutely in traffic. My New York license plates—those gold and blue Empire State beauties that marked me as special, not from around here—invited distrust, defensiveness, or even downright hatred from other drivers. I sensed the cars both wary of me and driven more erratically in my presence just to prove that being lame behind the wheel was a God-given right in Tennessee. Honking the horn—a basic New York survival skill—only made things worse, causing the other drivers to go even slower and wave their newfangled cellphones around. "I make *all* my calls from the driver's seat, it's great!" I could practically hear the other drivers thinking as they brandished their phones. Or maybe it was just paranoia. I doubt they noticed me at all.

"Don't worry, you'll get used to it. You might even end up loving it here," said Claire Mulally, as she passed around slices of homemade apple pie with ice cream. It was so nice of her and her husband Greg Trooper to invite Hazel and me over for dinner. Our move to Nashville was off to a shaky start.

When viewed from afar, as a two-or-three times a year visitor, Music City was a glittering whirlwind of breakfasts at Pancake Pantry (where I'd been thrilled to spot Grand Ole Opry star and Dolly Parton's former duet partner Porter Wagoner amble across the room, greeting half the customers by name); bagels and lox at the unfortunately-named Noshville (where I'd seen Chet Atkins holding court); and co-writing appointments and happening shows where I'd pressed the flesh with artists and writers whose work I admired. Publishers flung open their doors to me, the out-of-towner, and hinted that there were bags of money sitting around town, but you kinda had to "be here" to find out where they were hidden. Musicians eager for an infusion of fresh blood, and with seemingly endless time to hang out drinking coffee and meeting up for lunch, were just a phone call away.

But moving to Nashville was a different story. As a resident, I was shown an entirely other side of town, most of it lived in church, or at Kroger supermarket, or standing in line at the post office. Playing gigs locally was to be avoided as much as possible. Attracting an audience when you lived in Nashville took powers only a few possessed, the talent pool outweighing the concert-going public.

Claire and Greg understood. I remembered seeing Greg's name in *The Village Voice* back in New York City when he and Claire lived there. Greg often played the same places my bands played: Folk City, Tramps and Columbia University's Postcrypt Coffeehouse. He was a talented songwriter and touring performer who'd had his songs covered by song-writing giants like Steve Earle. Claire was a lawyer with the map of Ireland on her face, which I found comforting. The Troopers lived in a cute bungalow similar to our rental with their young son Jack, and had made themselves at home in Nashville. We would adjust, they said. Just give it a little time.

Hazel made everyone laugh around the dinner table, with her description of riding the school bus to Head. We'd initially thought it would be a real perk of life in this town: an actual school bus! Such convenience never existed back in New York, especially when you lived in Brooklyn and went to public school in Manhattan. We'd always been on our own with transportation. So the bus was technically helpful for picking up and dropping Hazel off at school when I needed to be at my temp job.

But it was also kind of a nightmare. The other kids on board had all known each other since toddlerhood. They were big, blonde, and raw-boned natives who'd taken an instant dislike to my petite, dark-haired daughter from somewhere else.

"Y'all talk funny," they'd pronounced, one of them smacking her fist into the open palm of her other hand.

As much as Claire and Greg liked living in Nashville, they humored us by joining in a little light bashing:

"Hey, I saw they have bagels at Bongo Java Coffee House now. They're actually pretty good..."

"Yeah, right." And we were off. Being opinionated and obstinate were traits we would do our best to hide down south—except around other New Yorkers. In New York, or living in its tentacles – which felt like they might stretch till the end of our time on earth – if you couldn't complain about it, you must not really care.

"...they call that PIZZA?" Hazel was saying.

Public transportation was a joke, the drivers were all insane or on Valium, downtown parking was a rip-off. It felt so good to vent. We finished dessert and said our goodbyes, then crossed the Troopers' tidy front yard in the warm September night. The New York license plates on our silver station wagon seemed to glow in the moonlight.

I had to believe there could be a place for me in our new town. I'd given up a cheap, spacious apartment in a rapidly-developing Brooklyn neighborhood one subway stop away from Manhattan; left behind a reputation as an established artist with critical acclaim, credibility, and decades-long friendships with fellow musicians and writers; walked away from a great school for my daughter, and well-paying office work when I needed it. Wait, I asked myself again—why exactly had we moved?

Our house was only a few blocks away from the Troopers', but we'd driven because that's what you did in Nashville. It wasn't like New York in so many ways, most of them infuriating. There were no sidewalks, no streetlights. Walking at night would be akin to a death wish, if there were any traffic to speak of. And during the day, it was just too hot.

We waved goodbye to the Troopers. I turned the key in the ignition. The engine came to life for one moment. Then a shrill whine.

I smiled at Hazel. Same old, same old—business as usual. Car trouble was our middle name. We'd broken down twice —three times—on the move south. All part of the artist path I'd chosen for both of us.

I turned the key again. Nothing. All we heard was the buzzing sound of cicadas, and a TV somewhere down the block playing the *Entertainment Tonight* theme. One more try. A whir, a snap.

The car was dead. It was early evening—maybe one of the garages on Charlotte Avenue was still open? I called from the Troopers' house (cellphones still such a novelty I hadn't thought to carry mine with me). I joked how it was always something, that it was probably no big deal.

A tow truck arrived. I got word next day from the garage on Charlotte that the timing belt had gone. The Pontiac was toast.

So Hazel was back with the bullies on the school bus, and I took the Nashville city bus (locals referred to it as the "ghost bus," as most people doubted its existence) to my new long-term temp job at Vanderbilt University Medical Center. As I stood waiting in the heat—it was already stifling at 7:30 AM, in October – I wondered again what I'd done.

My parents visited and my dad showed me his notes from our phone conversation of October 18, 1999:

"AMY CALLED—HAS NO CAR
GRAY GHOST DIED
NEEDS TO BORROW $
AMY—40 YEARS OLD!
Thoughts:
-Work on Music on Weekends
-Borrow $ from us to buy auto
-Get a Full Time Job"

I explained to my father I couldn't give in and turn music into a hobby. That would be some kind of defeat. Duane Jarvis loaned me his majestic old Continental sedan while he was out on the road. "I have friends, Dad—music friends. We help each other out. It's kind of like with neighbors in the suburbs when you need to borrow some hedge trimmers or a snow shovel, only it's our whole lives, not just weekend chores. My friends babysit my daughter; I drive them to the airport. We all know what it's like to live on a shoestring, to risk everything for no guaranteed reward." He tried to hear me.

I invited some of my Nashville friends over for dinner in the charming kitchen/dining room the owners had built on the back of the '20s bungalow, hoping to reassure my dad we'd be okay here. I hoped for a music payday, some day: a cover of one of my songs by a big-selling artist; a slot on a bigger tour; a publishing deal. These were achievable goals, weren't they?

My mother took her usual post-head injury position in the front yard, raking the few leaves that blew over from our neighbor's tree.

My old Brooklyn neighbors Kit and Ted came for a weekend, and we headed to the Ryman for a Grand Ole Opry show. The Opry famously vacated the Mother Church of Country Music back in the early '70s but returned occasionally, as Nashville began to celebrate rather than act ashamed of its homespun history. From up in the balcony, I watched Skeeter Davis take the stage to sing two songs and I felt that old pull, the one that attracted me to country music in the first place. There was magic in the way Skeeter projected humility, charm, and wackiness into her microphone, up and over the monitors and out into the audience. When Charley Pride sang, in "Is Anybody Going To San Antone," about wind whipping down the back of his shirt like he wasn't wearing one, I felt the cold chill and all the hard miles he put in, the prejudice and barriers he overcame to look so easygoing and nonchalant up on that stage. The country stars transcended reality through their realness.

After the show, we slipped across the alley behind the Ryman into Tootsie's Orchid Lounge, just like Hank Williams and Patsy Cline used to do. When current country star Lorrie Morgan appeared in the doorway in a big fur coat I hoped was fake—face so radiant it looked like she had her own private spotlight—the backroom bar exploded in whistles and cheers. Lorrie was from a whole other world than any I aspired to: commercial country, Music City royalty, and a tabloid regular. With her new husband Sammy Kershaw, she'd just opened a fast-food restaurant called Hot Chickens Dot Com that everyone joked didn't even have a website. It was a classic country star move, like Bill Anderson's PoFolks restaurant or Kenny Rogers Roasters. Country stars' lack of shame about trying to make a buck was endearing.

I didn't have designs on any kind of country music performing career. I just wanted to write songs. But I also wanted to keep making records and playing for people who appreciated what I did, people like me who grew up with rock music but also loved writing. When fans found me, we shared a bond, and they often became friends who supported me in ways it would take me years to fully appreciate, like Dave showing up from Chicago to take me to see Bruce Springsteen reunited with the E Street Band after the decade-long hiatus. Norma, a fellow mom and a pop music academic who'd emailed me when I was opening for Warren Zevon, inviting me to give the keynote speech at the International Association for the Study of Popular Music conference, in nearby Murfreesboro my first year in Nashville. Kate and Scott putting my entire band up in their house in Chicago. Dan and Liz hosting me for a concert in their Rhode Island living room—again and again and again. David bringing me to Middle Tennessee State University to speak and play my songs for his students in the Tom T. Hall Writers Series. It was the first time I'd ever heard the word "honorarium"—a payment as a gesture of thanks and good will— and the respect conferred in that word felt like confirmation I was on the right path, even if I had to accept charity when another friend David (are most Davids predisposed to being kind?) from New York City offered me the $1000 I needed to replace the Pontiac with a used Ford minivan called an Aerostar. It wasn't easy to explain to my dad how all of this added up to a great big safety net of support, because at the time it was hard for me to see it myself.

All I saw was the struggle. I wanted something to happen and fast. I'd turned the front room of the house into my office/studio, with the Tascam Portastudio on an old desk. I wrote at least a dozen songs within two months of arriving in Nashville, including "Balls," "Rode Hard," and

"Wait Til I Get You Home." Each song felt like the best one yet. Whatever it took to pay the bills, I needed to keep writing. That's the reason I was here, wasn't it?

Rode Hard

I could ruin my reputation around here
But this town don't know me from Eve
Somebody put something in the water
I swear I only had one beer, maybe I'd better leave?
I walk these streets with a dazed expression
"Hey ain't there somewhere you're supposed to be?"
Every prank phone call and minor insurrection
Sin, bad check - heck they could pin it all on me

Rode hard and put away wet
Driven round the bend
Got far down as I could get
But I'm going back out again

A woman could get her hand blown off reaching
There's some things you really shouldn't touch
A guy told me that I was asking for trouble
I had to kick his ass - I didn't like it much
A girl gets tired of doing all this for nothing
You look around and everyone's got retirement funds
They're all socking away saving for the future
While I buy shoes, shave my legs and see how fast I can run

Rode hard and put away wet
Driven round the bend
Got far down as I could get
But I'm going back out again

It's way too dark in this old stall
I can't find a pen to write my number on the wall

Yeah I got brains and a good hair conditioner
I wanna be ready when they take that aerial shot
Went by the parish house last night for dinner

Lively conversation but the food was not so hot
And what's there to look forward to but ice cream and TV
I'd like to meet the man who's giving milk a bad name
Peeking in windows at different happy families
While the lonely so and so's you know - we all look the same

Rode hard and put away wet
Driven round the bend
Got far down as I could get
But I'm going back out again

Chapter Six

I'd played precious few gigs since moving to Nashville. I'd go to my temp job at Vanderbilt five days a week and wonder when I could at least start recording another album. I came to Nashville to make more music, not less, but hadn't factored in the expense and readjustment of a major move. "Act now, worry about it later"—my general credo—had its drawbacks.

Then I got a call from booking agent Steve Martin offering me more gigs opening for Warren Zevon. The cantankerous genius might not have been many people's idea of a savior, but this was the second time he'd stepped in at just the right moment to make a positive difference in my life. I'm sure he wasn't aware how much it meant to me—it was just another round of gigs in a lifetime of endless touring for him.

Back in January 1999, I'd gotten the call to open a Zevon run starting in Minneapolis, through the Midwest and into the Northeastern US. I'd been struggling to find an audience for my own live shows, but opening for Warren was a way to play a concise solo set for a song-loving crowd and gain respect by mere proximity to a rowdy, beloved legend. It was no cakewalk—Zevon's audience was famously rowdy, and you needed to deliver sufficient goods to shut these people up and keep them entertained while they waited for their hero. I'd loved every show (well, maybe not the biker bar in Scranton). Warren had been kind and supportive ("My deli tray is yours"), complimenting me when he liked a particular song or outfit. I was surprised how into clothes he was: low-key Prada chic; quality fabrics in subtle shades of grey.

This time around, it would be southern dates and Florida. Touring for a few weeks meant giving up my full-time temp position and finding childcare for Hazel. Her dad had moved to Nashville and, as luck had it, Steve Earle was off the road for a few weeks. I gratefully accepted the gigs.

Walking into the Cat's Cradle club in Chapel Hill for the first show, I was overwhelmed by a sense of deja vu. Memories from shows over the years: Last Roundup with the Coolies who'd been having a moment with *dig..?*, their 1986 album covering Simon & Garfunkel before post-modern irony in rock was a regular thing. The Shams opening for Indigo Girls when they were climbing the charts with "Closer To Fine." Peter Hosapple & Chris Stamey of the dB's tour for their duo album *Angels*, and support slot on a Bob Mould solo tour in 1997. There were probably others my gig-clogged brain couldn't quite recall. When I started out, I felt sure I'd never forget a moment, but they pile up after a while.

The club relocated a few times as Chapel Hill grew from a sleepy southern university town to a wealthy strip of high-end stores and eateries, but the ambience of the place still brought to mind the early days of indie rock, when record labels and clubs were still making it up as they went along. Cat's Cradle was a scrappy way station in a scrappy world populated by survivors —lifers they called them (us? Did I include myself in that number yet?) and Warren Zevon was a poignant example. For all the respect and admiration he'd have heaped on him posthumously, he should've been playing in an arena or symphony hall instead of a gritty, graffitied shed in a strip mall. But he played where they'd have him, and at the turn of the century, that meant Cat's Cradle.

And for his audience, there was no better venue than the one they were in at that moment with their hero.

Zevon's audience loved lyrics and they appreciated mine. After months of uncertainty and feeling like an alien in a new place, when I walked out onstage and started strumming my Guild acoustic guitar, I remembered who I was and what I did. "Good shit," said Warren. "And by the way, nice pants."

We headed further south and made our way around the state of Florida. Warren was on the wagon and sticking to the straight and narrow. He had got a steady girlfriend back in California he referred to as the School Marm and had pledged to be faithful—unaccustomed behavior for him, even unprecedented. Maybe I acted out his urges for him, or maybe it was Florida, kind of like Las Vegas only with alligators—a place people move to escape reality. I met a guy at the merch table after a show, and we ended up in a bar where a band was cranking out old country hits. Two cocktails later, I found myself on stage singing "Help Me Make It Through The Night" ... and then he did.

"I want some of what you're having," Warren said, when he saw me looking bright-eyed in the dressing room the next night. I blushed and tried to explain this wasn't how I usually behaved out on the road, or anywhere for that matter.

"Yeah, yeah—save it for the judge," he said.

But maybe an unavailable man, a one- or two-night stand, was safer territory for a single mother with a daughter on the brink of puberty. Was dating back home even an option? I hoped it was and thought how wonderful it would be to find love—support, comradeship, somebody to share the ups and downs with and not just a good time.

I drove myself from gig to gig, listening to a Doug Sahm tape my ex-husband made for me, back when we were in falling in love and his compilation cassettes were our billets-doux, my developing feelings imbuing the music with an extra layer of depth and meaning. Then, tuned into the community radio station out of Tampa, I learned that Sahm had died, aged fifty-eight, alone in a motel room. I'd stood a foot away from him at the Broken Spoke in Austin, fixated on his big silver belt buckle, dying to talk to him, to tell him how his soulful voice and hybrid songs made me feel like there were no rules or boundaries with music. Out on the road in those pre-social media days, there was no immediate community to commiserate with about the loss of this one-off musical figure. So, I rewound the tape and listened again.

It wasn't all dingy rock clubs and beer crate-strewn stages in Warren's odd showbiz world. There were frequent cellphone check-ins from Don Henley and comedian Richard Lewis, and also good news: Meat Loaf was including his cover version of "Lawyers, Guns and Money" on a new live album. And every time Zevon took the stage, it was master conservatory time, from the perpetually-cocked eyebrow, wry smile that might be a wince, and first strum of his acoustic guitar like a cannon blast, through a catalog of idiosyncratic songs that turned a listener from reprobate to empathetic observer, and back again. I wished I could watch him every night for the rest of my life.

A few of Warren's author friends were at the last show of the tour, in the tony environs of the art deco Carefree Theatre in West Palm Beach. Carl Hiassen got up onstage to play a song with his sometime collaborator and Warren, who revered writers, seemed nervous around *him*. Kathi Kamen Goldmark, best known for masterminding the Rock Bottom Remainders – a ragtag band of best-selling authors including Dave Barry, Amy Tan, and even Stephen King – gave me a copy of her *Rock and Roll Joke Book* so I could add to my repertoire of drummer jokes. Kathi and her literary crew got a kick out of pretending to be rock stars for fun and for charity. I looked at her and Hiassen, so self-contained, not needing to show off in front of an audience except once in a while as a treat. Their bravado all happened on the page, and I thought, probably like Warren did, how great to not have that need for attention that made us performers—how much cleaner and dignified to just be a writer.

But when I'd leave the stage, covered in sweat from wringing out my soul, and was swamped by men and women wanting to talk to me about their lives, how they related to my songs, I knew it wasn't really a choice. Some of us are fated to play this game. In Zevon's case, it felt like a fight he'd never win but damn, he made the whole audience feel like he'd be taking them down with him, and they loved him for it. *Life'll Kill Ya* was the title of his forthcoming album. "And then you'll be dead."

When I returned to Nashville, I finally had money to deposit into my brand-new bank account at Bank of America's Music Row branch that occupied an old house—it might've been a church at one time—a driveway's width from the song publishers' offices on either side. This bank even had a writer's room—a small office with a couple of armchairs and a resident acoustic guitar, in case any brilliant ideas arrived when you were waiting in the very short line to either a) deposit all the money made the past weekend out on the road or b) talk them into a loan because of all that money you spent out on the road the past weekend. There were definitely weekends when I was in the second camp, spending more than I'd earned, paying a band, putting everyone up in hotels, buying gas and repairing my van. But the bank trusted me enough to buzz me in when I stood outside the locked front door, and being a customer had the odd effect of making me feel like I belonged in that town. Funny, the way we make puzzle pieces fit if we want something badly enough.

I never saw anyone actually use the writer's room, but Bank of America Music Row branch holds a place in my heart for the sense of possibility I got just walking into it. In Nashville, songs were currency.

I began to play regular gigs in my new town. Fellow ex-New Yorkers Kristi Rose and Tim Carroll were thriving in Music City; we joined forces for a night at the Sutler with a cross-dressing duo called Y'All, who'd traveled down from the East Village. There was a feeling of community that evening. I had Bill Lloyd on guitar, Byron House from Dolly Parton's band on upright bass, and Rick Schell on drums along with Pete Finney—who played with everyone from Bobby Bare to the Monkees—on pedal steel. There were endless numbers of great players in Nashville, and unlike in New York City, everyone had a car and even a garage or studio to rehearse in. I began to see the benefits of the place.

A friend took me to the Grand Ole Opry out at Opryland. We slipped backstage before the show, and I remembered from Last Roundup's visit back in the '80s how backstage at the Opry was almost like being in a high school locker room in advance of a big game. Meeting the fans was part of the job for country stars. I saw a trim blonde in a long velvet dress like you might wear to a Renaissance faire. Skeeter Davis, her smile as big and sweet as on her album covers.

I had to speak to her. "Hi Skeeter, I'm such a fan. I put your name in my song "Summer Of My Wasted Youth!"

"Are you from New York? Let's talk!" That voice with the heart-tugging catch sounded just like her recitation on "The End Of The World." We discussed Nashville and rock musicians. And relationships. I could see how maybe she was a little too much for Joey Spampinato, the bass player in NRBQ, who she married and was now estranged from; too much for Nashville in general. She went to her locker and brought out a copy of a children's Christmas book she'd written and signed it to me. Then she gave me her phone number.

In the next room, Garth Brooks locked eyes with anyone brave enough to look his way. He was right then the biggest star in country music. I wondered what makes a person want it so badly. Skeeter had once been country's biggest star. It's got to wear a person out. Now she was—had always been, which might make it harder—just herself.

Back in the rented house, I wrote a song inspired by what Skeeter told me about the breakup of her marriage that began with her and Joey making music together. Who knows the secrets of these things? I could only imagine how it felt and filter it through my own experience. She'd given me her phone number, so I called, hoping I could share the song with her. Maybe I'd be able to record it for real and have her come in and sing harmony. I didn't know she'd been diagnosed with the cancer that would kill her a few years later; I just figured she was too busy to return my call. I traced my finger over her name in my little leather address book, remembering back to studying her duo, the Davis Sisters, singing "I Forgot More Than You'll Ever Know" when I was just learning to write songs. Fairy tale princesses were mind-blowingly, heartbreakingly real.

Everything's Different Now

We used to laugh all the time
You'd give me your last dime

We were in love and how
Oh but everything's different now

When you walked through the door
I knew what hugs were for
We couldn't wait to...wow
Oh but everything's different now

Everything's changed, everything's new
I have to learn to stop loving you
I have to try to like being free
But I miss the way life used to be

Is there a set amount
Of happy days to count?
We got all they allow
That's why everything's different now

Nashville gave me these moments like gifts, acknowledgments that I was on the right path and had done the correct thing by moving there. So why did I keep being drawn back to NYC? The pull was still strong. Hazel and I drove to New York via Pittsburgh (hi Dad, hi Mom) for the final New Year's Eve of the twentieth century. I piloted the Aerostar into the metropolitan area forcefield via the good old New Jersey Turnpike, curving past Newark Airport through the marshes and massive parking lots, with waste and chemical silos gleaming against the spires of Manhattan. Enshrined in the HBO show *The Sopranos* (that my friend music writer Scott Schinder taped for me weekly), the glittering skyline was a beautiful, familiar sight that made my throat ache. "This, THIS is where we belong!" I thought—with the pollution and the traffic and car horns blaring. Sitting in the line of traffic at the tollbooth for the Holland Tunnel, I tuned the radio dial to 91.1 WFMU, the freeform radio station that hosted every configuration of any musical ensemble I'd ever been a part of. Its surprisingly strong signal crackled out of the airwaves and through the Aerostar's speakers: the sound of home.

"YOU'RE YOUNG, UPWARDLY MOBILE—AND STUPID!" I heard a vaguely familiar voice cut through the engine roars and brakes releasing on either side of us. DJ Terre T back announced: "That was, of course, our friend Wreckless Eric in the Len Bright Combo." I'd been playing the hell out of a CD of Wreckless Eric's greatest hits that Scott burned for me.

This Len Bright Combo was a whole other side of an artist who captured my heart with his 45, "Whole Wide World" b/w "Semaphore Signals," back in my days living in the NYU dorm over twenty years ago. Released in 1977 on the Stiff label, Eric's voice cut through tracks with a tempo all their own, removed from the frenetic pace of a lot of the records we picked up at Bleecker Bob's. The lyrics painted an exotic English world with their specific images. I felt sure he was a sympathetic spirit, like he should be my boyfriend. Breathing exhaust fumes, I wondered what he was up to these days.

I missed this feeling of serendipity that was built into New York. In Nashville, it felt rare to access the random encounters you became accustomed to when living in the city. Driving through lower Manhattan en route to the Williamsburg Bridge to Brooklyn, I cast a glance down West Broadway towards the spot where Tier 3, the music club of my youth, sat just uptown from a one-time German tavern that became a steakhouse, then artist project El Internacional, and was currently an on-and-off hot spot called El Teddy's, sporting a huge Statue of Liberty crown on its roof. The one thing you could count on with New York was that the city would keep on changing.

We were back.

Hazel and I rang in Y2K from the farthest reaches of Williamsburg with the Valentines, old friends who'd been fixtures in our Brooklyn life since Roberta taught Hazel at the Greenpoint YMCA nursery school, her husband Fred the painter always organizing community events: epic Halloween parties; art camp for the kids. They were stalwart urban survivors, rolling with every change, drifting deeper into the boroughs as rents climbed. On the eve of the new century, I felt safe enveloped in their latest building, a raw space that they made into a home, as always with resourceful spirit. We knew who we were with them. If the predicted chaos came and crashed the whole city—the entire world even—into darkness, at least we'd face it with friends we used to carpool with across the Williamsburg Bridge to the short-lived magnet Lower East Side School with the unfortunate acronym LESS.

The world didn't end. I played a few gigs with some of my New York musician friends that made me feel like I could still keep up with the harder, faster pace of the northeast, whether I needed to or not. *Having an edge*, they called it. I wasn't ready to lose mine, afraid maybe it was what set me apart from all the pretty girls with lovely voices and heartfelt songs. Back in Nashville, I was determined not to go back to temping. I wanted to work towards a publishing deal—the main reason I'd left the familiar behind for this new town—but I needed money.

I'd written a whole new crop of songs and there was an option for one more album on my record deal. If I found the right producer with his own studio and worked out a reasonable budget, I could use part of the advance to pay myself to stay afloat while I made a record.

I considered a few ideas, envisioning a record that was rough and raw, almost live. Jim Dickinson, who I'd met by phone when he was briefly my label mate—what a vibe he had. Was it myth or was it reality? It didn't seem to matter. He was a lynchpin for a certain kind of renegade music, with his own piano playing through Big Star, Alex Chilton, and the Replacements. Or RS Field, who'd recorded Billy Joe Shaver and John Mayall—accomplished men so idiosyncratic that their mere presence in a studio suggested art was being made. I wished I was confident enough for that approach. Dickinson was in Memphis, not Nashville. RS was in Nashville but more aligned with the rebel spirit of soul city to the west and his home state of Mississippi.

And there was a reason I was in Nashville, not Memphis or further south. I still aspired to fit into the music business and felt most comfortable crafting a pop landscape around my songs. Like with my first two solo albums, I still wanted to record a better-looking version of me.

Then I remembered Brad Jones, who I'd met when I'd opened gigs for Marshall Crenshaw—he'd been on bass. I'd met him again through engineer Roger Moutenot when he and Robin Eaton were mixing Jill Sobule's second album, that included her hit, "I Kissed A Girl." Brad was a pop music maven, his style an appealing mix of retro and immediate. He had a studio a few miles away in the Berry Hill neighborhood.

I played Brad a batch of new songs I was excited about. He said, "Why don't we make a record?" Sometimes things were just so simple in Nashville.

Chapter Seven

I think Brad was what you might call a mensch, if mensches could be cornfed, blonde-haired, blue-eyed boys from Iowa. He was always upbeat and positive, full of creative energy and ideas, but also hard-working and no-nonsense. He made me do vocal exercises and wouldn't accept any of my vague, half-baked ideas for keys and arrangements. Here was one of the reasons I'd come to Nashville that I hadn't thought through but instinctively knew: you couldn't fake it or bluster your way through there. Even the stuff that might seem like formula—songs about Mama and tractors and front porch swings—came by their clichés honestly, with dead-serious sincerity. If you wanted to be thought of as good, you had to legitimately be good, not just "interesting" or promising that aimed for good.

I walked around the house singing "A-ah-A-ah-A-ah-O; Ee-ooh-Ee-ooh-Ee-ooh-Ah" for weeks. Brad and I sat down and worked out all the songs' barebones, just me on acoustic guitar. This approach was not new to me, as it's been the genesis of most of my songs, but doing it with Brad as sherpa kept me from falling back on my sometimes-sloppy rock approach, where I relied on the energy of drums and electric instruments to cover up uncertain notes or sentiments. As well as tightening my performance skills, stripping things back opened up arrangement possibilities.

Brad and Robin Eaton's Alex The Great studio sat in the no man's land between Franklin Road and Berry Hill. The complex was cool and rustic, with a shady courtyard that was a cross between Spanish countryside and an industrial loading dock. The large live room was filled with vintage amps and keyboards, as was the tiled kitchen. It felt like somewhere Lee Hazlewood might hang out if he were a Nashville guy:

maverick but well-turned out with equipment in excellent repair; retro but homey, down to the earth-toned tiles in the kitchen. It looked like an easy place to spend many hours, and that's exactly what I was about to do.

The control room had a cozy couch with a large window looking out over the live room. For the first time, I'd be recording in ProTools, the mixing desk digital—jagged spikes of sound on a computer screen. All the recording I'd done up to then had been committed to tape, from my early song attempts on a boombox cassette player to the first Last Roundup demos on Tascam Portastudio; eight-track reel to reel; sixteen tracks and then twenty-four in Los Angeles. Mixing began drifting to the digital realm during the making of my last album in 1998 and now here we were two years later, no physical tape. I wondered how it might affect the process, all this flexibility and infinite choices. Digital recording was less physical—the snap, whir and whine of tape and the hands-on faders were from a world of the past—and more visual, with all the tracks and parts and even individual notes appearing on the computer screen in a kaleidoscope of colors and shapes.

"Remember to listen," Brad said. "Don't just stare at the screen."

It was mid-February, but spring comes early in Nashville. The air was gentle, and buds pushed up from bright green grass that rarely took a hammering from snow like up North.

Mornings I drove Hazel to school off Charlotte Avenue and then arrived at the studio where the coffee was good. Brad and I made a plan for each song. Some were straightforward rockers we tracked with a drummer (either Mickey Grimm or Ken Coomer who'd recently moved to Nashville after leaving Wilco), Brad on bass and Will Kimbrough and me on guitars. I'd been wowed by Will's playing when I saw him with Kim Richey at the Bottom Line in New York—deft and soulful. Kim had the type of artistry I aspired to. She was uniquely herself, no frills Ohio but spare and masterful with lyrics and melody. I lacked her effortlessly perfect voice. Hopefully I had my own brand of magic.

Each day we worked until three or four in the afternoon when I drove back home to meet Hazel at the bus, or picked her up directly from school. Sometimes I drove us back over to the studio, where she did her homework on the comfortable couch right in the control room. Having her there while I worked reminded me of Chinese restaurants in New York City, where the kids sat at a table with their books spread out while their parents filled food orders around them. Working moms and dads do what they have to do, and children have no choice but to go along with it. Even if she saw it as slightly annoying and would rather be at home where at least she could watch homemade VHS recordings of *The Simpsons*, the recording studio had been part of her life since Shams days when she was a toddler crying, "I want to play the piano!" from the control room. Maybe she'd go into the family business herself; as nonchalant as she appeared, Hazel was an avid music fan who'd already progressed from the pop princesses of the day (Britney, Christina, and Spice Girls) to current pop punk and rock of the past.

And she was, after all, the daughter of a drummer. She'd signed up to play percussion in band at school, and we even roped her into putting down a glockenspiel part on one track. She pulled it off easily in one take and, homework done, took out her Game Boy to wait out the rest of the session on the control room couch.

As the child of a working artist, it's not your job to take pride in watching your parent work at fulfilling their creative desires. It's probably more a threat to your own security, like if this one more attempt succeeds and creates more work and opportunities, more touring—there'll be less of your parent for you alone. I didn't worry about any of this back then, only thought how cool for Hazel to hang out at the studio.

I sat on the couch for many, many hours listening and looking at the computer screen. Sometimes we recorded vocals or put down an acoustic guitar right there in the control room, other times I played out in the big room with the guys. Brad seemed to be pals with every great player in the central U.S.— Ross Rice drove in from Memphis to play keyboards and Dave Jacques, who I knew mostly as John Prine's bass player, contributed Salvation Army horn parts.

The players were all adaptable and hilarious, easy to hang out with and could roll with any ideas that presented themselves. I felt like all the work I'd done up till then prepared me for this new experience: that first Nashville recording session with Last Roundup back in 1984, when we were so out of our depth the results never saw the light of day; recording our Rounder album, *Twister*, in Springfield, Missouri, or harmonizing with the Shams in Brooklyn with Lenny Kaye as producer. Then putting my first solo album together from the ground up—Pie Studio on Long Island to Los Angeles. Dozens of homemade demos recorded on the Portastudio—it all added up and I didn't question my right to be there as I might've in the past.

The studio was a playground of cool instruments and players that spanned eras and scenes. Singer James Nixon, a cohort of Jimi Hendrix in his early years, arrived to layer doo wop parts for "Cynically Yours."

He was dapper and gracious, dressed in a beautiful suit. Kayton Roberts, for decades the lap steel player in Hank Snow's band, was a little more prickly as he tried to make sense of my songs: "I don't get what's going on here," he said about "Rode Hard," and I wondered if the impressionistic lyrics I'd felt proud of were just a load of nonsense. Country singer Bobby Bare's son, Bare Jr, came in to sing a harmony and the recording took shape then. It was verse, chorus, verse, chorus, bridge – nothing crazy – and I thought how Kayton was simply from a different world. What did utility man Charlie McCoy think when he played harmonica on *Nashville Skyline*? Or Ween's "Piss Up A Rope," for that matter? It's all music and a gig is a gig.

One of my New York friends, Jon Graboff, a fine guitarist who'd helped me find my feet when I first started playing solo gigs, joined the sessions to add haunting guitar parts to a few songs and rocking out on others. The outro to "If You Won't Hang Around"—the closest I'd come to a rockabilly feel song since Last Roundup and early Shams days – lasted nearly as long as the song itself, we were having so much fun vamping. "I hope that's as much fun to listen to as it was to play," said Jon. Not a given. It was nice to have Jon's sharp New York wit, a little taste of home. My new friend Joy Lynn White added harmonies, and I almost couldn't believe this incredible singer – who until a few months ago only existed on her CD *Wild Love*, which I'd scavenged from the giveaway pile while temping at Sony Music – was belting out my lyrics a third above my vocal melody.

Brad Jones' arranging skills came to the fore with "Cynically Yours"— the humor and offhand vocal style underscored by arch backup harmonies—and "Happy For You," a song I'd co-written with Bill DeMain, with overlapping strings and pedal steel emphasizing the poignant lyrics and sentiment. It was a long way from the immediate approach I'd initially anticipated for the album, but like a plain girl presented with designer duds and stunning jewelry, it was hard to not want to outfit myself in pop transcendence and a crown of stars when it was offered.

In writing, or songs, on stage and in the recording studio, I possess way more hubris than I feel in real life. Back then, in the darkened studio with just the microphone in front of me, I could be honest and vulnerable in a way I couldn't get to with whoever I was obsessed with or romantically curious about.

I was forty years old and making my last sonic bid to create the come-hither allure of the ladies in a book called *Mirror of Venus* that lived on a shelf in the control room of Alex the Great. With text by Francoise Sagan and Federico Fellini and softcore black and white photos by panting prepster Wingate Paine, the women in the pages of the book offered themselves up as objects aiming to please. I spent hours looking at the photos, feeling the closing of that window fast approaching. From the grown woman, wife and mother themes of my first solo attempts, I'd moved on to the still-fertile (but not for much longer) terrain of a divorcée's psyche, with lyrics that mentioned birth control, balls, wet dreams, and sex tapes.

I felt a sense of freedom...also maybe a thrill at being able to shock or catch listeners off guard. It was a way to subvert the cliché of a pretty-sounding girl with a guitar.

But I still wanted to look pretty on the album cover. I'd come up with the title for the record during a Midwest run of dates. I was driving, with the three musicians I'd hired to back me for the weekend's worth of gigs in various reclining positions around the Aerostar. The configuration changed every time I made a short run—that was the game in Nashville because road guys took work that was there and unless you were working every week, you'd lose somebody: a drummer here, a bass player there. We stopped in Springfield, where Last Roundup recorded in the '80s, and I felt like I'd certainly come a long way from those early days. A road sign flashed by somewhere in Missouri: Sugar Tree, the phrase like a prayer to make the fruits of my labor pay off for this final disc of my record deal. Things were as big time as they were going to get professionally, but I didn't know that. "There's no way I'll still be riding around in a van when I'm forty," I'd thought when I was twenty-eight and had only been at it for five years. I couldn't have imagined how many more records to make, songs to write, gigs to play there were ... and that I'd need to keep driving the van myself.

I envisioned *The Sugar Tree* cover as one of those 1960s countrypolitan LPs you'd stumble across in a thrift store, with a soft color portrait in a natural setting. Photographer Jim Herrington—who looked like James Dean's brainy but slightly debauched older brother and had taken pictures of some of my heroes like Merle Haggard and Tom Petty— lived just down the street from East Nashville's Shelby Park. A little research (pre-Google, that likely involved asking one of my music writer pals) pinpointed this bucolic setting only minutes from the liquor stores and hot chicken places of Gallatin Pike as a frequent backdrop for country album cover shoots in the past.

Jim recommended a makeup artist, and she met me at his house on a hot afternoon to prepare me for the shoot. The April humidity made my face pour oil and frizzed my hair. I was okay in Nashville when it wasn't the sticky season, but since spring down south started in late February and summer lasted until about the beginning of November, I was finding there weren't many weeks out of the year when looking well-groomed was a possibility.

"Don't worry, we'll fix you right up," the gorgeous young woman said as I settled onto one of Jim's dining chairs. I'd picked up a fitted dress on sale at the mall, not realizing until I put it on outside of the air-conditioned store that it was 100% polyester, causing me to sweat and practically break out in a rash.

I'd been happy with hair and makeup people's work in the past, making me look like myself only better, so I relaxed as the makeup artist sponged, brushed, curled, and pencilled me. She applied lip liner and lipstick—the final touches—and stood back to assess her handiwork. Then she held up a mirror for me to admire the results.

I took a deep breath, then wondered why Joan Crawford in *Whatever Happened to Baby Jane?* was staring back at me. My brows were double their usual width, and my mouth looked like those wax lips kids used to wear at Halloween. I thought my eyes were pretty sultry but was too horrified to keep looking at myself.

Murmuring a few words of appreciation, I handed her a check and as soon as she'd driven away, went into the bathroom to scrub everything off and start over again with whatever was in my makeup bag. Maybe it'd be dark enough by the time we reached Shelby Park that my face wouldn't really have to show in the photo.

The sun was going down as Jim and I drove into the park and there wasn't much time to look around for a suitable spot before it turned into night. We found a wooded area above the Little League field where there was a game in full swing, the lights just coming on. I heard shouts and cheers from the young players and their parents as I sat down next to a tree. Do all other female artists go through this? I wondered. I thought how the successful ones had those perfect attributes of womanhood— the obvious boobs and beauty—to show off, while I was stuck with the flawed human bits like greasy skin and limp hair. Why couldn't I have just been a guy? I knew from having brothers and boyfriends, and even having been married for years to a man, that vanity and wobbly self-esteem aren't only for women. But I think of the cover of Crosby, Stills and Nash, the guys clearly rolling up as they were to lounge on a beat-up old couch. I aspired to self-acceptance, but for that moment just wanted to look attractive.

"Your legs look great," said Jim. I hitched my dress up a little. The field lights shone on the gold platform shoes a friend gave me years ago, swearing they'd once belonged to a Hollywood screen goddess. I gazed off into the distance like I was searching for love, success, anything to lift me out of driving all day to play for fifteen people, a grubby road atlas clutched in my right hand. I prayed for that magical combination of luck and timing that would send my songs—this latest recording— like a Little League home run, up through the air into the ears and hearts of people, lots of them, who'd see themselves in the lyrics and find some transcendence in the music. If I wished hard enough, it almost felt possible.

Chapter Eight

"Why was I looking forward to playing this gig?" I asked myself early in my set at the Association for Independent Music's annual convention. I stood onstage at the Cleveland Renaissance Hotel in a ballroom filled with round tables covered with white cloths. Low lighting shone on the name tags of several hundred music biz lifers. The din of an open bar should've been a clue the gig wasn't going to be easy—this was the first night of a weekend where indie label reps, salespeople, marketing folks, and record store owners gathered to schmooze and swap gossip. And—May 2000, dawn of a new century – talk about the looming threat of the file sharing service Napster and its potential to destroy the fairly small record sales that independent labels relied on to stay in business.

I strummed my acoustic guitar. There were a couple hundred conversations going on right in front of me.

"...and I said to him, let's just see how it does out there in the world." and

"...they told me, `You are looking at the next Fiona Apple'..." and

"Have you tried the popcorn shrimp? They're really good!"

I chose a quiet song, and the volume of the talking decreased—these were music folks, after all, they weren't total heathens. There were some smiles and nods, and people clapped when I finished the song. When I played louder, stomping on my Big Muff fuzz pedal for "Balls," the din rose. I thought back to checking into the Renaissance earlier that afternoon, how the plush lobby – all polished wood and brass – felt far removed from my past experiences as a musician coming through Cleveland. I'd stayed out near the Interstate in the Motel Six following sparsely-attended shows in blues bars crossed with barbecue joints that were a staple of this city. The Ian Hunter song, "Cleveland Rocks," was a little misleading: this city could rock and —given its post-industrial hardships—should rock. But sometimes the people just didn't show up, preferring to rock at home?

This time around I'd flown from Nashville, taken a taxi to the hotel, and luxuriated in a cushy room with a view towards the Rock and Roll Hall of Fame on the shores of Lake Erie. I'd first visited the Hall one morning after a gig in 1996, a year after the I.M. Pei-designed museum opened. My band and I marveled how rock music had earned itself such a glitzy home. I'd been thrilled to learn the museum waives the admission fee for artists who give them a copy of music they've released. Maybe they added it to the museum library, or tossed it onto a landfill pile— whatever, I appreciated this unexpected perk of being a musician who just paid some dues with a show in Cleveland.

Onstage at the convention, I worked my way through a few more songs, keeping it short. I didn't whine or complain as I might've done at one time, having learned to never blame the audience, whoever they are, for choices I've made in my life that have brought me to this moment. "I'm here because I want to be, and besides, they voted for me as one of their indie artists of the year," I told myself. "I'm Amy Rigby and that's 'Twenty Questions!'" I said, with a final rave-up strum. Now get me the hell out of here.

I caught a taxi east along Lake Erie and across the Interstate, into a homey neighborhood where an old Lithuanian dance hall was now a venue called the Beachland Ballroom and Tavern. Neon beer signs were the main light source in the tavern, with a time-worn wooden bar along one side of the room and a linoleum-tiled floor. The bathroom doors were visible directly behind the stage. I strapped my guitar on, plugged in, stood up in front of the twenty or thirty people who'd paid to see me and...

I felt at home. The other person I tried and tried to be, the one in my promo photo and new album cover, who smiled seductively over a bare shoulder, was set aside for a Cubist study of a woman in motion with sweat on her face, a song in her throat, and a buzz in the monitors. On this kind of stage in a room that size, you can't control the way you look or how you're perceived. You just do it the best way you can for the people who believe or are open to being persuaded.

And hey, I had my indie artist plaque, and I was in the Rock Hall, wasn't I? Somewhere on a shelf or in a bin? The records we pour our lives into, and shows like this one, are the bricks and mortar that helped build that glittering pyramid. I finished my set for the people, my people, sold some CDs and grabbed a ride back to my fancy hotel.

The school year ended early in Nashville and Hazel was out by mid-May. The heat and humidity came on and we ate ice cream and discovered Wave Country, Nashville's honky-tonk water park. My new record was coming out with help from the label: a smaller poster this time, and a hopeful feeling that one of the tracks might receive radio airplay. The replacement A & R guy was gone, and a new one came in; it turned out he was already a fan and was pushing the label for a bigger budget for tour support.

I was happy with whatever happened. I was just happy. Over the course of recording and mixing and getting all the parts of *The Sugar Tree* together, I'd fallen in love with a sweetheart of a guy.

It wasn't his fault he was a drummer.

Give The Drummer Some

He's cute, if a middle-aged man can be described as cute
He's alive, that's saying a lot,
You'd be surprised how many are not
He's real, sometimes I wish he'd try to be a little less real
He's broke, but he knows how to cook—
He always fixes a real nice meal
He's got a drawer of Zildjan shirts
And a bass drum in his living room
He hits the snare so hard it hurts
And he makes my heart go boom, boom, boom
So tonight I'm gonna give the drummer some
Tonight I'm gonna give the drummer some
He's sad, cause he's gotta go work a day job
 til somebody calls
He's pissed, cause the guy they chose
has Cheerios instead of balls
He rocks, when he puts the Meters on and turns it up to ten
He feels alone sometimes, he knows he's not like other men
Cause he's got a drawer of Zildjan shirts
And a bass drum in his living room
He hits the snare so hard it hurts
And he makes my heart go boom, boom, boom

So tonight I'm gonna give the drummer some
Tonight I'm gonna give the drummer some
His splintered sticks, his calloused hands
Stuck in the back, that head is broke
His hearing sucks, go load the van
Here comes another drummer joke

The first thing that attracted me to Paul was—his drumming.

I was in love with another drummer, after the first one and the one after that (that was a rebound romance, similar to a paradiddle where the stick bounces up, down, and back up again quickly). Like my ex-husband Will, Paul was a left-handed drummer. A left-handed drummer is its own brand of madness. House kits and backlines set up for the right-handed majority mean it takes a certain indomitable spirit to strike out left-handed on the skins. Left-handed drummers look at the world sideways, and that appealed to me.

I first noticed Paul's playing on Knoxville poet, playwright, and recording artist RB Morris's album, *Take That Ride*. The opening track, "World Owes Me," reached out through the CD player of Duane Jarvis' slick burgundy Continental on a late-night post-gig drive back to Nashville. Duane and I had played a poorly-attended show in a rustic Knoxville church, and the sentiment of the song spoke to me, about the world owing us a living, sung by RB with equal parts resignation and defiance while the drums kicked against the world and leaned back into it at the same time. That was Paul.

Part Welshman by way of Louisiana, Paul lived the kind of road life that looks romantic from the outside: full of vans and tour buses populated with journeyman musicians. Talented men living like soldiers in service of rocking country and poor white boy blues, they slept in bus bunks, stumbled out into truck stops in the middle of the night in the middle of nowhere to grab snacks and call home. They spent weeks away from loved ones for the glory of getting up on stage in roadhouses and fairs, backing up veteran guitar slingers and singers who held their players' fates in the back pocket of their Roper jeans. A gruff "Send him home" was all it took to end the gritty magic carpet ride and plunge the road guys back into real life. Along with getting to spend more time with their families – but was that really a consolation when you weren't working? – they'd have a chance to catch the leaves changing, or the glory of springtime in Nashville, where most of the sidemen lived.

I didn't know any of this when I first heard Paul's drumming, but I could feel it. At first, we encountered each other as fellow musicians who shared a passion for culinary experiences. There were musicians who ate whatever fast food the road put in front of them, and others – like Paul and me – who made finding decent barbecue a side job to their life's work. Pre-internet and smartphones, Jane and Michael Stern's *Roadfood* was as essential on the floor of any vehicle I traveled in as the box of cassettes and a *Rand McNally Road Atlas*. With Paul, I would explore the more obscure barbecue spots of the South. I'd finally taste oysters, raw on Saltine crackers with Tabasco, and enjoy dive burgers at Rotier's Restaurant and Brown's Diner in Nashville, always followed by cold beer, like sacramental hosts chased with sacristy wine.

The religion reference isn't random—in addition to being an ace drummer, Paul was a writer, contributing thoughtful book and film criticism to the local weekly, *Nashville Scene*. And he was, confoundingly, a doctoral candidate in the Divinity School at Vanderbilt. An avowed atheist studying religion, there was a contrariness to Paul I thought must stem from being born on the Isle of Wight, son of a Welshman and an Englishwoman, only to be plunked down in the bayous of Louisiana at an impressionable age.

He drove a black manual transmission Nissan pickup truck, and had a solid physical presence. The best word I could think of to describe Paul would be merry. He just had a twinkle in his eyes, cheeks, and crinkly hair.

Between the sheets, my divorce final, I tossed off the weight of Catholic guilt but heaped on a good bit of the parental variety to take its place. Hazel disliked the whole idea of Paul at first, but he was such fun and so charming that she came around eventually. Paul was a dad himself, with a son my daughter's age (who lived with his mother far away in Michigan), so he knew how important my kid's opinion was, how much looking out for her mattered to me. But when it came to sex, I was like a teenager myself: sneaking around, acting as if I invented the stuff.

Paul rented a room in a cool old cottage in the neighborhood where Granny White Pike gave way to Twelfth Avenue South, as crack houses were giving way to landscape design and tidy neutral paintwork. Every now and then, when Hazel's dad was off the road, I spent the night with Paul in his room and felt like I was in my twenties again.

He'd moved to Nashville years ago and, like many in that town, alternately loved and hated it. Maybe my impression of Music City was clouded by his experience, often expressed hilariously. Coming from New York, his critical eye and built-in cynicism, alternating with unbridled enthusiasm, felt like home.

Paul and I scored tickets to see Johnny Paycheck at 328 Performance Hall. Paycheck's 1977 hit, "Take This Job and Shove It," inspired me to write "File Clerk Blues" back in my early songwriting days—the working person's woes a rich thematic mine I never tired of. And Johnny matched with George Jones on "You'd Better Move On," from George's duets album, was harmony made in —well, not exactly heaven, more like the place around the back of heaven. He'd spent time in and out of prison—most recently for shooting a man in a barroom fight in Ohio. Word had it Johnny wouldn't be alive much longer due to emphysema.

We found a convenient parking spot for Paul's truck right near the venue. Even in the early 2000s, before development took hold of the desolate stretches near downtown Nashville, free or reasonable event parking was a tricky business. Sometimes it almost felt like the Music City powers that be didn't actually want people to go out and hear music. The place was a strange mix of license and moral judgment, with oppressive parking restrictions around nightspots where there was nothing but space—no residences, no other businesses, nothing going on but discarded pages of *The Tennessean* rolling down the street until the church bells pealed on Sunday morning.

The crowd in the wide, low-ceilinged venue was in high spirits. At times, Nashville was a tacky hellhole and you felt like you'd sold your soul to be there. Other times, like this night, you felt the energy and talent of every person in the room with you. I met Bobby Bare, a towering presence with a twinkling smile, by the side of the stage. I'd fallen in love with him from hearing his recording of Shel Silverstein's "The Winner."

The audience seemed livelier and scrappier just knowing Paycheck was there in the room with us. Everyone was smoking. Before he took the stage, I saw Johnny breathing from an oxygen tank. Then he came out in front of the packed house and sang like it was no big deal, in between hits of oxygen. His voice carried physical weight, even though his body looked slight and frail. Between the oxygen tank and barking out lines ("Friend, don't take her, she's all I've got"), Johnny smoked too.

When the show ended, Paul and I headed out into the night, the smokiness of the venue echoed in the mistiness of Nashville at midnight, the emptiness of the back streets stretching in all directions, interrupted only by interstate highways headed north, south, east, and west. Off in the distance, a neon sign for the World's Largest Adult Store flickered on and off.

Paul pulled the stick shift back to reverse the truck out into the street and—we couldn't move. There was a reason no one parked in this spot—a metal bar in the concrete gripped the truck's suspension. A small crowd gathered around us, everyone an automotive expert.

"Maybe put a little more air in the tires?"

"What about a couple of two by fours under the wheels?"

We tried to call a cab but ended up catching a ride back to my house with some friends. It was just the type of evidence Paul needed, further proof that this town was a low-class backwater that would never be a decent place to live. "Don't get sucked in," he told me, not for the first time.

Next morning, we drove to the Hermitage Cafe for breakfast. Southern diner food in all its Sunday glory, church attendance optional: grits, biscuits—you could even order pork chops with your eggs.

"Isn't this place the greatest?" said Paul. I drove us in my Aerostar through still-deserted streets to meet AAA. The truck sat just where we left it. Johnny Paycheck was on to the next town, maybe one where you could buy alcohol on a Sunday.

Chapter Nine

"You're not really obscure until you're nobody in someone else's country," I thought, as I leaned back in the shotgun seat of a right-hand drive council van. We were heading up the M1, or maybe it was down the M3 motorway through the middle of England.

For almost two decades I'd played in bands, and then as a solo artist. In my late teens, and then again in 1981, I'd spent time and even lived in London. I'd been an Anglophile since my parents bought me Talking Stacey, Barbie's "British Chum" from Swingin' London, who'd thrilled me with exotic phrases like, "I think miniskirts are *smashing*!" and "Let's have Barbie over for tea." Music (Elton John, the Who, and any punk record released between 1976 and 1982), literature, painters like David Hockney; TV shows (*Monty Python*; *No, Honestly*; *Rock Follies*), films, and fashion—I'd eaten up anything the British served even though their cuisine back then left a lot to be desired.

I wished I'd started touring there at a younger age. America was wide but Britain might be impenetrable. The mere act of covering lots of miles in the U.S. meant you were likely to catch on somewhere or at least look impressive trying. The U.K. was so small, you could go in and set the place alight immediately, or struggle for years thinking, "Shouldn't it be easier in a place this size?"

May 2000. With my new album just out, I'd flown from Nashville to Atlanta to London and headed straight from the airport to rehearsal with Western Electric, a British outfit led by American musician Sid Griffin. Sid was a forefather of alt-country with his Los Angeles outfit, the Long Ryders. He'd lived in London for years, played in various combos and wrote for music magazines like *MOJO* and *Uncut*. He had a thorough knowledge and deep appreciation for early American country rock (Byrds, Burritos) and Bob Dylan. I'd met him in what felt like another lifetime, back in Williamsburg at a party thrown by mutual friends who lived in an old funeral parlor near the BQE.

I'm not sure who hatched the idea for me to open shows for his new electro-country outfit, using them as my backing band, but I didn't have the necessary clout or profile to book a tour of my own in the U.K. and it seemed like a good way to test the waters. Even though I'd just done a run of shows opening for Warren Zevon, playing solo and going over well with large audiences, I didn't think people would take a chance on seeing me without a band, when my records all had full arrangements and impressive players. It's a common singer/songwriter's conundrum: you write your songs alone, but it takes a certain level of confidence to go out and play them that way, especially when some judge your worth as an artist by the level of player you attract.

I spent my first night in London at Gina Birch's flat in Monmouth Road, the very street where I'd lived in a squat back in 1980-1981. The area called Notting Hill was coming up, its once-grimy pastel-terraced houses sporting a sheen of new money. I'd kept in touch with Gina since the punk days; she was one of my early heroines with her pioneering all-female band, the Raincoats, who'd come and played Tier 3, our home-made Manhattan club way downtown. We'd put the band up and in turn she'd bequeathed her old room in London to me, and had been a good neighbor and friend my solo year in London. It was gratifying when Kurt Cobain rediscovered and spotlit the Raincoats to the world at the peak of his fame; and then I'd been excited to see her lead her own band, the Hangovers, in New York a few years back. Now she was married to Mike Holdsworth, a publicist for Matador Records, the Shams' one-time label. In the year 2000, the world of indie was still a small and cozy one. I felt like I'd come a long way, staying with Gina before I headed out to play gigs of my own in the U.K. Back in the early days of our acquaintance, I'd been a breathless fan who wouldn't have imagined being "on tour" and out "promoting my album." Now it was my life.

Sid and the band and I drove out of London in a van courtesy of the pedal steel player's day job with a London borough council. The perks of socialism, as renting a van of similar size would likely have cancelled out any tour profits. At least this way Sid and I could pay the guys and come close to breaking even.

First stop eight hours to the north, Glasgow had a gritty charm. Load-ing into basement club the 13th Note (I'd learn over the years it's almost all basement clubs in Glasgow), I thought how we could be in New York or St. Louis or any American city as I breathed the familiar smell of stale booze and bleach, and stepped around beer crates stacked at the side of the stage. We set up, soundchecked, and ate a hasty meal at an Italian cafe around the corner. Laura Cantrell, a radio DJ friend from New York who was just coming into her own as an Americana artist, was over in the U.K. doing her first tour and had come for the show. I played the first part of my set solo and then a half dozen songs with the band. Onstage, things magically gelled after only one rehearsal, and I felt a connection with the small audience: "They get me, they really get me," I thought. That feeling would keep me coming back again and again, playing the same-sized clubs to around the same number of people, for many years to come. I didn't know this yet. In my mind, I was paying my dues on the lower steps of the ladder.

"What are YOU looking at, fucking bitch?" In the ladies' room after my set, I made the mistake of catching a girl's eye in the mirror. I thought that's what I heard her say but couldn't be sure—the Glaswegian accent was impenetrable. The threat of violence was a shock, and it occurred to me I wasn't in New York or Philadelphia. I wasn't even in Boston. The world was a complicated place, and I knew nothing.

After Western Electric finished their set, we loaded our equipment out of the basement, and the guys dropped me at a bed and breakfast in the city while they headed off to stay with friends on the outskirts, where the van full of equipment would be safer. Glasgow was an edgy place, not the quaint land of tea and tartan Americans imagine.

A friend had collected the key for me from the landlady—no late check-ins at these establishments. I took the opportunity to use a pay phone in the front parlor room. I leaned against the red and black patterned wallpaper in my short skirt, tall boots and leather coat, guitar propped against the mantelpiece that might have once been posh. I felt almost glamorous for a minute: "Look at me, on tour, in Scotland!" I used my international calling card to dial a series of access numbers, pin codes and finally the area code and phone number to speak to my daughter for a minute; left a message for Paul. I made my way through a darkened breakfast room and up a rickety set of stairs to a back hallway. My room was simple and tidy: a single bed and kettle, sink and toilet, with shower down the hall.

Shortly after climbing into bed, I heard banging on the stairs. Heavy boots: two pairs, four pairs. Then female laughter and the sound of bodies slamming against the thin walls of the hallway. They were speaking something that sounded sort of like English, but I couldn't make out a word. I read my book and tried to ignore the noise of a party in its early stages.

A half hour later, they began pounding on my door, calling me "girlie" and "lass," shouting at me to come out and have a drink. Just a little earlier, on the phone in the hallway, I'd felt worldly. Now I was pushing a dresser in front of the door, feeling very alone and vulnerable. I didn't know whether the drunks in the hallway were serious or joking when they yelled, "We know you're in there!" but there was no way to call for help. I wondered if I could crawl out the window. I vowed to never return to Scotland—Glasgow, anyway. I put headphones on, covered my head with a pillow and cried myself to sleep.

Next morning, I avoided the breakfast room, afraid to face whoever had been terrorizing me in the night. I found a half-eaten Nutri-grain bar in the bottom of my bag and pictured my daughter at her dad's apartment off of Nolensville Road back in Nashville. Did she miss me like I missed her? I dragged my case and guitar downstairs at check-out time and complained to the landlady about how unsafe I'd felt in her establishment last night, and what was she going to do about it?

She chuckled. "Ah, the fooball," she said. "Scotland vs. Ireland today."

"But..." I sputtered. "I felt unsafe!" The woman walked off to clear plates from another table. Pre-Yelp or Trip Advisor, I imagined myself writing a strongly-worded letter of complaint to the B&B and pictured the staff, and maybe even the group of unruly guests, having a good laugh when it arrived all the way from America.

Scotch helped. So did beer. I couldn't understand why everyone drank copious amounts of the Belgian brew Stella Artois when the U.K. was known for its beer. (Stella was extra-strong, worked faster, more bang for your pound.) There was so much to learn. In Aberdeen, someone told me, "These people really like you! They don't usually laugh so much!" They were...laughing? In Hull, off in its own little cul de sac in the Northeast of England, I felt oddly at home. The people displayed a comfortable humility and deadpan humor.

The crowd at the Borderline in London groaned with amusement when I mentioned Hull, and I saw how that small Northern city might be the Pittsburgh of England. Preston, Nottingham, Sheffield. The audiences were small. Some people actually had one or two of my albums, which felt like a diplomatic achievement. Every club's schedule listed night after night of tribute bands: Think Floyd, the Rolling Clones. This was the stuff that packed these places. Original music felt like a niche endeavor.

Sid and I discussed how what we were doing might be anachronistic, like a tinker rolling into town. Did young people still want to do this? Did they still need to? We'd come of age when picking up a guitar was a statement of intent to be not like our parents; to be free. The gulf between their generation and ours seemed a lot wider back then. Now our heroes, the ones who'd survived, were old enough to be grandparents.

The glory they'd achieved was a far cry from the reality of Preston on a Tuesday night: loading into a cold room above a pub, setting up and soundchecking; eating whatever passed for dinner, and playing the show; selling merch and talking to whoever hung around after, loading out and standing around a convenience store for ten minutes deciding between biscuits and questionable sandwiches.

Or was it? On a night off, Sid took us all to see Chris Hillman— one of the architects of the country rock genre with the Byrds and the Flying Burrito brothers, and an early inductee into the Rock and Roll Hall of Fame— play a small room in Southampton. He was still movie cowboy-handsome with that thrilling voice. To sit just a few feet away for his solo performance, then actually meet him and shake his hand, felt precious, like we the audience were part of a privileged club. He'd climbed as far as you can go—reached the top of the mountain—but still had to find something to eat after the gig on a Tuesday night in Southampton.

It was enough to make you cry or laugh, and so we laughed, wondering how often did grownups get to have this much fun, even if it sometimes felt pointless?

When I said goodbye to Sid and the guys of Western Electric, I missed them before the van pulled away, even though a week earlier in Leicester I'd been convinced they were trying to ditch me. Maybe it was Leicester, but mostly it was me, the typical artist mess of ego and self-conscious insecurity. There is no easy way to come together as a band; loyalty has to be either earned or well-paid, or both.

I wrote none of this for the tour diary I'd begun keeping online in 1998, sending my updates to the fan who knew HTML and had offered to maintain a website for me. I remembered a fellow musician friend's advice when anyone asked how your tour went: "However many audience there were, double it." Yes, what happens on the road stays on the road— the people back home only need to know you were out there. I left out the Glasgow B&B, the fears and doubts. At the end of it all, what's important is I showed up and did my best. I toured the U.K.

Back home in steamy Nashville, through jet lag and a cold amplified by weeks of damp weather and smoky pub air (remember smoking in bars and pubs?), I pulled out my dog-eared USA road atlas. A new agent was offering to book fall dates for me. I wondered if it made sense to start in Cleveland, knowing how hard it could be to get an audience there. Not quite as hard as Preston, in the north of England, on a Tuesday night. Maybe New York? That was only a...seventeen-hour drive away.

Chapter Ten

"Could I get one of them junior dip top cones? Vanilla ice cream with chocolate dip and...let me see, a root beer float?" A woman's face loomed through the Dairy Dip window. She pushed a five-dollar bill across the counter. I gave her change and she dropped some coins in the tip jar. When she stepped back to wait for her order, I leaned out the window to catch a breeze. Early August in Nashville, and it had to be nearly a hundred degrees out there. Inside the Dairy Dip, it felt a good twenty degrees hotter.

I wasn't working a teenager's summer job because I couldn't get anything better. Back in the spring I'd helped my friend Claire with her refurbishment of the old ice cream place on Charlotte Avenue. Claire had taken a course at Ice Cream University; sought out the very best beef for her burgers and an authentic Belgian recipe for the French fries. The newly-painted pink, red, and mint green exterior of Bobbie's Dairy Dip was a nostalgic contrast to neighboring commercial chains Krystal and Burger King. I remembered stopping at the original Dairy Dip when Hazel and I first visited Nashville together and how captivated we'd been, saying, "Wow—this is America! So different from New York City!" I was proud of Claire and her vision, and thought it might be more fun helping out here than going back to temping in an office before I headed out to play shows in the fall.

Fun wasn't exactly the right word for hours of sweating, scooping, and slinging burgers and fries alongside my surly teenage co-workers. I commiserated and laughed with Juan the grill cook, a sweet-natured man about my age who sent his earnings back home to his wife and children in Mexico.

Twenty summers before, I'd been the teenager scooping ice cream at the original Haagen Dazs store on Christopher Street in Manhattan's West Village, handing cones to buff leather-clad gentlemen with thick mustaches and eyes only for each other. Maybe I liked the carefree nature of a summer job as a brief respite from adult responsibilities? When I tied on my white apron each day in Nashville, there wasn't that lure of temporary jobs in academia, real estate, or the world of business that said, "Why only be a temp? Give up your foolish music dreams and come work for us...FOREVER!" My music life had been so insecure and financially precarious that, at times, I was afraid the lure of a steady paycheck would just be too tempting.

I liked how scooping ice cream at the Dairy Dip was seasonal work that would end after Labor Day.

Another thing I appreciated about the Dairy Dip: ice cream made people happy. Children's eyes would shine; adults', too. Businessmen with their brick-like cellphones, sweating in dress shirts and voluminous khaki trousers, turned into beatific little boys when they gripped a cone and turned their heads sideways to lap up the drips. "Mmm, good!" they'd say, and I could almost forget they were probably Republicans.

I was still getting settled in Nashville. Anyone I knew in town eventually pulled up in their car for an ice cream or burger at the Dairy Dip, but unlike temping at Sony Music back in NYC—where I'd hidden in back of the elevator to avoid running into music biz people I knew—I didn't mind having this Charlotte Avenue window onto what began to take shape in my mind as a community: guitar players, fellow songwriters, and music publishers. I didn't mind if they saw me with hamburger grease and chocolate ice cream smeared across my front. I felt proud to help a friend realize an ambitious dream that benefited everybody.

Claire and her husband Greg Trooper hit on the idea of putting on live music in the parking lot. A P.A. system was set up next to the picnic tables for John Prine's birthday party. A friend and supporter of Claire and Greg's, Prine brought Greg on tour to open for him, a huge vote of confidence coming from an important folk performer. Prine had the dream singer/songwriter career: love and respect from fans and fellow musicians over his decades of crafting classic songs, for the simple act of being himself onstage and on record. He was kind of a patron saint of Nashville.

The summer humidity had lifted, and the air was full of fall energy: kids back to school, autumn touring starting up again. Folks grabbed burgers and Cokes, and musician pals started cranking out cover songs. "Get Amy out here!" somebody shouted. I came out from behind the counter in my apron and Greg handed me an acoustic guitar.

"I'll be back in about three minutes!" I shouted to my teenage co-worker who was struggling to fill orders alone. First, I played "Cynically Yours," a song I'd started writing as a temp in the CBS Legal Department in New York City, finished at a temp position at Vanderbilt Medical Center in Nashville, and recorded for *The Sugar Tree*. Working to make ends meet had been a big part of my artist life, and I'd tried to not let it ever stop me from creating. I hated to think financial challenges might even be the fuel that kept me creating, because that meant I could never stop scrambling. I wasn't thinking any of this in the parking lot, just "John Prine's here so I better be good."

Beneath the big yellow Krystal sign shining down from next door, I played my song and Prine laughed and cheered. "That's a good song right there," he said. I felt like he'd blessed me.

Next time the guys were set up for another night of covers, I asked if they knew Wreckless Eric's song "Whole Wide World." "It's only got two chords," I said. Like "Louie Louie," every musician sort of knew the song—garage, punk, and new wave records were a secret handshake for a certain type of musician drawn to Nashville. That place where the wit and simplicity of classic country intersects with the early rock and roll attributes of punk was a good, if slightly exclusive, place to be. Bill Lloyd; Steve Allen from Tulsa via L.A. power pop outfit 20/20; Dave Jacques who played bass with Prine—we chugged through the first two verses of "Whole Wide World" before things kicked into higher gear for the chorus.

We messed up the two extra beats in the chorus but redeemed ourselves and ended on a celebratory note. That song—romantic and rogue—had a magical power to lift an audience. I didn't realize when I started sticking it into my set, any time it felt like I could use a friend onstage, just where it might lead. For the moment, it just felt like the song and I were meant to be together.

Later in the evening, after locking up the Dairy Dip, I pedaled my bike a few blocks over to our sweet rental house on Nevada Avenue where Hazel was doing her homework, and I thought how living in Nashville was going to be alright.

A few days later, the landlord called to tell me they'd decided to sell the place. We had less than a month to find somewhere else to live.

One of the best things about the next place I found was that it had a front porch swing. If I could've sat on that swing forever, with my daughter next to me or at least in the house happily listening to music or watching TV, everything would've been perfect. Except I wanted more, so much more.

Grantland Avenue was a two-block long street in a historic neighborhood called Woodland In Waverly, bordered on one end by utilitarian Bradford Avenue and on the other by a mansion called the Demonbreun Inn. Franklin Road, a busy thoroughfare, ran parallel, with an alleyway shielding us from the noise. We moved our stuff across town in the Aerostar and a U-Haul with help from Paul—he and I were still casual enough for his help to feel like a favor from a friend and not the obligation of a partner. He clued me in to the hidden gems nearby: long-running music club Douglas Corner; Arnold's Country Kitchen, a well-loved meat and three; and also the seedy side that wasn't immediately obvious: a surplus of massage parlors fronting Franklin Road. Those establishments, shorthand for brothels, dotting the stretch between our house and downtown would soon be shut down for good by a city government primed for change. They looked almost quaint with their low-key signs: Dottie's; Menages; Sunny's. Another transitional neighborhood. The tawdry grit helped me feel at home.

Most of the houses on Grantland were early twentieth century wooden affairs: Queen Anne, classical revival, or Craftsman bungalows with gently sloping roofs, columned front porches, and walkways lined with spiky green monkey grass. A few of the neighboring houses were single-story brick duplexes, making the street a cross section of early eras of the town, frozen at about 1962. Our rental was a mint green duplex, and Hazel and I occupied the larger unit, with attic converted to a second bedroom and full bath. The other tenant was a polite single woman a little younger than me who worked full-time and kept to herself, making her the perfect duplex neighbor.

Birds—so many birds—sang in the morning. Next door was a mustard-colored two-family with mud brown trim whose inhabitants came and went at all times of the day and night. It wasn't a crack house, though a few of those existed just to the east. Our neighbors were trashy in a genial way, like the constant hum of I-65 just beyond the backyards one street over, and the weekend whine of Nashville Fairgrounds Speedway beyond.

Out on the front porch swing, the weather still warm though it was autumn, I read or wrote in my journal. *And swing*...Hazel was twelve, starting seventh grade at MLK Jr, Nashville's first secondary magnet school. It had to be better than Head.

Swing. I wrote song after song, played gig upon gig. Shopped at Kroger; bought a rake.

James the cat came into his own. He lounged calmly around the house when he wasn't roaming outdoors. We were frantic when he disappeared one day. Only in his absence did I feel his important place in our lives. He returned, badly beaten up, and Hazel and I wrapped him in a blanket and rushed him to the vet on foot. Our comrade fallen in the trenches, only James knew the life we'd left behind in Brooklyn, and the wistful, tentative joy we felt adapting to this new town. We were relieved to find out he would be okay, and chastened to learn he was hugely overweight. Through all my travels, the friends and acquaintances who'd stay for a week or two and help look after him couldn't resist his charms. We all overfed him.

My daughter took the upstairs bedroom at first — it had its own bathroom and loads of storage under the eaves. I was in the downstairs bedroom with a door that opened onto the backyard I rarely took advantage of, not sure how to make the outdoors nicer with lawn furniture or plants or flowers— and then there was the intense humidity and the bugs. Eventually we swapped; Hazel moved downstairs and I took the larger room at the top, which gave me space to set up my 4-track and writing desk. I loved looking out the window there onto Grantland below. I'd see my neighbor across the street start his car each morning by running alongside, and when the motor caught, he'd jump in and drive off. I cheered him on every time, and this made me feel part of the neighborhood, even though we never met.

Hazel and I still had the '20s enamel-topped table my mother gave me back in the early '80s. I'd moved it to the first apartment that was completely mine, the one on 14th Street in Manhattan where I'd made a family with Will and Hazel, and we'd brought it along to Brooklyn. Now it served as our dining table in the middle of the tall living/dining room/kitchen—part polished hardwood floor, part carpeting. Not gross carpet either, but classy Berber-style neutral, unthinkable in New York City. Look at us, I thought, living in a real grown-up kind of house.

Hazel and I rarely sat at the table to eat, preferring to bring our plates to the sofa and dine in front of the television, rickety metal folding trays in front of us. My mother gave me these trays from her antique shop, and like everything my mother scavenged and sold or passed on to me and my brothers, they had style beyond the use they were intended for. Each individual tray was a different vibrant color: red, chartreuse, yellow. They must have come from the '30s or '40s—pre-television. Maybe a posh family used them to hold peanuts and olives and cocktails as they sat around the living room listening to a radio program.

Me and Hazel's default shows were *The Simpsons*, *American Idol*, and *Seventh Heaven*, where a Midwestern reverend and his loopy wife wrangled a brood of seven kids. We loved to mock the warm, loving family with their everyday problems while we sat in front of the TV, our plates on the trays, screaming along to the acoustic guitar-driven theme song, shaking our heads at the smugness of it all. *The Simpsons* were so comfortingly *us*—they were every family—but the *Seventh Heaven* clan made us feel like we should be better.

For one night only, we sat down at the '20s table with our plates of chicken tenders, pasta, and broccoli.

"This is how the civilized people eat," I said. We chewed. I'd thought we could have a conversation, like the *Seventh Heaven* family did at their dinner table, noisily relating tales of their lives while they passed platters of food around. But Hazel and I had already talked about our days on the drive home from school. We talked all the time. Now, a knife scraped on a plate. I found myself looking longingly over at the television set.

Hazel saw me staring at the TV. "I'll get the trays," she said.

Well into fall, I walked in the early morning before heat and humidity set in. I drove out to Radnor Lake or traversed the alleys around Eighth Avenue, climbed up towards Twelve South past Dolly Parton's compound that looked like a girly Alamo and down around Sevier Park, breathing the sweet, doughy scent from Communion Bread Company on Gale Lane. I circled back past the Acuff-Rose building on Franklin and home. Maybe I'd imagined a different life for myself in Nashville, one where I was a professional songwriter, driving a better car, looking groomed and professional. Instead, I wore sweats and grubby old Keds and drove a thousand-dollar minivan. But most mornings I sat out on the front porch swing with a mug of coffee and thought, "Maybe today I'll write a song that changes everything."

Then, *swing*, early one morning the phone rang.

"Amy, it's your father." I set my coffee cup down on the cool wooden boards of the front porch. Ever since the phone call twelve years ago—my mother in a devastating car accident that shattered the security I'd been so lucky to have for twenty-nine years but never felt a drop of gratitude for, just assumed that's the way things should be—I always tried to prepare myself for bad news.

My dad said he was selling our childhood home and moving himself and my mother into an apartment at an independent living facility that could offer care for my mom if needed. He was, after all, in his mid-seventies. He was giving my brothers and me the chance to meet up at the old house in the suburbs south of Pittsburgh and take any meaningful items we'd like to keep—the rest would be tossed. I knew there were paintings I'd made for my parents that I felt obliged to hold onto. They weren't particularly good, but they'd become part of our family legacy and, in the way that paintings do, *felt* like they captured memories better than a photograph could.

And when it came to photographs, we had hundreds of slides. My dad was a decent photographer and Kodachrome was his film of choice, our childhood documented not with disposable, fading Instamatic snapshots but via color-drenched slides, carousels of them. For years, dragging out the slide projector and unfolding the metal pole and screen for a family viewing had become as familiar a part of growing up as the faux brick linoleum that covered the hallway and kitchen floors of a house I couldn't imagine another family ever living in.

So, one last time on Sleepy Hollow Road, we set up out on the driveway to project directly onto the back of the house. My dad had painted all the red brick white years ago, decreeing, "This way, there will always be a Republican in the white house." Haw haw. My dad was funny, when he wasn't pissed off. I'd eventually grow to appreciate his wit. Back in my forties, I felt nothing but impatience with him. Be sincere, I wanted to say. Be loving and warm. *Be like mom was.*

Someone grabbed a carousel and the show began. Slide shows were a kind of Russian roulette as nothing was catalogued, so we could get 1967 when I was still daddy's little princess, or any time after 1971 when I'd hit puberty and was the family pariah for my thick black eyeliner and wanton ways.

We were on the '70s. There were many shots of my brothers in Penguin jerseys and Pirate t-shirts, looking sweaty, throwing footballs and wiffle balls around the backyard. There were photos of them red-cheeked in the snow, building forts, or wearing hilariously short shorts and tube socks in summer. I finally shouted out, "Where am I? Wasn't I part of this family too?"

"There's your leg!" one of my brothers said helpfully, after a shot from a summer birthday party flashed larger than life on the back of the house. One of us dated the photo to be from about 1974, probably based on the number of rings on a tube sock. Back in those days, I was mostly absent, having just discovered sex and rock music. I had a boyfriend with a car, and when I wasn't sneaking into the house after a night of partying, I was nursing a hangover in my room or laying out at the public swimming pool working on my tan. Alongside my urgent artist dreams, maybe I had also always been deeply superficial.

When photos of me in a Jane Fonda shag or Farrah Fawcett waves appeared, the hoots of laughter made me sink down into my lawn chair as if I was sixteen all over again. I'd learned that going along with the joke was better than showing weakness and humiliation, but somehow back there on the driveway—where we'd all played together, shoveled snow, and I'd danced to Stevie Wonder at my first boy/girl party (where it had dawned on me I'd finally gotten my period)—I couldn't help regressing. I thought of the challenges and benefits of being the only girl with four brothers and a hard-to-please father, how many of my choices stemmed from that: men, rock music, bands.

My daughter kept supportively silent during the slide show except for an occasional muffled gasp. "You were a nice young lady," said my mother. I looked at the basketball net just above the garage doors, thinking how easy it had been to shoot baskets here with my brothers while we were growing up. I never realized until I left home that the net was a good foot lower than it should be. I wondered how many other things I'd thought I was better at than I actually was. And how useful a little self-belief would be in the areas where I actually deserved some and was lacking. Isn't life just so many adjustments for advantages and handicaps, real and imagined?"

One thing I did know, without any doubt, was that I could write songs. We drove back down to Nashville with my old paintings and a few choice pieces of family Pyrex and pewter in the back of the minivan. And just as I'd hoped for and staked everything on—enough to move me and Hazel halfway across the country—a few weeks later, I signed a publishing deal.

Chapter Eleven

One of the main reasons I moved to Nashville was the possibility of landing a publishing deal. It wasn't so much the money (though that would be nice) as the legitimacy I was seeking. A music industry vote of confidence that said my songs were valuable. I wish I'd thought creative accomplishments alone were enough, but I had a daughter to raise, and we needed money to live.

I'd tried back in New York, bringing tapes of my songs to Warner Chappell, one of the few major song publishers who'd even entertained the possibility of signing someone like me: that is, a singer/songwriter who wasn't likely to sell a huge amount of records, but might write songs other artists could record, and maybe even have hits with. And in the '90s, there were still those fluke moments where unlikely suspects hit the jackpot: Ben Folds, Liz Phair, Beck. All talented but uncategorizable. I'd received encouragement from Warner Chappell, but no deal.

In Nashville, songs opened doors. They were the lifeblood of the town, the engine that fueled the country music industry. Song publishing – that began with sheet music in the early part of the twentieth century and then encompassed performance royalties and mechanical licenses (the right to record a copyrighted piece of music) – was a legitimate business, and songwriters have long been drawn to Music City like hopeful starlets heading to Hollywood, to compete with the best.

I'd had a little interest from publishers so far: Reba's Starstruck, and an upstart company called Ten Ten, where I'd written with one of their writers, Stacey Earle, Steve's talented sister. I enjoyed artistic collaboration, had been happy in bands firing ideas off each other, and I liked writing with other writers. Co-writing was a huge part of Nashville songwriting, and not only for creative reasons. Two or three or four heads together could be better than one, but it also gave a song more parents to help the creation make its way out into the world.

Greg Trooper was the first person I knew who signed a publishing deal with Welk Music. Yes, *that* Welk. Lawrence Welk's song publishing company, run by the TV schmaltz king's son. I'd adored *The Lawrence Welk Show* when I was a kid, especially the dancing feet of Arthur Duncan. But all joking aside, Welk was a legitimate company, connected with the Vanguard jazz and Sugar Hill bluegrass labels. They had big success publishing writers like Kostas in the '80s, with his new traditional country songs like "Timber" and "Blame It On Your Heart," recorded by Patty Loveless, and "Oh What A Crying Shame," a hit for the Mavericks. Classic, undeniable songs any writer would be proud of. The kind I aimed to write.

Greg passed my albums on to Bob Kirsch, head of Welk's Nashville office, and Bob loved my songs. He was an old school music biz guy—wrote for *Billboard* before shifting to the business and publishing side of things. He had an intellectual bent that maybe made his belief a double-edged sword: would less cerebral types get what Bob naturally tuned into? Was he...too New York for Nashville?

I visited Welk's offices on 31st Avenue off West End, a mile and a half from the heart of Music Row on 16th and 17th Avenues. Maybe the oblique location was intentional, telling the town that Welk held itself apart from the commercial songwriting world. Perhaps here, artistry was king?

I was greeted in the front office by Tudie, the office manager. She was pure Tennessee from her year-round suntan to the Titans football jersey. Bob and I chatted in his office and then walked out to his Cadillac to drive several blocks around Nashville's one-way system to reach the Tin Angel, a block and a half away on foot.

This would become our monthly routine. In the car, Bob played me a disc he was excited about, usually a classic I might have missed like Fred Neil or Dion. He also handed me a book or two, asking, "Have you read this?" Bob was hip in a way that came from years of being in the music biz for the right reasons: he loved artists, words, and music. In Nashville, that love could be put to practical use.

I'd always heard, "Don't give up your publishing unless you really really need the money." I didn't know anyone this didn't apply to—chances were if you were looking for a publishing deal you DID need the money. I'd also heard, "Don't take the money unless it's a life-changing amount of money." When Bob Kirsch offered me a deal with Welk, I was in debt, renting a house I couldn't afford, and working at the Dairy Dip while trying to write songs and tour.

So, when Welk offered me a decent advance and monthly draw, that was most definitely life-changing. I typed up Schedule A myself on our home computer and attached it to the contract: the songs I'd already written, cataloguing a lifetime of struggles, hopes, and dreams in melody and rhyme. "All I Want" and "Don't Break The Heart" felt like pleas to the universe when my marriage was failing. Others—like "War Between The Sheets" or "You Oughta Be Against The Law"— never existed beyond my cassette and CD archive, but the titles alone had value and potential. As much as I could really use the money, I hoped Welk was signing me because they believed they'd earn it back through convincing other artists to record my songs. All it took was one song, I'd heard, and other cuts would follow.

I held the contract in my hands, the weight of all those pages and the legalese ("each party acknowledges and agrees..." etc.) familiar from my years spent temping in entertainment company law offices. This time it was my name listed as "party." I felt hopeful but scared. What if "the one" never came? I was agreeing to turn in a certain number of songs for the two years of the term (with option for a third). At least I did know of one artist who'd always be open to recording the songs I wrote: me.

In the Tin Angel, a comfortingly retro bar/restaurant with tin ceiling and exposed brick, everyone seemed to know Bob Kirsch. He wasn't the trendiest guy in the room, but he was a man of substance who believed in art that stood the test of time; artists and writers who created work both new and lasting. We toasted my deal with glasses of iced tea—gone were the days of the Nashville liquid lunch. Bob drove me back to my minivan, and as we said goodbye he handed me a CD of *Small Town Talk* by Bobby Charles, like a benediction. Go forth, write some potential hits but—be real; be true.

As I wound around the hills to pick Hazel up from school, I smiled and thought, "Writing songs is my job now."

So, five days a week I drove Hazel to MLK. The school sat in the shadow of a towering brick smokestack with freight trains running nearby; railroad tracks criss-crossed all the older parts of Nashville, but you couldn't actually catch a passenger train anywhere. Union Station downtown was an imposing stone structure boasting a posh hotel, but it hadn't seen a passenger train in decades. I appreciated the lost Atlantis mystique of old Nashville, the ghosts of what had been, but at the same time wished it possessed a few more benefits of modern urban living. They called Nashville a city, but in the early 2000s that felt like a stretch. The Pittsburgh Pirates farm team, the Sounds, played in a stadium well below the standard of every other ballpark in the country—but what other stadium had a guitar-shaped scoreboard? The balance between old treasures and big-ticket improvements was a precarious one I saw on full display any time I set out from the house.

After dropping off Hazel, it was time to write. Most working days started with coffee; there were two places in Nashville circa 2000. Bongo Java, situated in a cozy old house near Belmont University, was owned by a guy who'd relocated from Chicago, and was one of the few places in town where you could buy a copy of *The New York Times* (or better yet, find a free discarded one on a table). Fido, in Hillsboro Village, was a good spot for meeting up. It had a runway-length walk from the register to the counter, so more people could scope out who you were and who you were with. Getting coffee was social hour—a chance to run into people, share gossip, and tout any gigs you had coming up in or out of town. "How were the gigs?" and "When do you head out?" were standard conversation starters.

Random encounters were one of the highlights of getting coffee, but when it came to songwriting nothing was left to chance. Appointments to write were a regular thing. I managed one a day, starting about 10 AM, leaving time to grab lunch before I needed to pick Hazel up at school at 3 PM (no school bus at MLK Magnet). The hardcore pros might have two sessions a day. I told myself it was okay if my second appointment was with my myself.

Bill Lloyd was one of the first writers I met when I'd first visited Nashville five or six years earlier. I admired his tireless work ethic and positive vibe. Bill had written a mind-boggling number of songs. He maintained a running list with lyrics in a binder, and it made practical sense: songwriting is an art – it's magic and alchemy – but it was also a business that could pay the bills, and a methodical approach made sense. If you write what feels like an instant hit or classic, but find you can't remember the words or melody or chords, did the song ever even exist? I aspired to get a better filing system for my writing.

I was awed by Bill's guitar playing and the grown-up ranch house he and his wife owned just south of town. He was liked and respected by both the commercial country and more idiosyncratic pop contingents in town. When we sat down to write in Bill's office, we nearly always came up with something good: I recorded one of our co-writes, "Stop Showing

Up In My Dreams," for *The Sugar Tree*—such a fun song I couldn't have written on my own. If we were lacking in ideas, he always had a cool guitar figure or chord progression on standby. This kind of professionalism was part of what attracted me to Nashville. I wanted to bust out of my shambolic indie "Hey, if it happens, it happens" ways.

Bill DeMain and I connected through Bug Music, grassroots song publishing administrators who fostered relationships between their writers. He was a fellow Burt Bacharach fan and devotee of sophisticated '60s pop music and aesthetics. His band, Swan Dive, recorded with Brad Jones and he frequently wrote with Jill Sobule, a songwriter and performer I adored. Jill took the job opening for Warren Zevon after me—I saw the show when they came through Nashville and was stunned when Jill brought Warren out in her set to cover the Johnny Cash/June Carter hit, "Jackson." I wished I had that kind of nerve and chutzpah.

Bill was a master of melody, artful chord changes, and clever lyrics. When we'd meet up to write, usually at Bill's apartment complex off West End Avenue, the first half hour of our session was devoted to my rants about dozy drivers and the lack of Italian food in Nashville. Bill moved to town in the late '80s but hailed from New Jersey so he understood those challenges.

Next, we'd move on to romantic travails. Internet dating was still in its infancy, and so provided a fresh vein—the results didn't necessarily make it into our songs, but amused us so much that the downstairs neighbor had to pound on his ceiling with a broom handle to quiet our cries of laughter.

In the early part of my relationship with Paul I vented about L.A. Sam and what a jerk he was. Pillow talk conversation – how awful it felt to be used and taken for granted.

"Where is he? I'll kill him," said Paul, half-joking.

"I can give you his address," I replied. We laughed and laughed. The next morning, I met up with Bill and he had a chord sequence and the perfect bossa nova groove he'd been kicking around. We were both devoted fans of *The Sopranos*, then in its second season. Murder felt natural—hilarious even. The beauty of songwriting is you can exact revenge in verse and chorus to make other people—and yourself— feel better... over and over again.

Keep It To Yourself

You say you'd like to kill the man who broke my heart
You don't think he should be allowed to live
You say you want to shoot the dude who screwed me up
Me I'm trying so hard to forgive

But here's his address, here's his picture
Here's the make and model of his car
He works until four thirty
Then he hangs out at the topless bar
With a girl on each arm
If he should come to harm
Just keep it to yourself

Remember how he cheated and he lied to me?
You told me that it makes you lose your head
I hear they're pouring concrete on Route 33
I don't think you should do those things you said

But here's his address, here's his picture
Here's his pager number and his cell
He works out at the health club
And he really likes to watch himself
Flexing in the mirror
If he should disappear
Just keep it to yourself

I like the way that you take care of me
I like the way you say that you'll take care of things

So here's his address, here's his picture...

Some mornings I'd pull up in front of Joy Lynn White's house around 11 AM. It would already be hot, bees buzzing, birds going crazy in the trees on her street of '30s bungalows. No sidewalks, just metal mailboxes on posts; older cars. It was a short street just up the hill behind Belmont Boulevard, one of the nicest thoroughfares in town, the one newcomers used until they figured out the cut-throughs and shortcuts.

I'd grab my guitar out of the back seat of the Aerostar and approach

Joy's front door. No need to knock, as two dogs would start barking, a cat circling on the hardwood floor.

"Hey!" said Joy. She and I would talk about her visits to her mother's place in East Tennessee, or what was going on around town, as she heated up coffee in the microwave. The bright yellow walls and red trim of her '50s-style kitchen were a perfect backdrop for Joy's red hair and film star good looks. She was the perfect intersection of cute girl next door and dangerous femme fatale. "You got anything you wanna work on?" she'd ask. I'd think for a second, but then Joy would start telling me about this idea she had for a song.

It was hard not to be drawn in by her fiery mane and tough attitude on the cover of *Wild Love* when I'd first discovered Joy's music at Sony. It was impossible not to be knocked out by her voice; it hit right in the gut with hurt and power. As I'd gotten to know her, I'd learned she was also a genuine character who'd scored some commercial country success in spite of her outspoken, untameable persona. Lacking the calculating, level focus to play the game, Joy reminded me of that mix of indomitable spirit and vulnerability in artists like George Jones or Loretta Lynn that drew me to country music in the first place. Without a Mooney Lynn or Pappy Dailey, she had to fend for herself in a world that didn't always appreciate blunt honesty.

"How's that smart girl of yours doing?" Joy would ask. There were colleagues and co-writers in Nashville; collaborators and musicians you hired. And then there were people who'd loan you their car, babysit your kid, cry on your shoulder and let you cry on theirs. Joy and I wrote good songs together, and singing with her elevated my singing, but knowing I had a girlfriend in that town meant so much more.

Chapter Twelve

I'd achieved one of my biggest dreams, a publishing deal, just a little over a year after moving to Nashville. There were still gigs to play, though. I'd gotten a foot in the "Writer" door but was still pulled towards the "Artist" one. It had yielded just enough to keep me in the sometimes dank vestibule where booking the show was only the first step, and attracting an audience was never a given. The new album had come out and reviews were good. I had a run of dates booked for the northeast when a call came from the talent booker for *Late Night with Conan O'Brien* —their scheduled musical guest had canceled. Could I be in New York City at 2 PM on Thursday?

I was scheduled to start the tour in good old Cleveland on Wednesday night. Luckily Thursday's gig was in Manhattan at Joe's Pub—no need to cancel either show. (I hate to cancel when someone's had enough faith in me to book a gig.) We could stop and sleep for a few hours after the Cleveland show, drive the eight hours to NYC, setup and soundcheck, do the TV taping in front of a live audience, then head downtown for a line check and gig at 8 PM. No problem! Maybe it's best when opportunities sneak up on you, so there's no time to fret about them. Just a couple of tour stops: playing Beachland in front of thirty people, Conan in front of 2 million.

Business was as usual at the Beachland—a combination of "Why do I bother?" with "I love these people and never want to do anything else!" We drove a while afterwards, checked into a motel on the Ohio/Pennsylvania border and slept for a few hours. At 6 AM, Paul, guitarist Steve Allen, bass player Lorne Rall, and I were checking out when we saw a weary-looking Paul Cebar checking in. The Minneapolis-based musician was on his way to Chicago after a gig somewhere back east. We all wished each other well, and laughed blearily as we piled into the Aerostar. I'd

made a point not to gloat—yeah, good luck with your club gig, we're going to be on national television! Things could just as easily have been
the reverse.

We plowed across Pennsylvania and New Jersey straight to Manhattan, thankfully arriving between morning rush hour and afternoon
gridlock, the numbered streets and avenues, stoplights and taxi horns
greeting me like family. I stopped at my old bandmate Amanda Uprich-
ard's clothing shop downtown on Lafayette Street—the guys sat in the
van with the motor running while I ran in to pick up a dress to wear and
Amanda gave me an encouraging hug and wished me luck. We worked
so hard for such a long time to get somewhere with our band, the Shams;
wearing one of Amanda's creations on TV would feel like having her
hand on my shoulder.

There was a deluxe spread of sandwiches, fruit, and cookies backstage at the *Late Night* studio. They could only work one of my musicians into their studio setup, so I asked Steve Allen to accompany me on
"Cynically Yours." The Late Night band — Max Weinberg, Jimmy Vivino,
and company—had worked up a note-for-note recreation of the doo wop-
style backing on the album version of the song. I was amazed how good
they sounded when we did a brief run-through. What pros they were.

I put on the dress, sheer black chiffon with subtle pink polka dots,
then waited and waited backstage for hair and makeup—it felt like showtime was minutes away when I was finally called in. "And what was the
thinking behind this?" The hairdresser held a wispy piece of hair between his elegant fingers, as if bad layers were catching. He twisted it
this way and that, fluffed my too-short bangs, tried to pouf up the back
and let out a huge sigh. He widened his eyes at his own reflection in the
mirror: "I will do my best." I hadn't known when I got a bad haircut the
week before that I'd have to go on TV. It can take a while to find the right
haircutter when you move to a new town. Or it can take a while to figure
out who you're reinventing yourself as when you relocate. I was in a kind
of a *Malcolm In The Middle*'s mom crossed with Gram Parsons moment.

And in five minutes I was on television, holding a green Greco guitar
as Conan introduced me. We launched into "Cynically Yours" and I felt
magically composed, like I was in a trance. When the audience laughed
at the punchline at the end of the first verse, it was a sound I'd heard all
my life from the other side of the TV—the studio audience—and I had
them. For a second I felt like Rodney Dangerfield. I didn't think I could
ever experience anything so perfect again—or maybe I hoped that this
was only the first of many experiences on live television. Clearly, Conan

would decide to have me as a regular on his show. We glided through the song, and then he invited me to sit on the *Late Night* couch. I kept wishing my mother was still capable of watching late night television. When I eventually asked my dad if he'd seen the show, his only response was, "Why didn't you play one of your *nice* songs?"

We packed up after Conan admired the Greco and brought out his prized Gretsch to compare.

I told him how when my brother bought the Greco down in Tennessee, we'd been so clueless about guitars we thought it WAS a Gretsch, and the salesperson in the pawn shop hadn't done anything to dispel that notion.

Then it was down to Joe's Pub where I think we played a pretty solid show, never easy without a soundcheck. Afterwards, in Ray's Pizza on Sixth Avenue, I saw myself on the wall-mounted TV, strumming my green guitar in the black dress with pink polka dots I was still wearing. Another customer looked up at the TV. "Huh, that's you," he said, then turned back to the guy behind the counter. "Gimme a slice, make it hot." Just another day in New York City, where they see it all, all the time.

Later, back in the nice midtown hotel room I'd booked at a bargain rate through Priceline, Paul and I lay next to each other in strained silence. Out on the road, beyond the bubble of Nashville where he was the old hand and I was the novice, the balance was tipped, and it wasn't exactly an aphrodisiac to be your boyfriend's boss. I felt bad he didn't get to play drums with me on TV, and maybe we weren't comfortable enough yet as a couple to roll with the weird workplace dynamic, but it felt like something shifted, and before we'd even fully started—been through Thanksgiving, Christmas, his birthday, my birthday together—our romance was doomed. By morning we were laughing and joking. Paul was a truly funny, entertaining guy, but my awkward ambition crossed with his occasionally brooding Welsh temperament spelled trouble ahead.

My band and I played Boston, Philadelphia, and then suburban DC with Sid Griffin and Western Electric — it had only been a few months since I'd toured with them in the U.K. We greeted each other like old Army buddies: "Remember Preston? And Sheffield! God, that was hard, and cold, but...I still wouldn't trade it." It seems the more underwhelming the gig experience, the more profoundly musicians relish the memory. When you were suffering, that's when you really knew you were alive.

Out west to California with a completely different band, and back through the Midwest with Paul and the guys, and then a southern tour with Will

Kimbrough and his band. They were all great players—younger than me but with years of experience. Will hazed me one night by offering to change the broken guitar string on my acoustic mid-set, and returning the guitar with one of my gold slingback shoes hanging from the headstock. I was developing a few necessary survival skills: don't take yourself too seriously, and be prepared to laugh through the embarrassment— things I should've learned but hadn't quite gotten the hang of growing up with four brothers.

New York City, January 2001. West 3rd Street was covered in snow. Not the bright, pristine blanket that cheers up the whole city, but the crusting-with-grey kind that's sat around for a few days too many. I didn't mind, though. I was just so happy to be back in New York. There were seasons down south, but the winters weren't cold enough to really punctuate the beginning of a new year. I missed the enforced camaraderie that followed a good snowstorm.

I pulled the Aerostar into a loading zone outside the Village Underground club and put my flashers on. I could imagine Bob Dylan and Ramblin' Jack Elliott hanging around on the sidewalk out front, and remembered meeting Odetta at Folk City just next door back in the early '80s, when Last Roundup played one of the Music For Dozens nights there. Even twenty years ago, I'd gotten the feeling we were just one more layer in the musical strata of the city. There'd been folk and punk and new folk and indie and anti-folk all right here on this street. I still liked to think I was part of that continuum.

My band—Paul, Jon Graboff, Pat Sansone, and Joe McGinty— had begun this run with a rehearsal in the city, then worked our way up to the New York gig with shows in Northampton and a ski resort in Vermont. We had clicked as a team now and easily started unloading equipment and hauling amps, guitars, and drums downstairs into the club. Then the manager led me upstairs to the dressing room at the back, enthusing about the incredible Patti Smith show the night before.

"Patti and her band, here?" I asked. The last place I'd seen her was Central Park in the mid-'90s, her onstage return to New York after years in Michigan as a wife and mother. Newly-widowed, she'd held the crowd spellbound in heat and humidity so intense Patti stopped her set on hearing a baby cry out, to ask if baby and mother had enough water to drink. I'd realized seeing her back then how much I'd missed her. As an artist and performer there was really no one like her: poet, rocker, shaman, and also a mom. Artists are markers for our own lives. Could I ever be that for someone else? I hoped so.

I carried my suitcase upstairs to the dressing room and was stunned by the gorgeous floral arrangement—white roses, hydrangeas, dusky greenery. For me? And there was a deli tray: cheese, bread, cold cuts, and a massive fruit bowl. I grabbed a banana, thinking, "At last—I've arrived." All those years playing shows while living in New York, it took moving away to merit such a luxe spread. I deserved it, didn't I?

Then I noticed the meat seemed to be curling at the edges. The flowers drooped slightly, and the assortment of chocolates looked picked over. The manager swept in with a bus boy and started removing the trays.

"Sorry about all this," he said. "Like I told you, Patti Smith was here last night. Whoever was working the show didn't get in here to clean up after, so let me just—" He dumped the deli tray into a big black trash bag. He saw me looking wistfully at the fruit bowl and the bouquet. "Hey, you can keep the fruit and flowers if you want. Oh, and there's some bottles of water for you in the fridge."

I parked the van in a garage, gasping at the big city prices. Locals prided themselves on knowing every side street and regulation so they'd never have to pay for parking. I remembered how having your vehicle towed for not paying the inevitable tickets that piled up was almost a badge of honor—in New York, life was always save a penny to spend a dollar. Or save a dollar to spend twenty.

My band and I set up and later that night played a great set to a full house. The warmth of the New York crowd wrapped around me like a favorite thrift shop overcoat. When they called us back for an encore, we winged our way through a version of Kirsty MacColl's "They Don't Know." It had been hard to come to grips with her tragic death just a few weeks before. I was still young enough that losing people I looked up to hadn't become a regular occurrence. I'd always felt a kinship with her through the humor in her songs, and the mix of strength and vulnerability in her voice. Reaching to hit that falsetto note in the bridge of her song—"Ba-aby!" – was like a salute to the heavens. It was one way to say thank you.

After the show, I stuffed fruit from Patti Smith's rider into my bag, but left her flowers behind. What was I going to do, prop them on the dashboard of the van? We had a long drive back to Nashville.

Heading out of Manhattan late that Saturday night—just Paul and me, having left the rest of the band there in the city where they lived—the stop and start of traffic into the Holland Tunnel felt as familiar as breathing.

When we climbed the approach to the turnpike in New Jersey, I took a last look at the Statue of Liberty, the lights of downtown, and the Twin Towers, and wondered if I'd ever get used to seeing them in the rear view mirror.

Chapter Thirteen

I parked the Aerostar in the nether regions of Queens near JFK to fly over to the U.K. for another solo tour. It was not exactly convenient to Nashville, but I'd coordinated a short run of Northeast gigs on either end of that overseas trip. After the U.K., I'd finish up with a festival in Rome, then fly back to New York to open shows for Richard Shindell, a deep and acerbic singer/songwriter with a devoted following on the folk circuit. I was always scrambling to make this connect to that.

My excitement about the upcoming gigs almost paled next to the promise of a Business Class flight, courtesy of a frequent flying fan who'd become a friend. The ticket even included access to the British Airways lounge—I checked in, ready to assert my right to be there in jeans, boots, guitar case, and scraggly hair—in amongst the business-suited and well-heeled. I marveled at the comprehensive buffet, comfy chairs, and couches; bottled water everywhere you turned and a FREE BAR. I settled into a freshly-upholstered armchair with my plate of food, glass of sparkling wine, and cup of coffee, and practically swooned at the pile of crisp daily newspapers and glossy magazines of every description artfully splayed on a coffee table. I leaned forward to load up on reading matter.

Then everything felt like a sad cartoon. The *New York Post*, *Times*, and *Daily News*, and the British papers the *Guardian* and *Independent* featured headlines like a sock to the gut: "Punk Icon Joey Ramone Dead at 49."

Joey, gone. Not yet fifty, he'd felt like an elder since I'd discovered the Ramones back in 1976, when he was twenty-five years old to my seventeen. To say we all looked up to him was true and an understatement: at six feet six inches, literally everyone looked up to him, but his stature was broad and wide too, as catalyst and frontman for what many considered the first punk band, fast and loud but with wit and a calculated aesthetic. I'd never known him but seeing the Ramones at CBGB had been my portal to the developing New York scene of the '70s. My treasured memory of an early '90s in the round show at the Bottom Line—A Bunch of Songwriters Sitting Around Singing—is Joey sitting next to Lucinda Williams, singing "Be My Baby" with an acoustic guitar, his sweet, gawky fandom and sincere croon on full display without the buzzsaw of the band.

I'd even met him once, in the lounge of Coyote, the rehearsal and recording studio in Williamsburg where the Shams recorded our album *Quilt*. He'd been cute and shy, or maybe I'd been the shy one, and all I could think and remark on at the time was that he resembled Amanda, the cool, six-foot-tall, black-haired siren of my band.

In the airport lounge, I read about the lymphoma that killed Joey, and details of his young life I'd never known. A few businessmen (the only other woman in the lounge greeted me from behind the check-in desk—Business Class felt like a boys' club) sat engrossed in their papers or prepared for meetings. In 2001, the BA Lounge wasn't a great place to find a kindred spirit to share the news with. The Ramones were icons to a certain type of music fan; they had yet to become t-shirt shorthand for alternative. "Long live Joey Ramone, gone too soon," I wanted to speak or shout out loud, but I just thought it.

On the plane, I snuggled into my private fully-reclining seat in free socks, eye mask, and earplugs after spritzing myself with the complimentary Molton Brown toiletries and silently toasted Joey with my champagne flute.

After a run of gigs in England and Scotland, I was on my way to Rome. I'd been accepted to play a festival of Women in Music, put on by a former British opera star who married an Italian count and started a foundation to support female musicians. A week before, she'd emailed to ask if I could bring a few items she couldn't find in Italia (pre-Amazon): two Spode teacups in a particular pattern available at Harrod's or Fortnum & Mason's (not exactly frequent stops for touring musicians); a particular type of Cadbury's chocolate bar, and as much Berocca Vitamin C tablets as I could carry. She promised to reimburse me. I thought the opera world must be a lot different from the troubadour game and did my best, but the Spode would have to wait.

I landed at an airport way outside of Rome, without lire or even an Italian phrasebook, having arranged to be picked up by the Contessa's driver. He didn't materialize and the only way I could manage to travel to Rome was via taxi. The rogue took me the long way around; I gasped when the Coliseum came into view. The Contessa—regal, tall, and pale with once-lustrous red hair coiled into a chignon—met me at the hotel and was aghast at the fare on the meter. She demanded to know why I hadn't waited for her driver. He'd only been delayed an hour or two... Welcome to Italy.

The next day I played for a fabulous crowd in an ancient courtyard while the Contessa stood to the right of the stage acting out my lyrics for the Italians. The women in the audience mobbed me when I finished. There are days in life as a musician where you get confirmation that you're on the right path. It might not lead to anything—I never played Italy again, the Contessa passed away years ago, I doubt anyone remembers that day—but right then and there you have to enjoy the moment as its own reward. I was taken all around the city, ending the night with gelato and a peek at the Vatican dome through the keyhole of Santa Maria del Priorato on the Aventine Hill. I felt it was my birthright, or at least my Italian mom's, to enjoy everything about Rome: I drank wine, I bought shoes, I bought sunglasses, not knowing how much I was spending and not caring. All those lire felt like play money, worthless except for what it paid for in the here and now.

But then I came down with the flu. I was feverish; delirious even. I managed to catch my cheap flight back to London, where I'd booked a Paddington hotel to spend one last night in England before catching another flight to New York. I'd imagined myself strolling around this familiar part of London, visiting old haunts from when I'd lived near Queensway twenty years before, enjoying one last curry. The best I could manage was to find strong cold medicine called Night Nurse and crawl back to lay shivering in my sad room like a desperate character in a Jean Rhys novel. It was scary to be alone and ill so far from home. I suddenly felt very vulnerable and American, in spite of my chic sunglasses.

The British Airways flight attendants tucked blankets around me on the return flight to JFK as my teeth chattered, and I wondered how I'd make it through the next week of shows with Richard Shindell. I managed to score some Prednisone from a doctor in New Jersey and carried on playing, wondering if Joey had done it this way—working, not letting the cracks show. I felt pretty certain he had. This was the life we'd chosen. What didn't kill you made you stronger until... maybe it killed you.

Chapter Fourteen

I must have settled in. I was about to buy a house in Nashville.

I hadn't intended to buy a place so soon, or to be a landlord. But just like with our first rental, my landlords needed to sell—and it hadn't even been a year since Hazel and I moved in. I saw our possible future of moving vans and working out the layout of Kroger after Kroger until we'd lived in every part of Nashville. In New York City, tenants usually had some protection, but the Nashville rental market was a free-for-all. Who knew how much rent would cost for the next place we found? Between that, utilities, and frequent pricey repairs to the Aerostar, I was barely scraping by. Not to mention catching up on years of lax dental care. I'd never been great at money, so why start when I actually had some?

"Can't you find a cheaper house?" my father asked when I sought his help with the down payment. The owners/sellers had offered to finance—even though I had the first steady monthly paycheck of my entire working life, I still didn't qualify for a mortgage through the bank. Everyone said the cheapest places were over in East Nashville, past the new stadium where the Titans played football. But the schools in East Nashville were even worse than the ones on the west side of town. It would still be another year or two before voters amended the state constitution to allow a lottery to raise much-needed funding for schools in Tennessee.

My dad made a good point, but I was so used to battling with him I didn't bother to consider looking around. So then—I owned a house. But I didn't know anything about owning a house. This one had been beautifully renovated and maintained by Mark and Donna, the previous owners, and rent from the attached unit would help with my monthly mortgage payments and loan payment to my dad. My tenant was so sweet, quiet, and employed that it never occurred to me to raise her rent even a little bit. I never asked to see her small, tidy apartment until I needed to get in to make a repair. When the air conditioner malfunctioned, the repair guy waved a gummed-up, fuzzy filter at me. "Y'all need to change these once in a while," he said.

"Umm...what do you call that, just so I know what to ask for?" Decades of New York City apartment living left me ill-prepared for all the issues that go along with owning a house with a yard. It was a big day when I found my way to Home Depot for the first time and bought a lawn mower.

Being my own landlord was a lot to balance with frequent touring. Flights, drives, and gigs were a lot to balance along with parenting, but at least we had a secure base at last. Nobody could kick us out, unless I fell behind on the payments. So, I needed to work harder, push more.

A tour on the west coast tested me and Paul to the breaking point. Somehow, we were okay back in the cozy confines of Nashville, but touring as a couple – when I tried to be road manager, bandleader, and artist all at once – was a brutal test of our generally easy-going relationship. I felt like Paul was on my side, but it felt hard for me to be on his when I had to keep putting myself first. We arrived in L.A. and the rental car I hired at LAX immediately broke down on the way to the soundcheck that was meant to serve as rehearsal with guitarist Tony Gilkyson and bass player Kip Boardman. We ran through the songs at the Silver Lake venue Spaceland, then sat and waited for Budget to deliver a working car while I felt all my dreams of a perfect L.A. show evaporate: no time to return to the hotel to shower, change clothes, or put on makeup. I bitched, fretted, and complained to Paul before and after the sparsely-attended show until he turned on me, unleashing venom and fury I never suspected lay bottled up inside his gentle exterior. Back at the hotel we sobbed and held each other. Were we breaking up? We still had a week of shows to play.

The second gig went better, and we headed towards Reno, checking into a Super Eight outside Bakersfield. I'd sprung for plane tickets for the other guys, convinced I needed to treat musicians as well as possible, maybe a result of being married to a sideman for years—I'd heard every complaint and failing but forgot the artists Will worked with usually had management, tour managers, real label support behind them. Maybe I was afraid the guys wouldn't think I was worth working with if I didn't pamper them a little—what was that I said about loyalty either being earned or bought? I didn't figure out till years later that part of a musician's reward was playing good songs with an artist they respected.

I flailed around sleepless in the motel bed, worrying about Hazel back at her father's depressing apartment complex in Nashville, and what the rest of the West Coast gigs would be like. We needed to start driving in a little while – Bakersfield to Reno was a seven- or eight-hour drive. Oh, why hadn't we flown too? But then I would've needed to find amps and drums up north. There was no easy way. Through the thin motel wall, I heard the same two bass notes over and over again. Music was tormenting me. I couldn't stand it any longer.

"Paul, the person in the next room has been playing this same Waylon Jennings song for over an hour. I'm losing my mind!"

"That," said Paul, laying on his back and smiling up at the ceiling, "is the sound of a man snoring." We laughed and laughed, and my angst faded. The rest of the trip was a success: gigs full, magic onstage as Tony, Kip, Paul, and I clicked in the van and as a band. Paul and I made up.

I was losing money out on the road, what with airfares, renting vans, and paying a band, but I was making progress, too, connecting with audiences through new songs that were almost eclipsing the old ones I thought were my classics. Nashville was having a positive effect: not quite twenty years since I wrote my first song, I felt like I was beginning to develop as a songwriter.

How lucky was I, though, to have been a part of that freewheeling '70s, '80s and '90s New York City scene that gave me the confidence to push my ideas out there without any technical ability? I owed New York a lot.

Then I ached to get back there like you'd rush to a loved one in a crisis.

It was September 11, 2001.

I'd flown from LaGuardia Airport to Nashville the night of September 10th, in love with New York City and happy to still feel a part of it. I'd played a good short run of shows backed by local musician pals, finishing up with a rocking show at Maxwell's in Hoboken. The one thing I couldn't help noticing and remarking upon at the end of the trip was how kind everyone had been. Maybe it was the happiness I felt connecting with old friends and fans through music—not for where it would get me. Just to be where still felt like home.

On that familiar stage, so hot and unventilated I'd had to take off my shirt and play in a camisole, I'd found a moment of clarity: this, just this.

Chords, volume, and melody. Words, rhythm, and harmony. Smiles, sweat; tears. Let me hold onto this.

And it was the way the city turned optimistic when summer was over and anything felt possible, even the Mets in the playoffs. I'd bought a pair of knee-high boots at one of the shoe stores on Broadway, the sales clerk working me, sharp and funny in that only-in-the-city way. Picked up a few cosmetics at Ricky's next store, entertained by drag queens parading in the false eyelash aisle. It had been one of those days New York gives you sometimes like a gift: you look good, you feel good, and even catcalls appear almost like a blessing: "Looking *fine*, mama!"

Back in Nashville buying coffee at Bongo Java the next morning, a barista said one of the twin towers had been hit by a plane. I said, "That's not funny, don't joke like that."

"I'm not joking," he said. Hazel was at school. When I got back to our house on Grantland, I knelt in front of the TV to watch the second tower fall. Two of my brothers lived in the city. I tried to call them and the lines were jammed. Another plane crashed in Pennsylvania, seventy miles from my dad and mom and brother Patrick in Pittsburgh. Another in D.C., just up the road from my oldest brother in Fredericksburg. I felt like my whole family was in harm's way. The school called to tell me they were sending the kids home and to come pick up my daughter.

When I used to temp around Manhattan, I was amazed by the varied lives people led outside of the office. Determined bohemian that I was, I had mistakenly presumed that someone who held a "real job" was defined by their working life. When I stayed at a company more than a week, I'd get to know people —diverse characters with outside interests: boats, gardens, children; pasts, hopes, creativity. I'd done a stint on the 101st floor of the World Trade Center when I was pregnant in 1988. All those elevator rides, buying lunch in the mall underneath the towers, crossing the immense plaza to get to the subway. For the next few months, I'd read the *Times'* "Portraits of Grief," capsule bios of many of those who died in the attacks, and felt like I knew them all.

A week later, I wondered if it was okay to leave home for a run of dates, opening for Richard Shindell in the Northeast. Supporting better known, more established artists was how I spent a lot of my time on the road. This tour had been all set to be business as usual—but everything had changed. I left Hazel with her dad and set out from Nashville in the Aerostar. I was only halfway to Knoxville when I had to pull over and rest—it was going to be a long drive and the psychic toll of putting myself out in the world in the middle of such grief and uncertainty was heavy. But it felt like playing music might help someone now—maybe even me?

Somewhere in Virginia, I popped a mix tape in the van's cassette player. Elvis Costello singing, "What's So Funny 'Bout Peace, Love and Understanding," the Nick Lowe song I'd thought I was intimately familiar with, never sounded so urgent, so deep and meaningful. That was life just after 9/11. What we'd perceived as truth before rang even truer.

The mountains of Virginia go on forever traveling north on I-81, or so it seemed with my effort to get back to where I'd come from. (Heading down south has always felt to me like rolling downhill.) As I climbed a steep section of highway approaching Lexington, I felt the Aerostar's engine straining. I thought I smelled smoke. Hello car trouble, my old friend. I tried not to worry about it.

Suddenly, I heard honking. A couple passed me on the left and gestured frantically. I flipped them off, a New Yorker's preferred defensive driving technique. The next driver matched my speed and motioned to roll down my window. I remembered the World Trade Center and how we were all going to get through this together.

"You're smoking, bad! You better get off the road!" the man shouted. I pulled off at the next exit, and the lady behind the counter at the gas station directed me to a nearby garage, her accent a softer twang than the Tennessee one I was becoming used to.

The mechanic looked like Father Time. He popped the hood of the Aerostar. "Where you headed?" he asked. He clocked the guitar case and box of merchandise in the back of the van. I'd planned to stop for the night somewhere in New Jersey and drive into Manhattan early the next morning, like you'd go visit a dear friend in the ICU. I wasn't trying to meet up with anyone in New York, not even my brothers, their trauma too recent and raw to intrude on. I just felt the pull of the city—my city. Once I saw it, felt the energy and assured myself life would continue there, I could carry on up I-95 for the first gig.

"You can't drive this van," the mechanic said. He saw the look of disbelief on my face, and said, "Take that blue Chevelle over there. Just worked on it, drives great. Bring it back when you're done and we'll see what we can do about this Aerostar." I started calculating costs in my head. When I asked how much to rent the car, he told me to just give him one of my CDs. "Your favorite—deal?" Asking a musician to choose their favorite album is like asking a mother to pick her favorite child. I probably just gave him the one that was hardest to sell, The Sugar Tree. Why oh why had I let someone at the label choose that font? And the artwork was just way too dark. Still, I was stunned by his kindness.

Next morning, I lined up in traffic at the Lincoln Tunnel. Police were checking inside every truck. I had no business coming into Manhattan, but it was too late to turn back. I felt guilty for being there and guilty for not being there when the unthinkable happened. I'd turned my back on New York, choosing a softer, easier place. I'd rolled on downhill to Nashville, but still wanted to keep my claim on New York.

Coming up out of the tunnel into midtown, I'd never heard the city so quiet. No honking, just a hush. The air was dank and foggy. It was a whole other New York from the one I'd flown out of a week ago. I headed downtown towards what felt like a giant void, a smoky gap between buildings. I crossed Canal to the Manhattan Bridge and took the usually hateful BQE like I was running my fingers over the face of an old lover, remembering this pothole and that curve and *this feeling*. Tears rolled down my cheeks.

Up in New England, Richard and I played to audiences hushed and reverent, who then suddenly let go with laughter and cheers. Everyone was punch drunk on grief, and we helped them career down to the mat. In Shelburne Falls, MA, I sang the Nick Lowe song, feeling it so much that the people in the old Memorial Hall felt it too. Richard sang the old Stephen Foster song, "Hard Times," and the audience sang along, gradually joining voices until the hall was filled with a hushed block of sound. I imagined a crowd in this hall at the turn of the last century, facing whatever trials bound them together. Looking back, it seems we were living the end of an innocence we hadn't realized still existed. The Y2K everyone fretted about had finally arrived. But the joining together made everyone a little stronger.

In the local coffee shop the next morning, strangers came up and thanked me for playing. I sat on the rocks by the Deerfield River and thought, "What a beautiful place in this awful but still somehow perfect world." I was thankful I'd come out on tour, even if I wasn't sure how I'd get home when it was over.

Driving back down through Connecticut in the alien Chevelle, I heard the Kennedys singing "Life Is Large" on WPKN. How wonderful to write a positive song, I thought, one that celebrated life. My songs were mostly laments, or at least a little pissed off. Feeling good never motivated me to create the way feeling bad or uncertain did. I wished I could share the feeling of love I'd felt in Shelburne Falls. I had to pull over at the next rest area because a song was coming to me, the words and melody like dictation I needed to take down.

The next show was held at a school auditorium in a commuter town in New Jersey. I finished the second verse of "Don't Ever Change" in the classroom used as a dressing room, while I waited for my soundcheck. The town lost dozens of people at the World Trade Center. I thought of kids saying goodbye to their parents as they left for work, not knowing they'd never see each other again. I thought of my daughter back in Nashville, and how much I wanted to get back there.

The mechanic gave me the bad news over the phone that the Aerostar was not capable of making it the five hundred miles back to Nashville. He offered me a little money for it: "One of them Washington & Lee students can use it for a runaround," he said. Paul offered to drive from Nashville and pick me up when the gigs ended.

He was waiting in the parking lot of the auto shop in the shadow of the mountains when I pulled up, his curly hair tied back in a ponytail. Sometimes I felt pissed off about the things that attracted me to him: that he was a drummer; that food was the only thing he took seriously. But he wrapped his arms around me, his wooly oatmeal sweater scratching my cheek, and I felt safe. He'd driven eight hours north and I'd driven eight hours south. I emptied the blue Chevelle of my guitar and nearly empty merch box and put them under the tarp in the back of Paul's truck. I checked the Aerostar for cassettes and grabbed my tattered road atlas.

When we'd made it home to Nashville, I wrote the last verse of the song and tried to hold onto the faces of people in little halls across the Northeast. I remembered Shindell's sonorous voice, the acrid smell of New York City, an aching wish that my daughter be safe. The love I felt for Paul. After a few weeks the song was all I had left. Like many things from that era of my life, I was so fixated on getting somewhere that it was hard to appreciate the beauty of what I had. But every time I play the song, the feeling comes back.

Don't Ever Change

I took a walk in a small town Sunday morning
Just to see what was going on
Sat watching two guys fishing in the river running through
Like there was nothing wrong, nothing wrong
They had their lines in the water ten feet apart
Beer guts, t-shirts

Me with my heavy heart
I don't have religion, but I'm trying to pray
And I never liked fishing but I wanted to stand up and say
Hey I love you, you're perfect
Don't ever change

I picked my daughter up at school last week
She had her headphones on, she barely said hello
And all I wanted was to hug her, smother her with kisses
But I was cool, like "Hi there, how did it go?"
She had chipped nail polish, writing on her hand
She was nodding her head to hear favorite band
Staring into space like she was all alone
But I didn't take it personal, it meant that I was home
And I said hey, I love you, you're perfect
Don't ever change

I'm holding on to everything that's good in this world
There's a lot that's good in this world

I saw my baby sitting there at the breakfast table
His hair a mess and he forgot to shave
And I wished that he would get up, make it all better
Stop drinking so much, learn how to behave
Then the radio was playing a Chuck Berry song
He was looking at me asking what was wrong
I made a list of the things I could say
But he gave me a wink and it all went away, I told him
Hey I love you, you're perfect, don't ever change
Don't ever change

Chapter Fifteen

I received word from the record label that all three of my solo albums were going out of print: *Diary Of A Mod Housewife* (1996), *Middlescence* (1998) and *The Sugar Tree*, which had come out only the year before. The hatchet I never knew existed had fallen—I'd bought cheap discs in cut-out bins before, but hadn't known the feeling of being cut out myself. Cartons of my unsold CDs were slated to be smashed by a machine they kept in the Koch warehouse for expressly this purpose—to free up space on the shelves for albums deemed to have a future. Like an old horse being sent to the glue factory, but without any byproduct to show for it. The smasher would reduce the music I'd poured my sweat, tears, and probably actual blood into, to useless shards and finally, powdered crystals.

I remembered one other time when I thought the record business might actually kill me: when the album Last Roundup recorded in Nashville back in the mid '80s was deemed not worthy of release. The disappointment was so intense, the injustice felt so grossly unfair at the time, even the physical pain of childbirth couldn't compare, because at least there'd been the miracle of baby Hazel at the end of that. The label had done Last Roundup a favor—years later, I saw that this shelved album wasn't the lost classic I'd imagined it to be, but rather the sound of a band in an awkward phase between charmingly primitive and fully realized.

I'd learned some hustle and survival skills since those early days. The best way to handle the pain was spring into action mode. I worked out a deal to buy my discs back from the label for one dollar a piece.

One day in early 2002, in the middle of a run of northeast gigs, I drove out to Long Island and liberated my discs from the Koch warehouse.

I was hungry and thirsty by the time the exit for Port Washington loomed. I'd passed the Jones Beach exit what felt like an hour before. Jones Beach, where in 1988 Will and I took a ten-month-old Hazel to see Bob Dylan, with Steve Earle opening. Now, Will played drums in Steve's band, Hazel was almost a teenager, and Will and I were officially divorced. Things change, time moves on—but Bob was still on the road, a stable point we could measure everything else against.

I stopped at a deli: Tropicana orange juice, coffee regular; Poland Spring bottled water, plain bagel with butter—New York in a brown paper bag. I wound my way around the office park roads that lead to the Koch complex. I remembered coming here just before my first album release. I'd met the folks who worked for the label and together we'd hashed out a poster and CD single artwork. Now Koch mostly worked hip-hop and Pokemon releases to cash in on the video game craze. I'd joked with Hazel that I would no longer be label mates with Pikachu.

I backed the van up to the warehouse, and a helpful employee who happened to be a fan lead me to the pallet where my discs were stacked up in cartons. I wrote a check, and as I pulled away from the massive warehouse I half-expected two guards to come running after me in flak jackets and rifles, trying to stop me from taking control of my own destiny. But there was only a bored seagull watching from a lamp post.

So, this is how dreams end, I thought. Not in a burnt out blaze of glory, like Kris Kristofferson in *A Star Is Born*, old and washed up, smashing his sports car in the desert. Just a practical move by a middle-aged lady in a minivan.

A moment that felt like a defeat was actually a step towards liberation and self-sufficiency. Too bad I couldn't see it yet.

Koch asked me to put together a "Best Of" album — a little embarrassing because, well, three albums don't exactly demand a career retrospective. Still, my trio of solo albums wasn't a bad run, and I came up with a decent list of songs to include, though are any of us the best archivists of our own material? I added the original demo of "Magicians," which captured the essence of the song better than the full-blown production on *The Sugar Tree*. There was also the demo of "Keep It To Yourself" — those two added up to the bonus tracks that are supposed to lure in fans who already had my albums. I gathered up photos from the last half-decade for the CD booklet. I was still young enough to think five years was a long time ago.

Another photo session for a cover pic, this time with photographer

Brydget Carrillo, whose husband, songwriter Gwil Owen, was a frequent David Olney collaborator. I loved taking pictures with Brydget. I liked how she saw me through her artist's eyes. But when I look back at the photos, I wonder if I was looking for artistic success or...a date? Hair colored and flipped, lips glossed, I pose on couches and beds, or plop down on a grassy bank and gaze yearningly into the camera. I'm in a camisole or halter top here, a slip dress there. A few times I tried for something more businesslike: a pin-striped jacket; a trench coat! Was it fashion in the early 2000s, or just me, that didn't know who or what it wanted to be?

If only I'd realized that the best way to feel cool and strong was to pretend to be a member of the Velvet Underground, I could've saved myself so much agony. Early 2000s fashion was fitted on top with low slung jeans. Shoes were spindly, feminine: pointed toes, kitten heels. Back in New York, I'd wanted to stand out. In Nashville, all I wanted was to fit in and not call attention to myself. I was afraid of appearing to be a freak, an outsider, even though those were attributes I used to aspire to.

So much time and expense on my appearance, trying to look a high enough level of good. I tried this chic new salon that an artist I admired recommended, thinking maybe if I got my hair right, the success part would follow. Oh, the ego rush when the owner of the place told me she loved my music. She cut and styled some of the biggest names in Nashville. After she gave me the coolest haircut I'd ever had in my life, she told me to take a deep breath and then handed me the bill.

Was it worth it? It was without a doubt the most I ever paid somebody to look like somebody.

For certain women in Nashville, beauty and haircare were practically a religion – they were perfect-looking, even on the hiking trail at seven in the morning. I'd catch a whiff of perfume and hair products and then jump out of the way of two or three ladies who looked like they'd gotten up an hour early to shower, shampoo, blow dry, apply light makeup, and choose coordinated exercisewear. I felt like a mangier, greasier species. The women's voices sounded like expensive birds in the Radnor Lake state park. I envied them. They never walked alone.

I did find more friends, though. Sherry Rich was an Australian rocker who landed in Nashville and married one of the best musicians in town, Rick Plant. She made punky, garage band records back in Oz, and had recently made a solo album with Jay Bennett from Wilco. When we met, she'd just had a baby and that inspired the first lines of her song idea, "Are We Ever Gonna Have Sex Again?": "Life's become one great big list, of things to do and buy and fix."

I remembered the feeling so well, from back when I was married. The rest of the lines flowed out like dictation from my past, but the idea was all Sherry's. We got a couple other songs going that we never finished, but aside from "Sex," the best thing we did together was form a cover band called Apple Scruffs: Sherry and me on guitars, Audrey Malone on bass (she was married to Dave Roe, who played bass with Johnny Cash, then on a roll with his American Recordings) and Dave's son Jerry, Jerry Reed's grandson, on drums. That was Nashville, pedigrees everywhere you turned in addition to pure talent. Jerry Roe was just a kid but so good. We covered Teenage Fanclub, the Ramones, and Flamin' Groovies, and only played a handful of shows that were amazingly well-attended. A sure way to attract a crowd in Music City was to play covers. Guilty Pleasures and the Long Players were a couple other groups who filled rooms with the writers, artists, and sidemen who were often just too busy or tired to go out to shows.

"When I need some time to myself, I book a gig in Nashville," the great songwriter David Olney said. We were all carrying the weight of our dreams, and maybe listening to original songs was too much pressure. Apple Scruffs rocked without the need for validation – "Like me! Accept me!" – that overcame me when I played my own gigs in town. It could be hard to find an audience who weren't all busy doing it themselves. Apple Scruffs recorded a few tracks before becoming too busy with our individual projects to carry on.

There was no doubt living in Nashville was a sure way to get better at writing, playing, and singing. You couldn't help but absorb something from the mastery all around, and if you were competitive, feel spurred on to improve. And co-writing was fruitful and fun. I was supposed to turn a modest number of new songs in to Welk over the course of the year, and they did begin to pile up.

There were eighteen tracks on *18 Again* but the double meaning of the title wasn't a coincidence. I may as well have been a teenager, I was that hormonal and self-conscious. My skin even broke out again.

Maybe I was regressing as Hazel was growing up. We'd been a team: shopping at Target, splashing together in the fake surf at Wave Country. But as any parent prays and wishes for, she was making friends and starting her own trajectory in life.

I took my daughter to her first big show, dropping her at AmSouth Amphitheatre to see Blink 182. She'd been to so many gigs with me and/

or her dad, but this night was her choice, her friends. Way before every teen or tween had a cellphone, I worried how she'd let me know if she needed me.

I drove the twenty minutes back home, entered our empty house, and thought, "Great! At last, some time to myself." Then I was immediately at a loss as to what I was supposed to do. I walked around the place like a zombie. Should I do a little cleaning?

Then I remembered back when Hazel was a toddler who still took naps. I disciplined myself to take advantage of that time to work on music.

I picked up my guitar and a line I'd written in a notebook popped into my head: "We've been circling each other like a couple of planes at O'Hare..." I channeled my yearning for love and my detachment—why couldn't I make it work with Paul?— into a feel and a melody until there was an entire song. And then it was time to drive back to AmSouth.

I found Hazel in the dark, crowded parking lot full of youngsters and their parents. She'd lost her shoes at the show, so carried away by the excitement of her time, her band, that she flung them high into the air. It wouldn't be long until she turned her back on punk lite and got into the real, serious stuff and beyond, but I'll never forget her happiness, and how I felt a new mix of pride and sadness: oh yeah, she's growing up! Oh no—she's growing up!

O'Hare

We've been circling each other like a couple of planes at O'Hare
With nowhere to land and if we did, no place to go from there
And you're talking to me like you're handling the Dead Sea Scrolls
Do you think we're gonna figure this out before we both get old
Tick tock, they're closing for the night
I'm shellshocked, giving up the fight

Come on and hold me, what are you waiting for?
You can't break a heart that doesn't work no more
And I'm tired of trying like I did before
I wanna lay down

Well, you can take off the kid gloves now, lose the finesse
There's no secret technique to separating me from this dress
I swear we've been here before, but in another life

I was a Conquistador, you were a pretty good wife
Something's moving in my chest
It's nothing, I just need some rest

And I need you to hold me, what are you waiting for
You can't break a heart that doesn't work no more
And I'm tired of trying like I did before
I wanna lay down
I wanna lay down

Chapter Sixteen

More gigs: the West Coast with Richard Shindell; a Texas jaunt; a mid-western swing. On Focus, on Lancer, on Saturn, on Stratus (they were running out of names for cars) to the Gulf of Mississippi, Glacier State Park, and the San Joaquin Valley. I traveled to Alaska to open a few shows for Todd Snider, who was sort of the diametric opposite of Shindell. Where Richard was almost professorial (Michael Douglas in *Wonder Boys*), Todd was stoned surfer (Jeff Spicoli's older brother: blonde, barefoot, and hilarious with his shaggy dog stories). Todd was John Prine's protege, a slacker golden boy tarnished by life. I'd fallen for him as an artist the first time I heard him, in a hotel room at Folk Alliance in Vancouver. So, any chance I could, I'd open a show for Todd.

The point where the artists I opened for intersected was that they all appeared to be completely comfortable in front of an audience. They knew who they were, onstage at least. I felt like I was still looking for that ease. When would I reach the moment of believing I had a right to be up there on that stage? Would I always be most at home as the opening act?

I lost count of broken guitar strings. I slept on floors, futons, comfy beds, lumpy mattresses, and velvet couches. I flew Southwest Airlines so often I ended a show with "I know you have lots of entertainment options out there, thank you for choosing me!"

I was always coming and going, traveling somewhere. That's what musicians who lived in Nashville did. If you wanted to play gigs, you couldn't just hang around town like musicians in New York did. In the early 2000s, there really wasn't enough of an audience to go around.

I checked out of a hotel in Dallas and headed for the airport in my rental car. It was a familiar feeling, looking for a place to fuel up at the last minute so I could return the car, hike my guitars and bags onto a shuttle, check in to the flight, and get to the gate on time. Post-September 11, flying had become fraught, the waits at security long, moments of indignity more frequent.

It was impossible to drive to the airport in Dallas without thinking about the motorcade of John F. Kennedy. I might've been distracted by those thoughts, but soon I began to feel desperate, driving up one side of the airport highway and down the other in search of a gas station.

This was touring, part of what made it different from driving to the same job every day. The daily actions of touring were always the same: finding your way in and out of town, keeping a vehicle working or hiring one, finding food and shelter. But you also needed to navigate the culture of every single place you passed through. Boston had students, bad weather, and Revolutionary War history. L.A. had jammed freeways and great Mexican food. In Dallas, the JFK assassination was part of its DNA.

Touring artists are chameleons. At the same time, we're the tourist in loud shorts at the Acropolis, only instead of cameras we carry guitars that loudly proclaim, "I'm not from around here."

Finally, I saw a gas station on the other side of the divided highway. I doubled back, pulled up to the pump, and jumped out of my generic white compact. Shoved the nozzle into the gas tank after determining which side of the car it was on, then flipped the notch to begin fueling. Nothing happened. True, I'd practically knocked over a bright orange cone that was blocking the pump. I ran into the store to find out what was going on.

"No gas today, ma'am!" the clerk said. No gas, in Dallas? I thought Dallas was nothing but oil and gas.

I jumped in the car and drove madly out of there, feeling a bump as I exited. Maybe I hit the orange cone again?

Up on a hillside I saw another sign for gas. I raced along the highway, cars honking at me, drivers gesturing and waving. I flipped them all off. Squealed up the hill into a Sunoco and around one of the islands. I jumped out, grabbed a nozzle from the pump, and went to shove it in my tank, but—

There was already a nozzle in there, and about ten foot of hose trailing behind me. That bump I'd heard had been the sound of me ripping the entire hose from the empty pump.

A guy stared open-mouthed from beside his pickup truck one pump over. He shook his head admiringly and let out a low whistle. "I'll be damned," he said. "I always heard about that happening to people but ain't never seen it...'til now."

At last, I'd made an impression in Dallas. Getting more than ten people to one of my shows there had proven impossible. Articles in the *Dallas Herald* or *Weekly* raving about my work looked great in a press kit, but had no effect on the general public. Either potential concertgoers didn't read the paper there, or they took a look at any article about me and immediately made plans to be somewhere else that evening.

But now—finally—they'd be talking about me. "You won't believe what I saw at a gas station out by the airport today," the pickup truck guy would tell the man next to him when he grabbed a beer and some barbecue later that evening. Soon the whole bar would be laughing, whooping and hollering, celebrating that hapless stranger who'd snapped a rubber service station hose.

I threw the hose behind some bushes. Filled the tank, returned the car, and managed to make my flight.

Compared to my U.S. touring, with frequent domestic flights, rental cars, and decent hotels (thanks, Priceline), U.K. dates were a much leaner affair. I'd tried to put Bob Neuwirth's advice into practice— when we'd played in the round at the Bluebird a few years back, he'd said, "Go by train, with just your guitar." That approach wasn't possible in America, but elsewhere—why not? I traveled with an acoustic guitar on my back, a rolling suitcase full of CDs to sell, and a duffel bag of clothes over my shoulder. I was in reasonable shape at the start of the run, but after only a few days on and off trains and up and down station stairs, I was a giddy combination of fit and exhausted, like a recruit after the first week at boot camp. On board the trains, I fell asleep, my bangs cushioning my forehead when it bumped against the train window. Shouldn't I have been enjoying the scenery? Newcastle, Leicester, Nottingham, and Brighton— green fields and sheep. I spoke to no one until I arrived in whatever town I was playing. Sometimes the promoters met me at the station, usually a freezing, cavernous antique structure with birds swooping around the ceiling. I was shocked the first time a promoter took me to the venue by bus, then felt like a spoiled American brat for assuming everyone drove or owned a car.

Andy Richardson met me at the train station in Hull, in the northeast of England. Andy had promoted the show I played there with Sid Griffin—was it really just a little over a year ago? The Hull audience seemed to like the humor in my songs. There was a definite lack of pretension there that reminded me of my hometown of Pittsburgh. It was a city of underdogs. Underdogs like underdogs.

We ordered tea and biscuits in the Station Hotel bar to warm up. From what I could tell, Hull was almost always cold and wet, but this day felt colder and wetter than usual. The newspaper announced snow was coming.

We took the Beverley Road bus along to the hotel where I'd stayed my last time in town. Run by two brothers, it was an old school, bare-bones B&B, with toilet and shower in the hallway and a sink in the room, along with twin bed, small TV, an electric kettle, teacup, and...more biscuits. I appreciated the biscuits—you'd never get those in an American budget motel. There were modest perks to playing in Britain.

I showered down the hall and blew my hair dry in my room—the lightbulb couldn't have been more than 40 watts, but I aimed for as much glamour as I could muster because that night, a genuine pop idol would be in attendance at my gig. Wreckless Eric had his own performance scheduled the two following evenings there in Hull, and had agreed to spin records before and after my show. Andy the promoter was aware that Eric's classic "Whole Wide World" had found its way into my set. The underground romantic anthem possessed magical powers to turn things around. It also had a way of signaling indie credibility—that secret handshake again. The sharing of music via the internet was a new idea, so finding old cool stuff still took a certain level of commitment. Playing Eric's song—shrugging into it like the leather jacket and shades he wore on one of his record sleeves—let me display a different persona: the willful misfit. That was the beauty of a cover song.

So that night in Hull, in addition to the snow, he was coming. The guy who wrote and recorded that song, along with other classics like "Semaphore Signals," "Reconnez Cherie," and "Take the K.A.S.H.," all dorm room favorites back when I was an art student in New York. I put on a glam gold '70s shirt and treated myself to a taxi down to the Bull Hotel.

When I arrived at the venue, Eric was running late. I set up my equipment and grabbed a quick curry at the Indian restaurant next door. Gigs started earlier here than in the U.S., and in Hull dining choices were limited to curry, kebabs, fish and chips, or pizza. The only other option was to grab a bag of crisps at the bar and settle for a packaged sandwich from the petrol station after the gig.

People entered the function room above the pub and found seats on the short red velvet stools around little round tables. A hooded figure entered. He was covered in ice and snow and carried a crate of records.

Eric pulled the hood back, revealing snow in his greying brown hair and eyelashes that began melting down his cheeks as he told a story about being the last car allowed across the Humber Bridge. He described sheets of ice falling all around his car; how a final shard descended just before they closed the bridge entirely. He made it sound like a wonderful adventure and supernatural act of gallantry.

Eric had history with Hull, having attended the art college there back in the '70s, and played early gigs right in that very room. People of Hull considered him one of their own. He began setting up turntables.

"He just moved from France. I think he lives on a boat," said Andy. I heard Eric drop the needle on "You're The One That I Want" from the *Grease* soundtrack. He wasn't too cool to think Olivia Newton-John and John Travolta were cool? My interest in him was sealed.

I played my set, and with the snow falling outside and it being a weeknight, the show felt like a meeting of a secret society. I asked Eric to come up on stage with me to play "Whole Wide World." He unpacked his Microfret guitar, which was the same horrible but wonderful green color as the Greco electric I used for band gigs back in the states. I felt I'd met a kindred spirit. I started playing the song and saw Eric craning his neck, looking at my hands on the frets. I'd transposed the song's key from E to A.

"This song has two chords," he said to me, "and both of yours are wrong."

We made it through okay. I apologized afterwards for ambushing him. After almost two years in Nashville—a town that owed a big part of its identity to people who wrote songs—I would've felt weird not inviting the songwriter of a classic up for everyone to celebrate. Eric was amused. We made a vague and general plan to meet up again, hopefully soon. I said goodbye and headed back to my room at the Mayfair Hotel, where I slept in my twin bed accompanied by the snores of a man on the other side of the wall. Next day, I caught a train to Doncaster and another to Newcastle, then the train down to London, where I said I'd been in Hull the previous night to elicit a guaranteed laugh and nod of respect from the audience. I didn't play "Whole Wide World," thinking it was being played as well as it possibly could be that night, by the man who wrote the song, in the room where he first played it. I hoped I could get to know him better—it didn't seem that crazy to imagine. If a song brought us together the first time, maybe gigs or friends or the internet would intervene and make it happen again. The world wasn't *that* big.

Another U.K. tour under my belt, some shows better attended than others. I wasn't playing to big audiences in the British Isles, but I loved playing for people over there, enough to keep going back. Then I finally had a gig in Ireland, a country that embraced a certain kind of singer/songwriter. It was cheap to fly to Dublin from Glasgow after playing a few shows in Scotland. Part of the beauty of touring in this part of the world was the relatively short distances, even from country to country.

I often stayed with friends, and friends of friends, in Scotland. It was a different country up there with its own press and BBC Scotland who loved me. After my shaky start at the Glasgow B&B, former Cramps fan club president and fanzine editor Lindsay Hutton often hosted me at his flat, situated right between Glasgow and Edinburgh, in the glow of the BP oil refinery. It helped having a man on the ground in a foreign land, a support network. My last night on this trip I stayed at BBC producer Richard Bull's house in Glasgow. We left for the airport in the darkness of early morning, allowing me plenty of time to catch a 9 AM flight to Dublin.

"Good thing you're not flying out of Prestwick," said Richard.

"But I *am* flying out of Prestwick!" I looked at my ticket. "I didn't know there were two airports for Glasgow..." It was my first time flying Ryan Air, whose rock bottom fares were mainly possible because they used airports in the back of beyond, miles away from the cities they claimed to fly to. What you saved in airfare you inevitably made up for in train fares and taxis.

Richard dropped me at the train station, my best chance of reaching the airport in time for my flight. "Run, Amy —run!" he said with those beautifully rolled r's.

I was always running in those days. I was either chasing a gig, or running from the fear that I hadn't done enough, or would never be good enough.

I missed my flight and paid another hundred pounds for the next flight to Dublin, which didn't leave until four in the afternoon. I spent a long day in the airport's Graceland Bar. According to a plaque there, Prestwick was the only spot in the U.K. Elvis ever set foot, changing planes after his army stint in Germany. I loved Elvis, and it made me sad to think The King never knew the joy of playing outside of North America. But there are only so many times a person can read a plaque.

Inebriated stragglers from a weekend football match clogged the waiting area at my gate, along with a step dancing team returning home to Ireland in triumph. Rosy-cheeked ten-year-olds with hair scraped

back in tight buns broke into step routines at the newsstand, in the ladies' room, and across the jetway as we boarded the plane, their feet and
arms moving as if possessed.

"So what brings you to Ireland?" the tousle-haired immigration of-
ficer asked when we'd landed in Dublin. He nodded at the guitar on my
shoulder. "Will you be playing a little music?"

I tried to gauge whether he wanted me to have a gig so he could nail
me over my lack of a work permit or, because he was Irish, believed everyone should have a gig. Work permits were a constant source of stress
and expense when playing the U.K. Maybe Ireland was different?

"Sure," I said. Then, hedging my bets: "With friends."

"Grand," he said, and stamped my passport.

That night, in a room above a pub, I played a set following a performance by actress and singer Maria Doyle Kennedy. We had friends
in common back in the U.S. She was a fan of my songs and had kindly
offered to set something up. She'd starred in, among other things, The
Commitments, a film that was part of the Irish cultural canon. She introduced me to the crowd, who'd mostly come to see her, telling them they'd
love me. And they did.

Next day, I boarded a Delta flight back home to Nashville, via Atlanta.

"Why, look at you!" said the steward as I carried my guitar ahead of
me, hoping for a closet to stow it in up front. "Let me help you with that,"
he said. "You might be riding in economy, but honey, your guitar is going
first class all the way!"

A little later, another flight attendant stopped by my seat. "Are you
the lady with the guitar?" she asked. I nodded, worrying she was about to
tell me there was a problem and they'd removed it from the plane. "Our
steward in first class is SO excited to have you on board. He's been brag-
ging to everyone that you're with us today!"

I sat taller in my seat, wondering how word of my transcendent show
in a room above a pub had reached the crew of this Delta flight. It was
only sixteen hours since I'd landed in Ireland and here I was, practically
famous already. The flight attendant leaned in. "I would love to get one
of your CDs! What exactly do you sound like?" I started to explain how I
wrote songs about real life that working women just like her could relate
to, when she cut me off—"Oh, just a minute, hon, be right back."

Two other flight attendants, also women around my age but way
better groomed than I could ever hope to be, stationed themselves in the
aisle next to me. "We want to know all about you," they drawled. "This is

just so exciting, such an honor! What's your name again?"

"I'm Amy Rigby," I said, trying not to make it sound like a question.

Then the first flight attendant came back down the aisle, waving her hands at her co-workers: "THAT'S NOT HER!" she shouted. Turned out they'd held the Eurovision semifinals in Dublin the night before. The audience favorite was a dark-haired girl with a guitar. Rumors spread that she was on this very flight. My new fans dropped me as quickly as they'd discovered me.

When the flight attendants came back around to serve the meal, one of them practically threw a foil-wrapped container of pasta at me. "We're out of chicken," she said.

"But—do you still want a CD?" I said.

When I collected my guitar from first class at the end of the flight, the steward who'd been so thrilled to host me was busy helping another customer. I reminded myself the Dublin gig had been a success; magical even. Eurovision was a jokey spectacle, wasn't it? Art was made to last, even if nobody was interested unless someone told them they should be.

Chapter Seventeen

Nashville made it easy—essential, even—to go out on the road, but being a mom made it imperative that I come right back. Having a kid makes it hard to be rudderless. There was a built-in structure—the 3 PM school pickup—and feeling of working towards the greater familial good that provided a sense of purpose any time I lost faith and asked myself, "Why am I doing this?"

Why was I still asking myself why? I'd achieved what I'd come to Music City to do—found a publishing deal. A legitimate company believed in me enough to advance me a regular amount of money to keep afloat while I continued to write, record, and tour.

I knew that my publishing advance was essentially a loan I'd never pay off without a hit song, or at least a song on an album that sold in the hundreds of thousands. A cut—another artist covering one of my songs—was proving elusive. I'd heard that Welk's song plugger, the person responsible for keeping tabs on who was recording and pitching songs, considered my work too edgy. But wasn't that edge part of the reason they'd signed me?

Once you'd gone from dreaming of Nashville as a possibility to living there—getting up every day, buying groceries at Kroger and bottles of wine at Frugal MacDoogal; sitting in the round at the Bluebird or selling off CDs at Phonoluxe to make extra cash—there was no going back to how you were before. It was boot camp, spring training. Once you threw your lot in with the fraternity and sorority of songwriters, musicians, and artists—whatever happened and however long you managed to stick it out—elsewhere in the world you'd forever walk a little taller.

The downside of the career protein shake that was Nashville was you wanted to see results. And you couldn't help but compare how you were doing with the guy or gal next to you.

I'd heard Dolly Parton interviewed on the radio when her 37th album, *The Grass Is Blue*, came out a few years back. "I would just love a chance for another hit," she said. She'd been without a record label, out of step with current country radio, and had the idea to relaunch herself with a bluegrass album. "But she's Dolly Parton!" I thought. Hadn't she already done everything? Yet she was still looking at younger artists wondering where and how she fit in.

I kept a PO box at the Melrose Post Office in Berry Hill. It helped to have one, so you didn't have to share your home address with the world. Email was still almost a novelty, and social media hadn't been invented yet. I'd started selling a live solo CD as well as my cut-out albums via my website. Pre-Paypal, that meant buyers actually paid by *mailing a check*. It felt good to take charge of that record-selling part of my artist career, the retail channels proving to be pretty fickle when left in someone else's hands. It was satisfying packing up discs and writing a note to buyers. One fan sent me a photo of my first few albums at the top of Mt. Everest. There were many levels of success, and I tried to appreciate the modest wins, even if I kept hoping for the bigger score I felt sure was my due.

They had my picture on the wall of the post office—not a mug shot, but an autographed 8 x 10. I was in good company with friends and neighbors and even legends represented. The postal clerks got to know everybody with a PO box. When the branch manager came to my gig at the Sutler, a nearby club, I felt like I'd achieved a small level of status in Nashville.

Across town, the Acklen Avenue post office had an even bigger wall of photos of instantly recognizable big country stars, but I liked to think of Melrose as more like an underground club.

I was a cult figure who appealed to a small group—I constantly asked myself whether it was worth continuing. Even with a publishing deal. Even when the local weekly paper *Nashville Scene* called me 2003's Songwriter of the Year—in the city of songwriters. The fraternity of excellent music writers in town appreciated me: Michael McCall, Bill Frisck-is-Warren, Robert Oermann (one of the first to write about Last Roundup); Craig Havighurst, Peter Cooper at *The Tennessean*; Jim Ridley, and Jonathan Marx at the *Scene*. They all wrote about me as if I belonged there and even added something to the place.

But any artist will tell you there's no there there. I remembered when all Last Roundup wanted was to put out an album. It took four years; when you're in your twenties that feels like forever. In retrospect, I could laugh about quitting my day job the week before we left New York for our first U.S. tour, thinking, "I'll never need to work again!" What a rookie move that was.

Maybe I'd come to Nashville with the same kind of faith—call it naivete—that a publishing deal was the answer to everything. These goals are the necessary carrot on the stick to keep pushing. No need to blame others for constantly moving the goalposts—artists are perfectly capable of doing that for ourselves. We make a life out of it.

I wondered how I could access the magic formula that let you be yourself as a writer—think Dolly songs, or Deana Carter's "Did I Shave My Legs For This," or any number of Shania Twain hits of the time—creating work with an individual point of view, the ring of truth, and popular appeal. Sometimes I wished I could look like me only more generally appealing. And sometimes I wished the same for the songs I wrote in Nashville.

I thought there might be a bigger artist who could use my help to finish their songs. But I didn't know how to make something like that happen, and wasn't good at asking for help. The few times I tried to "write up"— work with more commercially successful artists/writers— the humbling aspects stung.

There was the glamorous hitmaker who had her people call minutes after my arrival at her writing studio, "Yeah, it's fine. Nope, no worries." I guess there was fear a potential co-writer (me?) could be a freak or stalker. Instead of joking about it to break the ice—"What makes you so sure I'm not an axe murderer?"—I spent our appointment constrained, wishing I had people too. Who was checking to make sure *I* was okay?

And then there was the artist whose people needed "to run it by him and get back to you" if it was something he'd be interested in. I thought he was a fan of mine like I was one of his. But there was a hierarchy to these things and critical success like mine was pretty low on the ladder, a little too "Well, I love her work but, yeah, most people probably wouldn't get it."

Maybe I just wasn't tough enough for the game.

But like Paul cautioned, Nashville had a hold on me. I was only just getting started here, wasn't I? Angelo, a bona fide hit songwriter so successful folks knew him by one name, invited me over to write. He'd also invited Chuck Prophet to work on a three-way. I'd never done one of those before—three songwriters putting their heads together instead of the two I was used to—but it seemed worth a try. Chuck was famous for being in the band Green on Red. We'd traveled some of the same paths back in the days of cowpunk. He was passing through town on tour with his band, the Mission Express, and when I watched them rocking 12th & Porter, I thought they must be one of the finest bands out there.

Angelo started out as one of us (played in bands, slogged around on the circuit of small clubs, made rock albums) but was getting songs cut and even having hits writing and producing: Kim Richey, Patty Griffin, and Trisha Yearwood. Chuck was always putting out great records and touring—he was both an artist and road warrior. Getting together with the two of them was a little like that old Mystery Date board game. Did I want to go the Angelo route, settle into a Nashville life of co-writing, aiming for cuts by bigger artists, and let touring fall by the wayside? Or was I more for the Chuck door: live it, breathe it, BE IT—a genuine rock star if on a smaller scale than we'd ever imagined could exist back when we'd fallen in love with rock music in the epic, grandiose early '70s? It was that old Artist Door vs Songwriter Door thing all over again.

I didn't worry about any of it when we got together in Angelo's nice house off Belmont Boulevard. Angelo was cool, Chuck a ball of energy, and I probably wanted too much for them both to like me to feel comfortable enough to do anything more than talk a lot and find common ground: friends on both coasts, barbecue, the beautiful production on Chuck's latest album. We didn't come up with a song, but it was a start.

I think when I moved to Nashville, I'd hoped to find other female musicians who were also moms, but music was still a man's world, and you needed a certain toughness to survive. I met Rosie Flores, Lucinda Williams, Allison Moorer, Jonell Mosser, and Joy Lynn White—all unique artists and incredible singers with an edge. I sat next to Gail Davies at a dinner party at Rosie's house. Gail was one of the only female country artists to produce her own albums. Her son, Chris Scruggs, just out of his teens, played every instrument phenomenally well with everyone in town. Gail was the only mom I met who made music for a living, and I wished I could ask her, "How did you do both?"

"You guys hungry?" I asked Rosie and Lucinda. Hazel was asleep when we came in from the Gold Rush bar. She was old enough to stay home on her own for a few hours now. I tried not to make too much noise, but definitely felt a little wobbly, a little worse for wear after a couple of drinks.

The three of us gathered around the kitchen island. I felt proud of my house, simple as it was. Hazel and I kept it tidy, fairly sparse. Tall ceilings with windows up high.

I felt a little starstruck —two musical heroines right there in my kitchen. Rosie Flores first caught my attention with her L.A. country punk band, Screamin' Sirens. I'd adored her solo country debut, loved her voice with a catch in it on Harlan Howard's "God May Forgive You (But I Won't)." Now she was my neighbor and even helped me out babysitting Hazel sometimes. She was a killer guitar player, great vocalist, and fine songwriter with a flair for colorful western style.

Lucinda Williams was a mix of uncompromising artistic credibility and touching vulnerability. I'd been aware of her since her Rough Trade debut back in the '80s, through my one-time benefactor and A&R guy Nick Hill, and then Duane Jarvis, who'd played guitar in her band. Paul had done a stint as her drummer. I'd never gotten to know her. I always felt too in awe and shy around her to fully be myself. But she knew Paul and I had broken up and she knew heartache, and we were all a few whiskeys along the road to comradeship. She murmured words of empathy and understanding in that *voice*—"I know, hon, *I know*."

I made quesadillas. These women had been putting themselves out there and on the line for years and I looked up to them. What did I have to offer? I was a mom. I could crank out meals and melt cheese even with a buzz on.

Motherhood made it hard to go to other people's shows, hang out, and network. It was also a blessing, a life raft, a place to ground the lightning rod that is the necessary equipment of being an artist. Even though Paul and I had called it quits, I'd never be all the way alone—even if I wanted to. I had my daughter, so even though I'd lost my boyfriend (or sent him away with my sulky uncertainty), I still always had a reason to get up and make breakfast in the morning. I may have floundered trying to navigate song publishing that wasn't really happening, touring that rarely broke even, the challenges of home ownership and keeping a vehicle running. But Hazel was a good kid who excelled at school. As a mom, I wasn't doing too badly.

We were still most definitely living down south, but sophistication was beginning to creep in. Provence, a French artisanal bakery, opened in Hillsboro Village. Provençal fabrics and yeasty loaves were a welcome alternative to the endless wait at down home Pancake Pantry just across the street. Still, it was hard to picture the old country stars you spotted in the traditional places even registering these newfangled locations. I wasn't sure I wanted to see Porter Wagoner clutching a baguette and a copy of *The New York Times*, but progress comes at a price.

They said Nashville was a five-year town: if you lasted that long you'd stay forever. I'd been there for three.

Chapter Eighteen

It was time to come up with another album. I wasn't signed to a label anymore, but I'd written a lot of songs since moving to Nashville and knew I wanted to release them somehow. I'd connected with Jim Olsen, whose Western Massachusetts-based label, Signature Sounds, was a good fit for a touring singer/songwriter, but I had to come up with an album they considered worth releasing before we could work out a licensing deal. A useful thing about being signed to a publishing deal was the publisher would pay for a certain number of demo recordings per year (all recoupable, of course —that is, they footed the bill up front and added it to your tab to be paid off... possibly never, if nothing ever gets licensed for film or TV, played enough times on the radio or covered by another artist). I'd made demos of a few possible contenders for the new album, and for the rest decided to work with engineers who owned their own studios. I'm making it sound way more organized and thought-out than it was. Like with anything—writing, painting, cooking— you just have to start...somewhere.

Sheryl Crow had a big hit the summer of 2003 with her single, "Soak Up The Sun"—catchy as hell with a surface sheen and irresistible chorus. I felt pissed off listening to Sheryl's song, and couldn't avoid it because they were playing it everywhere. Her hit plagued me with questions like, "Sheryl Crow, why can't I be you?" I thought if only I were a) better-looking, b) harder-working and c) could sing and play better, I could be where she was. It hurts facing the truth but can also be good motivation.

So I wrote "Why Do I" as a response, the lyrics asking myself all the questions it hurt to face in real life. Why had I broken up with Paul? He'd been an excellent boyfriend! There was absolutely nothing wrong with Paul and that was probably why he had to go—I wasn't sure I deserved a good guy.

And why did I make life harder for myself than it had to be? Maybe I could blame Catholicism for turning me into my own worst enemy, but it wasn't possible to go back and start over without the stain of original sin and agony of the confession booth reinforcing the idea that I was basically bad. If I wrote truthfully—and when it comes to songs, or anything really, there is no other way—perhaps I could move beyond those feelings of worthlessness that didn't serve me or anybody.

Why Do I

I'm tired of being tired of being
Why am I always disagreeing?
Why am I always giving in to my evil twin
I don't know why
I'm making trouble just to make it
Why can't I just lay back and take it
Why am I never satisfied just being satisfied
I try to suck it up
But then I always fuck it up

Why do I pull wings off butterflies
Look for things that hurt my eyes
I kiss the boys but I'm the one who cries
Why do I get off on misery
Loneliness feels good to me
I'm happy when I'm all hung out to dry
Why do I?

I look sweet but deep inside I'm awful
I'm colder than a frozen waffle
I'm always looking for the rip in the silver lining
Here it is
I'm busy being so downtrodden
I'm just a peach that's going rotten
I wanna save the other peaches so I roll away
I'm careful where I land
Does anybody understand?

I recorded "Why Do I" in New York City, with the New York musicians who'd often backed me for Northeast shows: Steve Goulding on drums, Joe McGinty on keyboards, Jon Graboff on guitar. We worked in bassist Brad Albetta's studio down near where the World Trade Center once stood. Richard Barone, whose band, the Bongos, had been a staple of Hoboken and lower Manhattan pop music in the '80s and into the '90s, produced the recording, his pop sensibility giving the track a polish that countered the darkness of the lyrics.

I was happy with it, but decided I didn't want to continue down this route, with a producer overseeing and helping shape the aesthetic—I just needed to gather a group of songs together myself. I hadn't been ready for that approach before, but this time I was.

In Nashville, there were recording studios in basements and garages all over the town. I don't think it's fair to characterize them as "home studios"—these aren't the domains of hobbyists but important tools of the musicians' working lives that just happen to be attached to the places they live. Steve Allen's was a walkout with hot tub on the patio looking out from a hill high above Granny White Pike. Steve's wife, Linda, had survived a brain tumor—nothing fazed her. She had stared down death and was minted. She would bravely stand up front at even sparsely-attended shows in Nashville, reminding everyone on stage that what we were doing up there mattered. Recording at Steve's was fun and easygoing, and I liked knowing Linda was right upstairs.

Bill Lloyd's basement was a den of pop records and musical ephemera. It adjoined the garage—a garage where you could park your car and keep the lawn mower, just like when I was growing up in the suburbs of Pittsburgh. When I'd first visited Bill, back when I still lived in NYC, I'd been stunned: music...could buy you a house? With a yard, and a driveway? Space and peace? It had given me hope and something to aspire to in my future as a musician—that kind of autonomy.

George Bradfute's basement was cozy and atmospheric. George lived on the outskirts of Nashville in a town called Madison. The house was a cool mid-century ranch, and the linoleum basement floor featured musical notes and motifs: a G clef, quarter notes. Back in the late '50s through mid-'60s the house belonged to pop country superstar Jim Reeves. Local lore had it the distinctive floor was visible in blue movies of the era—that when Jim was on the road crooning worldwide hits like "He'll Have To Go," his house was an occasional erotic film factory.

A big reason country music appealed to me in the first place—that it was music made by people who seemed like regular folks except they were blessed with real talent and drive—was evident working at George's studio. He'd recorded dozens of great Nashville artists: David Olney, Webb Wilder, Jason Ringenberg, but was humble and self-effacing. Because he owned the studio—engineering, mixing, doing everything himself including making coffee—the working atmosphere was relaxed; affordable but always focused and professional. We managed to arrange, record, and mix several songs over the course of a week or two: "Til The Wheels Fall Off," "Are We Ever Gonna Have Sex Again?," "Believe In You," "Breakup Boots," "All The Way To Heaven," and "Don't Ever Change."

Even though Paul and I had broken up, he came in to play drums on the tracks I recorded at George's. I'm glad Paul could play on one of my albums—I'd learned so much from him. He was a hell of a musician and knew not to take any of it too seriously, which may have irritated me as a girlfriend but served things well in a studio situation.

The title song, "Til The Wheels Fall Off," was inspired by Bob Dylan's "Brownsville Girl"—not musically or even lyrically, but that image of Ruby in the backyard with her red hair tied back, asking a couple how far they were willing to take this thing. My song felt like a statement of intent, that there was no turning back from the life I'd chosen. I'd made it this far, hadn't I?

In Scotland, I recorded a couple of tracks with David Scott in East Kilbride. Davie, best known for his band, the Pearlfishers, and sometime membership in BMX Bandits, had an affinity for '60s-style pop music, and I'd played some solo gigs with him around his wee corner of the country. His studio was in a state-funded Arts Center outside Glasgow—with Davie and drummer Jim Gash, I knocked out three tracks over two days, including "The Deal," a song co-written with Bill DeMain that took its title and refrain—"It's Optional"–from, what else, a Seinfeld episode.

When I met up with Jon Graboff in London on *my way* back to Nashville, I told him I'd gotten an album together, somehow, but I didn't know how I could keep up this pace of traveling and parenting. "I'm just so tired, Jon," I said. I'd never admitted that to anyone before.

But I planned out the artwork, the car theme of *Til The Wheels Fall Off* a nod to my endless driving and touring, and by April 2003 I was heading back to the U.K. and Ireland to tour for the new album. Things were complicated by the fact that Hazel's dad, Will, had a European tour with Steve Earle planned for the same time period.

With both Will and me living in Nashville, there were times it was fairly straightforward working things out as divorced musician parents. Will often toured for many weeks with Steve, and I made whatever arrangements I could to ensure Hazel had some supervision when I needed to be away for a night or a weekend. There were a handful of friends we relied on, most of whom had kids. Sometimes Hazel arranged sleepovers at her school friends' houses, but that might involve her having to attend some kind of church service if it coincided with a weekend or a Wednesday night, this being Nashville. (I'm sorry, Hazel.) She told me one family brought her along to an opening day screening of *The Passion Of The Christ*—the film gory, bloody, graphic; the audience mostly Jesus-loving parents and their kids, gathered to show support for their number one guy. "Look, Mommy, it's Jesus!" Hazel heard a small voice cry out with delight. Then, a gasp: "What are they *doing* to him?"

I tried to fit my gigs around Will's touring schedule. But this was the rare time we both had overseas touring plans, so I okayed it with Hazel's school for her to be away for two weeks. Hazel and I flew from Atlanta to Heathrow, then took a train to Bristol. I remember exhaustion after the overnight flight, and the taste of Ribena, a fruit-flavored children's drink with questionable nutritional value. Our foreheads against the train windows as we journeyed westward: the green hills a whole other color from the Tennessee and Georgia dark piney green; clouds the color of Regency stone houses; sheep the fluffy white of clouds. We crashed a few hours in a Bristol hotel, then gathered up Hazel's suitcase and knapsack and walked to Colston Hall, where Steve Earle and his band were soundchecking. We ate dinner backstage with Will and the other Dukes—Eric Ambel, who I'd known back in Brooklyn, and Kelley Looney, Steve's long-running bass player. I stayed to watch the show, enjoying the reverent but fervent atmosphere so particular to a British roots music audience. Steve was a great artist—his songs always pushed the boundaries while remaining simple, straightforward and uniquely him. Afterwards, I accompanied Hazel out to the tour bus where she'd be living for ten days. The band was Channel Tunnel bound, heading for gigs in Belgium, the Netherlands, and Switzerland. I waved goodbye to my daughter as she bravely climbed aboard a busload of touring musicians like she was walking onto a pirate ship, only she knew them and they were all decent guys and one was her dad.

I went back to the hotel by myself and caught a train the next morning. I wondered what my touring life would look like to my daughter, in contrast to her dad's.

Nottingham, Leicester, Newcastle, Hull, London. At the end of the dates, I arrived in Ireland, where I planned to pick Hazel up at Dublin Airport. Her dad had dropped her at the airport in Paris. No international mobile phones yet—there were internet cafes where you got change and logged in to a computer surrounded by other travelers. An email from Will arrived letting me know Hazel was on her flight. There wasn't a lot that could happen to her in the sky between Paris and Dublin, right? But that feeling of having no control over my daughter's fate, that she was out there in the world and not in my charge anymore, had me pacing and desperately peering over strangers' shoulders as the passengers from her flight came through immigration and customs. *Please don't let her have been abducted to some country I've never heard of...*

And then she was walking towards me, looking taller and more capable than I remembered. We dropped her bags off at the promoter's flat and wandered around Dublin and ate oxtail soup in a pub while she told me about all the gigs and venues in Europe, and I wondered how my fourteen-year-old daughter had gotten so much more worldly in just a few days?

Back in Nashville, one hot Saturday evening in June, I drove us out to AmSouth Amphitheatre to see Steve Earle and the band open for Jackson Browne. The Lumina minivan I'd bought to replace my Aerostar broke down on the way home. I called AAA and when the tow truck arrived and we climbed up into the cab, Hazel said, "Huh, this is the second time I've been in a tow truck today. Dad broke down bringing me over to your house this morning." The driver turned and said, "I *thought* y'all looked familiar."

It wasn't all broken-down vans and cobbled-together childcare arrangements in Nashville. I had good nights there, nights I'll hold onto forever:

Playing Bob Dylan's "Hurricane" at a Bluebird Freedom Sings event, remembering all seventeen verses with no lyric sheet. The night, supporting Nashville's First Amendment Center, was made up of performers playing songs that had been banned at one time. Pre-camera phone, I wish I'd busted out my Olympus 35 Trip to document Dobie Gray tearing the place up with "Drift Away"—never censored but a powerful anthem to the importance of what most of us in the room were driven to pursue: rhythm, rhyme, and harmony.

I remember hanging on every word as Randy Newman leaned against a lectern at Vanderbilt University, talking to a small crowd about songwriting...Lucinda Williams and Pat DiNizio of the Smithereens trading songs in the round at Tin Pan South. "I just wish I could write a rocking hit like you," Lucinda drawled after Pat played "Blood and Roses."

In New York, a lot of sweat and hard work went towards survival—parking, subway, dodging crime and crazies. There was inspiration there, sure. Life's rich pageant any time you stepped out of the front door, whether you wanted it or not. The easier lifestyle in Nashville put the focus on what I'd come there to do: writing and recording, and going out of town to play gigs. Passing a guitar around Greg and Claire Troopers' dining table, or a clothing swap at Rosie Flores' house down the street; walking the hills around Belmont with Joy Lynn White early in the morning, this sense of community I hadn't expected. I sat there in awe of the talent around me, but it pushed me to raise the level of my own writing. I wanted to fit in; I wanted to compete. I'd knock out a birthday song for Brad Jones ("Who Built The Pyramids?") or play a funny song like "I Hate Every Bone In Her Body," or hush the room with "Don't Ever Change," and feel like I was holding my own.

There were Neil Young tribute nights and frequent Beatles ones. Good chances to learn from the best. I saw Laura Cantrell open for Elvis Costello at the Ryman, and she played my song "Don't Break The Heart" right there on the stage where Hank Williams once drove the crowd so wild they brought him back for six encores. It felt like a supreme songwriter honor, almost as good as being up there myself.

I kept performing Wreckless Eric's "Whole Wide World" in my solo set. The pulsing rhythm of the verse and mix of hope and defiance when the chorus kicked in always connected. I wondered what Eric was up to. Last time in the U.K., someone had mentioned he might come see me play, but he never showed up.

I learned Welk weren't going to pick up the option for one more year on my publishing deal, and it stung but wasn't a complete shock. They hadn't pitched my songs to anyone, but I'd gotten a few cuts anyhow: Joy Lynn White titled her latest album, *On Her Own*, after one of our cowrites, and Jonell Mosser, another of the best singers in town, covered "Wait Til I Get You Home." *Til The Wheels Fall Off* was well-received, raved about even. The local music press seemed proud to have me as one of their own. Just like Paul had promised—or cautioned against—the town had a hold on me. It wasn't perfect, but nowhere is. I was gaining momentum.

Sometimes I wonder what I might've made of myself in Nashville, if I hadn't met Charles.

Chapter Nineteen

If I hadn't been up on a stage, he wouldn't have looked at me twice. He was the type of man who measured his self-worth by the kind of woman he was with. I was definitely not that kind of woman.

If I hadn't been a singer-songwriter, he wouldn't have thought he knew me when we'd barely met.

If I... if only... why do things happen the way they do?

I landed another gig opening for Todd Snider, this time in Birmingham, Alabama. My experience playing the Pittsburgh of the South was scant, starting with Last Roundup's barely-attended 1987 gig at the Nick, a lovable toilet of a club. I'd played there again solo in 2000 with similar underwhelming results. I mostly remember the smell of beer, and a dank freezing space too meager to be called a dressing room. Todd was classier than that, on a higher singer/songwriter level, so we were playing a decent establishment called Zydeco.

I checked into a hotel on the outskirts of town after the three-hour drive from Nashville. I had a little time before heading over to soundcheck, so I worked up a Louvin Brothers song in my room. "The Angels Rejoiced" always moved me, but I wasn't sure whose version I preferred: the Louvins or Gram Parsons and Emmylou Harris. I felt so much for this song and the story it told in a few minutes. It connected me to my discovery of country music in the early '80s and also to the man who'd become my husband and father of my daughter. Will loved the Louvin Brothers so much, we danced to their song, "Kentucky," for our first turn as a married couple—and neither of us was from the place. I wanted to share my appreciation of the hillbilly harmony duo right there in the song's originators' home state, even if there was only one of me. Maybe music's ability to help fill in what's missing—love when there isn't any;

words where there were none—is what draws me to write and play songs. I'm not here to impress anyone—just share a feeling.

It was February but already warm, the air slightly humid and smelling of hydrangeas crossed with hickory smoke. I played a good set for the largest assembled crowd I'd seen below the Alabama border. They seemed to really like me. I don't know why that was a surprise—it must be a byproduct of years of less than impressive audience numbers at my own gigs; one or two hundred in a room make a lot more noise than twenty. I'd done well opening for Warren Zevon and found a new level of relatability with my last two albums. Songs like "Cynically Yours," "Don't Ever Change," and "Are We Ever Gonna Have Sex Again?" felt personal and universal, and grabbed listeners whether they knew me or not.

After Todd's set, where he was his usual hilarious, engaging self, I stood behind a wooden counter selling my CDs and signing them for anyone who asked. The night had been a success. In retrospect I wish I'd basked in it, packed up my merch case, loaded my guitar into the Lumina and driven back to my comfy hotel room to enjoy some premium cable channels we didn't have back home in Nashville.

Instead, a man approached the table. He looked a little like the actor Stephen Collins, who played the reverend father in *Seventh Heaven*. Nice-looking. Sandy-haired, clean-cut, straight.

"You're funny," he said. "You don't usually hear women who are funny." Okay, so kind of an old-fashioned guy. He continued. "I said to my friend, 'I bet she gets the joke." He told me his name. I signed a CD for him: *TO CHARLES. I GET IT.*

I felt flattered. A normal person thought I was funny. He probably even had a job. I mean, I'd played on *Late Night with Conan O'Brien* and gotten a big laugh, several times, from the studio audience. Maybe even from the million or so viewers at home, many of them normal, with civilian jobs. But Charles was right here, in front of me.

Maybe he could be my boyfriend? I thought.

It was just that fast, that simple. I handed him a pen and asked him to sign up for my mailing list.

I emailed Charles a night or two later, assuming he was married and that would be that. No more married men, ever. I'd learned as a gullible twenty-year old that scenario never works.

He emailed back: he was divorced, living and working in Birmingham.

Did he like barbecue? I asked. I said I wouldn't mind driving back down that way for some Dreamland. I'd tried their legendary Tuscaloosa location back when Last Roundup toured the south and could still taste the smoke and tang of those perfectly-charred ribs. The Birmingham branch was supposed to be nearly as good.

A week later, at one in the afternoon, we dined together, chastely carrying our trays of ribs and cornbread and sweet tea to a table in the noisy, crowded barbecue place. It was a sea of chinos and pastel polo shirts, and Charles fit right in. Not a tattoo, band t-shirt, bandanna, or hip haircut in sight. The normalcy felt downright exotic.

We swapped stories. He was recently single after twenty years of marriage to a "knockout" who also happened to be really nice and still came around weekly to clean the house that had been theirs. He, the one who knew how to spur their children on to succeed, stayed in the family home to keep pushing their high school-age kids to be the star athletes they were destined to be.

He ogled my freeform life, an eager tourist urging me to tell him about the sex and drugs I no doubt indulged in as part of the musician lifestyle.

"Umm—I drink wine with dinner?" is about all I had to offer. My mundane striving was not the stuff to inspire vicarious thrills. Charles made it clear he wasn't a Republican and didn't go to church. I asked him what the hell was he doing in Alabama?

His job. He was all about his career and the kids.

A clean-cut guy with an actual job. I'm embarrassed to admit, it turned me on.

And when we walked back to his car through the broiling Alabama afternoon sun and he unlocked a sleek, dark green Series 7 BMW, I was smitten.

Looking back, I wonder, was I really that shallow?

The answer is, unfortunately, yes.

So, Charles looked like my savior for a minute, if a savior wore polo shirts and khakis and shopped at Costco.

Clean-cut is something I hadn't had much experience with. Khakis felt comforting, neutral fabric indicators of someone who had it all together—who was moral, upright, and true. Here was a man with hair cut by a barber. Aside from my dad, I don't think I'd met a man with that kind of haircut before, let alone slept with one.

Maybe meeting Charles felt like a sign I should throw in the towel on my bohemian life. I'd had what felt like my big shots: a record deal, and a publishing deal in Nashville. But I was still struggling away, trying to make my quirky records and play gigs for an audience I wasn't sure how to find. In certain respects, I felt I'd failed.

I didn't realize these were all just steps along the path. I still thought there was a destination you reached that said "winner," or a point where you called "game over." If I didn't qualify for a manager (Why didn't I qualify? Was I too old, or just too intent on doing things myself?) or an agent (I'd had agents willing to work with me, and I inevitably decided they weren't finding me enough work), was that their fault... or mine? Even Lawrence Welk's son's publishing company couldn't interest other artists in recording my songs. Was it time to just call it quits?

If I was only capable of attracting men like me—artists, bohemians, dreamers who struggled and suffered and woke up some mornings wondering what the hell they were doing—well, that was the equivalent of having my own stamp of approval, and what was that worth? Like Groucho Marx, sort of, I didn't want the member of any member of a club that would have me as a member.

So here was a man with a closet full of suits and dress shirts. Maybe if I had the attention and approval of that man, I'd merit the attention and approval of my father. For a person well into middle age, I had a lot of misconceptions about "normal" people—how they had it all figured out. I still held onto the belief that I could go straight any time. I still clung to the notion that not being an artist was a choice I could make.

The barbecue lunch was a tentative fishing expedition. The first real date was dinner, in Nashville. He arrived at our door in a dark grey pressed shirt and dark blue suit jacket. I dressed up in a silky top and low-slung bootcut jeans; kitten-heeled shoes.

"You're not as good-looking as I remember," he said. Not the first thing out of his mouth, but nearly. "I'm not usually seen with a woman as... how can I say this ... flawed as you." My mouth was probably wide open at this point. "But you're so talented, I'm willing to make an exception." My mouth closed.

Remember that early 2000s guy with the awful ponytail and top hat who was featured on every TV news show for teaching men how to capture a woman's heart by insulting her? I think his name was Mystery. His patented technique was called negging. Charles hadn't studied his teachings—he just came by this behavior naturally.

In a matter of weeks, he'd given me a BMW of my own. I loved that car. As ashamed as I was of what it might mean to accept the gift of a car from a man, when I was driving it, I felt about myself all the things I wanted to feel out there in the world and only occasionally felt on stage:

deft, capable, powerful.

I'd always had problems with low self-esteem. Maybe it was growing up in close-knit, provincial Pittsburgh—feeling like an outsider. Probably it was the acne I suffered as a teenager and again and again as an adult—too-visible evidence I was bad inside. The wounds that spur us to create are the same ones that make us doubt ourselves. Like a child, I took everything Charles offered, alternately doubting his intentions and thanking God for my good luck.

I wanted to be adored, to be worshiped, to be noticed—and here was a man who seemed to be offering that kind of attention, every minute of the day, every day of the week, whether we were together or apart.

"You're so talented, you're so smart—you deserve the best!" He said the words I'd longed to hear all my life, especially from my dad. Would I give up my autonomy to be treated like a princess?

I felt a genuine attraction to his clean cut looks, confidence, and intellect. But within two months he was talking about marriage, claiming betrothal was the only way he could legally sleep with me in the family home he shared with his teenage daughter and son.

My daughter felt deeply uncomfortable about the whole situation. Charles insisted I take Hazel to a psychotherapist to get to the bottom of why she was barely civil around him. To keep him off my back, I agreed. The therapist was a friend of Charles'.

"She's a spirited, intelligent young woman. I don't see any problem," said the therapist. Charles was furious, deciding his therapist friend was a quack.

I wished Hazel could understand how I was trying to make a better life for the both of us, at the same time wondering how she could have any respect left for me.

I was up in the Northeast playing a few gigs. Early spring, and Bob, my first New York boyfriend from back in art school days, and I made a plan to meet up in the last old-fashioned coffee shop on University Place in Manhattan. This type of establishment was becoming a thing of the past in the city, giving way to a whole new kind of deli with banks of bright flowers out front, healthy nuts and fruits inside.

I wondered when University became a one-way avenue that flowed uptown only. I'd been away from the city less than four years, and as I crossed to the opposite corner of 12th Street, sense memory caused my head to swivel left, right, left in search of that rarest of things in Manhattan—two-way traffic. I reminded myself how one year in New York was like a decade in other places. The large empty rectangle of sky over downtown, until two years ago neatly intersected by the Twin Towers, seemed to flash on and off as if outlined in neon, saying, "You're an outsider now. Remember when the towers came down? Sure, you do—you saw it from a distance—but YOU WEREN'T HERE."

The city had changed: it was cleaner, brighter-lit; traffic and subway signs easier to find. I wished I could've frozen everything in 1999, gone out and raised my daughter and returned a more successful version of myself to a gently-spinning carousel that kept one painted horse open and waiting for my inevitable return, with permanent access to the brass ring.

I was in a reverie and then Bob—denim jacket, olive skin, and slim build, just like when I'd met him in 1976—appeared out of the past, or the 14th Street and University exit of Union Square subway station, the one you could only enter if you already had a token or, more recently, a MetroCard. Tokens had been retired last year, yet another piece of my New York they'd chipped away. If it was true our bodies regenerate every seven to ten years, it was only a short amount of time before the me that existed here would be replaced by another me, and one day I'd arrive through the Holland or Lincoln Tunnel and New York City and I would greet each other as complete strangers.

"Amy McMahon!" Bob said, using my maiden name. We hugged and told each other we still looked exactly the same. Since we were only in our early forties, that was actually close to being true. Inside the door of the coffee shop, the manager, dressed in classic white shirt and black suit jacket, directed us to a booth. We exchanged current biographical details: he was back out on Long Island living at his mother's house; I was doing my best in Nashville but found myself caught up in a relationship that was getting serious—we were somehow talking about marriage. I'd only known the guy a few months. "Oh, that's Charles calling me right now," I said, as the familiar number appeared on the screen of my flip phone.

"I'll call him back later," I said, sounding more confident and in command than I felt. I knew from experience that ignoring even one phone call from Charles now meant interrogations and harangues later. But the familiar formica-topped table distance between me and Bob, and the space around our leatherette booth, created a shimmering force field of NYC energy that cloaked and grounded me in the past Bob and I shared.

As we ate our patty melts and fries, I felt like myself in a way I couldn't get to down south. There were gaps all around the space I inhabited in

Nashville, places I felt I just didn't fit the way I fit there in New York, and maybe that partly explained how Charles found his way in.

Bob and I talked about old friends and family (Me: Hazel, tenth grade in a Nashville magnet school; my four brothers sprinkled through NYC, Pittsburgh, and Virginia; Dad looking after my mother in senior living; Bob: His mother, same as ever) and music—good old Lou Reed's new release, *The Raven*—Hhmmm... did I have another hour? We hadn't caught up like that for almost a decade. I gave Bob my latest CD, work I felt proud of.

"We call this the Nashville handshake," I said. Bob, one of my oldest friends, and my first musical mentor, laughed at the idea of me promoting myself to him. We hugged goodbye on the street corner and my phone rang again.

"Why didn't you pick up before? I've been calling you for an hour!" Charles launched into a diatribe: I was a slut with loser friends and Bob was the worst. If it hadn't been for him, I'd have gotten a lot further in life. I wondered when I'd started dating my dad. Actually, Charles made me appreciate my father more: his basic decency and humanity. Yet lately I'd found myself distanced from my family, the same way he had no contact with his, who were sprinkled somewhere out in the Midwest. Like all the other red flags, I kept telling myself it was all okay. He insisted that if I couldn't accept his love—the purest, deepest love I'd ever have—well, I was surely flawed beyond repair and even he, my truest believer, couldn't help me.

I stood outside the Mental Health Building on East 12th Street, two dozen therapists' offices a short elevator ride away, wondering how I could make Charles disappear. I should shut my phone and ignore him completely. But I played my side of the sketch—arguing, denying, reassuring—while New York swirled around me. I could allow the flow of the city life I still longed for and dreamt about to pick me up and deposit me in the stacks of the Strand bookstore half a block away, where I'd happily lose myself. Instead, I leaned against a cool stone wall as Charles kept talking. "Are you going to sleep with him? You'd better not sleep with him."

The thought hadn't occurred to me for many, many years, but I argued my virtue like a lawyer defending a client on trial for her life.

"You are so busted," a young woman said to me outside a venue in Atlanta. I'd just sung my heart out for over an hour—stories of struggle, of trying to make ends meet as a single mom. So, what was I doing loading my guitar and merchandise case into the trunk of a silver BMW?

The girl reminded me a little of myself twenty years earlier: slightly bedraggled, with reddish brown lanky hair falling into her eyes; pert breasts and friendly hips in a calico thrift shop dress under a dingy leather jacket. Boots, guitar case a little grimy, but her face was dewy and so alive she was giving off sparks.

I was forty-five, still relatively pert myself. Maybe I was cleaner than I'd been back in my twenties when I lived in a roach-infested Manhattan apartment with a bathtub in the kitchen. The Red Light was a humble singer/songwriter joint, the type of place I'd gotten used to playing over the years of writing songs and putting out records. I was too old to play the ingenue, the promising newcomer. I wanted to tell the girl to come see me after twenty years of running a marathon in cheap used sneakers. Maybe by then she'd understand how a woman gets tired sometimes and doesn't think so clearly. Instead, I just chuckled grimly.

A late breakfast in Birmingham—wasn't this the life I always dreamt of for myself? Gigs on the books for weeks or months ahead, a man on my arm on the way to brunch, the wherewithal to pay for it.

Charles and I ordered eggs, bacon, and biscuits in the cozy cafe where a fancy mostly-white part of town turned into the racially-mixed neighborhood that felt way more comfortable to me than the big houses and well-maintained lawns of the tony area where Charles lived. He tutted when I added grits to my order, adding a knowing chuckle like, "You're just trashy enough for grits."

I picked up a copy of *The New York Times* at the counter. The cafe was a rare establishment this far south that carried the Yankee paper of record. The edition was dated Monday, September 8th, 2003. Leafing through stories about George Bush and Tony Blair, I found an obituary for Warren Zevon.

I knew it was coming, like everyone knew it was coming. He'd been so open about the cancer that was going to end his life, joking wryly on the Letterman show about death and enjoying every sandwich. That still didn't make it right, or easy to accept. I hoped he'd had an endless array of perfect sandwiches. I thought of how generous he'd been with his deli tray, like a Jewish mother—"You need to eat," he'd say. "Eat."

Beyoncé sang about being "Crazy In Love" through the deli speakers, and I shared the news with Charles about Zevon's death—and Charles was thankfully reverent and even managed to refrain from saying something crass and offensive as was his default setting. I wondered to myself,

"Is this love or just... crazy?"

Some might say Warren Zevon wasn't the greatest model of how to live. He'd even called himself "Mr. Bad Example." I think his droll fatalism could've made some sense of my current situation, just as he'd done with the School Marm, the partner he'd been keeping himself in line for a few years earlier. He'd had the School Marm and here I was with Charles, as if allowing a person with the attributes furthest from our own can bring our self-defeating traits into line.

As we walked back up the hill towards Charles' car, he pointed out the house he'd lived in with his first wife, before they'd moved to a posher neighborhood. This was a good time to remind me how beautiful she'd been and still was, how lucky I was to have someone with his excellent taste and professional position interested in the likes of me. And, by the way, in case I'd forgotten, I had a big ass.

Sweat poured down my face and back, and my hair began to frizz. I was amazed this didn't lead to more derogatory remarks as Charles cranked the air conditioner in his BMW.

"You'd be prettier without those acne scars," Charles said. "My ex-wife has a good plastic surgeon." He was hitting me where I lived. I felt like anything that didn't happen in my life the way I wanted it to happen was due to those scars.

"What scars?" my friends said.

I seesawed between panic that things were moving way too fast, and a sense of security that issues like college for my daughter, house payments, and my loneliness would all be taken care of. In spite of Charles' demands and behavior that alienated my friends and family, this man believed in me. After decades of barely getting by, I felt lucky to dress up and go out to eat in Nashville places I'd longed for but hadn't been able to afford: Sunset Grille, Zola, F. Scott's. Arrive, be seated, glance around, wondering who were these privileged folks and could they tell I was just pretending to be one of them?

A martini or a glass of wine, some appetizers—why not? He was paying and he never tired of telling me he'd retire a millionaire. A little light conversation and then:

"I know you slept with that guy we saw out the other night. I can just tell. Didn't you? Admit it! You've never had a good boyfriend until me, just these losers. Why have you always settled for losers?"

My thoughts careened between "He's right, no one decent would want me" and "Why are you sitting here listening to this?" My hands gripped my knife and fork, my lip trembled. I tried to ignore him. "These crabcakes are delicious," I said.

"You're not only a slut, you're a liar," he said. My hands were on the sides of my large white dinner plate. So big, so heavy. So beautiful, the way they'd arranged the food—

And then, the plate was across the table, the contents spilled in his lap, which was unfortunately covered with a heavy white cloth napkin.

"Fuck you!" I shouted. All the diners around us turned. That was a word you never heard in Nashville, let alone shouted in a fancy restaurant.

He laughed. He looked happy. He'd gotten what he wanted, me acting like a child, recipient of his abuse and largesse. They were a package deal. The low lights of the dining room twinkled off his glasses. He reminded me of my dad all of a sudden, my dad who had nothing to say to me while I was involved with this man who I thought would please him, make him proud.

Isn't this what you wanted, Dad? Didn't you hope I'd find somebody in control like... you?

Chapter Twenty

It hadn't been an easy tour, but then what tour was ever easy? For this one, I'd traveled with two other American artists—Amy Allison and Neil Cleary. We'd all released albums in the U.K. through the Scottish label Shoeshine, and a co-bill idea had been devised where we'd each play a set, sharing a guitarist, and work up a song or two all together. It was an idea that sounded better on paper. Only the most focused, discerning music fans pay attention to record labels. Touring was a challenge as a solo artist, and the package idea took those challenges—finding an audience, the right night, and the right venue—and multiplied them by three.

The tour started in Ireland. I arrived in Dublin via Aer Lingus from Atlanta to the news that all the Irish shows had been cancelled. The reasons were vague. It was like that old game of telephone: promoter talks to the label, who shares the news with the tour manager, who takes us for a meal in a pub to explain that she doesn't know what happened.

I didn't mind hanging out in Dublin for a few days, spending money instead of earning. The money part was nebulous anyway —who knows how the shows would've done? Now the pressure was off. I was several time zones away from Alabama, and Hazel was safely at home with her dad.

I shared a room with Amy, one of my favorite people in the world. Amy had a voice like no one else, wrote wonderful songs and possessed a tart sense of humor befitting the daughter of Mose Allison, one of the great musical wits of the twentieth century. The two of us snuggled into our twin beds like sisters who shared a first name. I imagined life would've been different if I'd had a sister to share secrets with, instead of four brothers.

In Dublin, I learned that Jack Emerson, who'd created the Praxis label in Nashville with his friend Andy McLenon, had passed away. Praxis was the first label interested in any music I helped create, bringing Last Roundup to Nashville to make a record back in the mid-'80s. I found out about Jack's fatal heart attack when I logged onto a public computer in an internet cafe and saw his name in capital letters in my AOL inbox. None of us had a cellphone that worked overseas, and I'd left my unwieldy laptop back home. There was no Facebook or Twitter; there may have been MySpace, but I hadn't heard of it yet. I was still young enough to feel disbelief along with a deep sadness, that someone so vital and—shockingly, I discovered only upon reading his obituary, a year younger than me—was gone. He'd been the authority that blessed my band with a memorable chance to record in the shadow of giants like Johnny Cash and Cowboy Jack Clement, with the great Jim Rooney producing. He'd also infuriated us all, deciding to pass on the results, but he'd been nothing but encouraging since I'd gone solo and moved to Nashville.

Later that first night, I walked to a payphone on the corner outside the hotel to call Charles. I wore the engagement ring he'd bought me, a diamond set in a platinum band. I'd chosen it myself, feeling like a floozy.

I stood in the rain just across from the American Embassy, a striking circular sixties building that had the odd effect of making me feel safe: imagination, courage—*remember, you're an artist*. I focused on the building while Charles ranted. How dare they cancel our shows? It was ridiculous that I was stuck in Dublin with no gigs while he was made to suffer without me back in Alabama. Once we were married, he'd see to it that I never had to waste my time again (not sure when he became a booking agent with a magic wand but)...

Hadn't I wanted a man to love and think about me when I was out in the world playing my songs? I pulled my coat tighter and hoped my friends back in the hotel had picked up some beer and snacks. We needed to rehearse and make the best of the U.K. shows.

In Manchester, the venue got switched at the last minute. In Sheffield, our van was broken into. In Glasgow, we replaced the van and played a decent show. Newcastle went well. We drove and drove, listening to CDs of the Strokes' newly released second album, comedian Mitch Hedberg live, and Laura Nyro. Everyone got a turn to play their favorites. Our date in London at the Borderline felt successful enough. We performed in Brighton and Hull. I wondered what Wreckless Eric was up to.

Fighting off exhaustion and a cold, I dialed my number back in Nashville from a payphone in Heathrow to retrieve my messages. I was happy this tour—cancelled gigs, low turnouts, van break-in, lousy weather balanced with a few good shows—was over.

I listened to a voicemail from my brother Riley: "I heard from Dad, Amy. Mom had a stroke. She's in the hospital. I hope you get this message."

The slick airport lounge floor rotated beneath me, and I felt a stab of guilt. I hadn't spoken to my parents in weeks; months even. Did they have any idea I was out of the country? I thought of my own daughter back in Nashville, how it would wound me to hear that she'd flown across the Atlantic Ocean without my knowledge. It would be like a part of my own soul had set off from the earth, leaving me with a void inside and not knowing why.

I felt guilt for being out of touch, even though it's possible my dad hadn't even realized we'd been out of touch. We only talked on the phone when it was absolutely necessary.

I dialed the calling card access code and pin, then entered the childhood phone number I would never forget, to let my father know I'd be there in Pittsburgh the next day.

"It's up to you," he said. "She might pull through...or she might not." What must he have been thinking and feeling? All those years of taking care of my mom. He was seventy-five—how had he survived fifteen years of parenting his wife? It hadn't been easy for him to parent actual kids when I was growing up. He'd never been the tender, caring kind of parent my mother had been, but he'd done his best.

As soon as I landed in Atlanta, my cellphone rang. "When are you coming to Birmingham?" Charles asked, wanting to see me immediately. I told him about my mother.

"She'll be fine," he said. "What about me?"

I drove straight to Nashville and picked my daughter up from her dad's apartment.

"I think I need to go see my mother," I told Hazel. "I'm sorry, I know I just got home from tour."

"You should go, Mom," she said.

I collapsed into bed and in the morning drove to Pittsburgh, north through Kentucky, east at Cincinnati, skirting Columbus, and hitting Wheeling, West Virginia as it was getting dark. Charles called often to pout. "How can you do this to me?" he said. "You're selfish!" The BMW glided powerfully, silently over the hills into Pennsylvania. Why had I let him give me this car? And worse, how could I love it so much? After years of breaking down on the side of highways, it worked well. It was something to rely on.

I drove straight to the hospital I was born in and met my dad on my mother's floor. He showed me to her room and told me he'd see me back at their apartment, where he'd found her slumped on the bathroom floor a few days before. "I feel awful I wasn't there when she needed me," he said, breaking my heart and reminding me how human he was beneath the stern exterior.

My mother looked like a child in her hospital bed. She lay on her back, a breathing tube in her mouth. Her eyes were closed and she didn't appear to be conscious, but I felt sure she knew I was there. I held her hand and sat with her, watching her chest rise and fall. My mom. "I'm here, Mom," I said. "I'm okay." That's all I wanted her to know, because I'd learned as a mom it's all that matters, that your kids be okay.

I arrived at my parents' apartment in Senior Living at one AM and took half an Ambien. I fell into a real sleep, the one you can only get to when you know you've made it home. An hour later my older brother, John, called. "Mom's gone, Amy."

What if I hadn't come? Would she have held on? I felt sure she waited until after I arrived to let go—her last act of caring for me.

John and I told our dad his wife was gone. We sat up all night, figuring out what we needed to do. We decided she would've wanted the simplest pine box coffin. Then we hit on the idea she would have loved it if we painted the coffin in folk art bright colors and rustic designs. Country crafts and antiques and collectibles had been her life after we kids left home. A country coffin! We were sure of it—it's what we needed to do.

Then we were screaming with laughter, picturing neighbors and relatives and family friends' looks of shock and dismay at a *Country Living* casket. We calmed down and, when morning came, called the funeral parlor and asked for something standard.

John and I walked up and down hills through old familiar neighborhoods to the funeral parlor. I flashed on a high school-era joyride with my older brother and his buddies, drunk on beer, taking the steep narrow cobbled streets at a crazy speed while I screamed at them from the back seat to slow down. And here my family always called me the rebel. Wasn't I just a good girl whose hormones occasionally led her astray?

We brought an outfit for the director to dress my mom in. When the undertaker finished, I looked at her and she looked very wrong. He'd applied pink lipstick to her lips. My mom's overbite framed by Revlon Fire and Ice had been one of her standout features, part of what made her

her. To see her in pink lipstick was jarring. I decided this moment was the reason for my existence—to correct a ghastly but honest error that negated everything my mom had been and done and stood for. She WAS red lipstick, plain and simple. Classic.

Charles phoned again, asking when I was coming back. He sent a beautiful floral arrangement, because the best he could offer was the things money can buy.

My ex-husband Will brought Hazel to the funeral. Will loved my mother.

When all the relatives and friends were in the room with my mother laid out looking peaceful in her red lipstick, my brothers, sister-in-law Karen, our kids and I hung out in a den of the funeral parlor. There was a basket of old VHS tapes and a TV with a VCR. Patrick pulled out a tape.

"Hey, look, Tim Conway!" Our mom loved Carol Burnett's TV show, and all Carol's co-stars: Harvey Korman, Vicki Lawrence, good old Tim. This tape was called *Dorf On Golf.*

Dorf was a grown man who hobbled around with shoes on his knees to make him look especially short. Genius, in a silly way. We sat around the funeral parlor TV and laughed hysterically, taking turns crying. Other mourners approached the room and fled immediately, unsure what was happening around the TV but knowing they couldn't penetrate our circle of memory and despair. We watched Dorf tee up on a bright green golf course, shoes on his knees.

"Dorf, look after our mother!" we screamed, choking on tears and guffaws. "Dorf knows! Dorf knows all!"

Later, up in the apartment, we went through Mom's clothes and entertained ourselves trying them on. Somebody found a CD of '40s big band music and we jitterbugged and jived in colorful scarves and plaid jumpers, just like our mother would have done. This was my family.

My phone rang. It was Charles again. Michael was mincing around the room with shoes on his knees. I silenced the ringer.

Chapter Twenty-One

I met another singer/songwriter who was also a mom. Shelley had a crystalline voice and made flawless bluegrass records. She'd been raised Catholic like me.

Turned out we had something else in common—she had a civilian boyfriend too. Jeff was a doctor, some kind of surgeon. Divorced, with a big house in Memphis. Three hours to the west, just like Charles was three hours south.

When Shelley or I played in the round at the Bluebird, or had out of town gigs where the audience sat rapt and blessed us with applause, Charles or Jeff could stand proudly by after the show, within earshot of the merch table as the kudos rained down: "You were wonderful!" and "I love your voice/songs/that record you made!" These men took some credit for the work we did, work we'd been at for years before ever laying eyes or anything else on them, because now they were helping sustain us, weren't they? By believing in our talent; by loving us. Female artists often think they have to choose between work and love, unless they're married to fellow artists or musicians, and that's its own balancing act. It's rare to find another artist who will always be on your side, no matter how their own work is going. But, thanks to the generous nature of our exceptional men who weren't artists but lovers of the arts, Shelley and I could each HAVE IT ALL.

Except, just like Charles, Jeff demanded to keep tabs on every aspect of Shelley's life away from him. Who was that male fan spending extra time looking at all her CDs? What exactly did she talk about with a certain male co-writer? Sure, the one who seemed gay wasn't a problem, but that recently-divorced guy, wasn't it a little intimate spending time in his apartment? And did she really have to meet up for lunch with a male friend, I mean, what kind of message did that send?

Was this love, or patronage?

Shelley and I wrote a few songs together, warily keeping in touch as her guy and my guy made us each increasingly uncomfortable. We could see what was happening—clearly something was off—but we were like two drowning people shouting "HELP!" at each other.

As if he knew I was on the edge of slipping away, Charles doubled down with the gifts: a sleeker, faster laptop ("They practically give these away at work"); ProTools interface and recording software. I'd been happily making demos on my old Tascam Portastudio, but the new standard was digital. Nothing but the best for me, Charles insisted.

And wasn't it time I replaced my Guild guitar with something better? The blond acoustic was a part of me, but held a flaw, a warp to the neck no luthier had ever been able to solve. I was always breaking strings. It was such a frequent and unwelcome part of my show that I'd even titled a live solo CD, *I've Got the World on a Broken String*.

For thirteen years the Guild had been my guitar, although I also enjoyed playing the green Greco semi-hollow body electric my brother Michael found in Tennessee. I loved the unreasonable power of an electric guitar.

I'd had a moment of kismet and possibility out west in 2002. Guitarist Tony Gilkyson brought me to meet a guy called Fat Dog in Berkeley. His shop, Subway, was a warren of guitars and old gear, a hovel, but it felt like magic in there. I picked up a cheap hunk of plywood with a striped silver pickguard, sat on a chair and plugged into a little amp and felt immediately at home. I took my gig money from playing at the Freight and Salvage, opening for Richard Shindell, and bought it. A Teisco del Rey. It was cool to look at and cool to play.

But it was nothing but trouble. The first time I played the Teisco in public, in 2003 at the AAA radio convention in Louisville, the pickup collapsed inside the body during my second song. The first song sounded incredible, but I'd had to stop in front of the crowd and borrow Buddy Miller's guitar. I thought I was cursed when it came to guitars, having yet to learn that mechanical challenges come with the territory of playing an instrument, especially electric ones.

So, when Charles said I should treat myself to a better acoustic guitar, I took him up on his offer to pay for it. I searched all over Nashville, trying out acoustics and eventually ended up at Gruen on Lower Broadway. The place is a temple to wood and steel, six strings, twelve strings.

There are humidors for the finest specimens and racks and rows of every color wood from every type of tree that can be shaped into the body of a guitar.

The salesman was patient and knowledgeable, and when I finally walked out with a Gibson J45, I felt confident I'd found the guitar that suited me like no other.

That night, I slept alone in my room upstairs on Grantland Avenue, the guitar sitting in its open case. I swore the room smelled different with the Gibson in it, the sound hole giving off a slightly acrid woodsy smell of cut rosewood and varnish. A new guitar smell I'd never known before. When I woke up the next morning, I transcribed the dream I'd just had, where I was dancing with Joey Ramone.

Why had a new Gibson guitar, built in Montana and bought in Nashville, brought me a dream prince from Queens? All the radio memories of my years spent living in New York City, listening to CBS-FM, the same music Joey Ramone loved, danced around in my head and came out as a song. It hurts to say I don't think I would have afforded myself this beautiful instrument without Charles telling me I deserved it.

Dancing With Joey Ramone

He walked into the party looking just like he had in the past
He came up to me and he didn't even have to ask
I tried to say something he said Girl shut your mouth
They're playing Papa Was A Rolling Stone
Last night I was dancing with Joey Ramone

He was cool in his leather jacket and his little dark shades
We started dancing around I tried to copy every move he made
When I reached for his hand he kinda brushed me off
Then they played Hanging On The Telephone
Last night when I was dancing with Joey Ramone

They played The Worst That Could Happen by The Brooklyn Bridge
He Hit Me And It Felt Like A Kiss
Glad All Over, Needles and Pins
Be My Baby again and again
Gloria by The Shadows of Knight
He's So Fine and I Feel Alright
Charlie Brown, Can't Sit Down

We were dancing around and around
Well I closed my eyes for a minute and then he was gone
The room looked different but the music kept playing
On and on and on and on
When I woke up today I had a song in my head
I Wanna Wanna Wanna Go Home
They played it last night when I was dancing with Joey Ramone
Last night I was dancing with Joey Ramone

Of course, these gifts weren't free. "Where's *my* song?" Charles started asking. He wanted to hear himself immortalized in my music, while picking apart songs written years before I met him. "Who were you thinking about when you wrote this one?" he said again and again. I talked myself hoarse trying to explain to him it doesn't work that way, that songs are fiction shaped by real life.

When I wrote "Dancing With Joey Ramone," it was like I reclaimed a part of my young self—the pure fan, in love with music. A feeling I climb inside any time I play the song.

It turned out the guitar I shopped for all over town was the same make and model played by pretty much every rocking singer/songwriter in town. Lucinda Williams had one. So did Steve Earle, I realized the next month when I opened shows for him. "Wait, what's he doing with my guitar?"

I saw Steve had solo tour dates that spring. "You need to call him," Charles said. "Tell him you'd like to open the shows." I've never been good at pushing myself forward, asking for what I want. I'd written with Stacey, Steve's sister, and for years my ex-husband Will had played drums in Steve's band, The Dukes. Steve was close with Jack Emerson, and maybe the death of Jack made him feel warm towards me. Even though Jack and his partner Andy had turned me down as a solo artist, Jack probably talked me up to Steve for years. For whatever reason, Steve said yes. I'd do a good job, certainly. I was good at being the support. On and off in thirty-five to forty minutes. Maybe the audience doesn't expect much—oh, great, a lady with an acoustic guitar—and then I'd play "Balls" or "Cynically Yours," or "Give The Drummer Some" or "Don't Ever Change"—and catch them off guard. They'd laugh. They'd cheer. Steve offered me a berth on his tour bus for shows in Kentucky, Ohio, and Pennsylvania.

When Paul and I were together, he'd entertained me with stories of tour bus life, and I'd imagined I'd reach the point as an artist where I might even have my own bus. It sounded like a perfect cocoon, transporting artist and band from show to show without breaking the forcefield. That alternate reality didn't show signs of happening anytime soon, but it'd be nice to have the experience anyway.

Steve's bus picked up our touring party in the middle of the night at a bus depot way out in the wild north of Nashville. Like the massive Soundstage rehearsal complex, or mastering genius Hank Williams' sleek lab on Music Row, or any number of music execs' mansions I'd spied through fences on the outskirts of town, there were occasionally glimpses into the music business that served as reminders it wasn't an impossible dream. Mere mortals did reach the heights.

North of Nashville, there were acres of black asphalt and stars in the sky, and the very important instruction, "Don't poop on the bus," conveyed mere seconds after I'd climbed the steps and met the bus driver. One of Steve's sons, Ian, was along as guitar roadie, and there was a road manager, a good guy named Patrick. We played nice theatres for attentive audiences, middle-aged folks filling every seat and swarming the merch table after our sets to buy CDs and have them signed. I was lucky Steve was between albums and his fans already owned everything he'd put out, so I sold every CD I'd brought.

The thought of playing in front of such a large crowd was intimidating, but once I walked onstage, all my gigs' worth of experience kicked in and I felt confident, knowing I had songs people responded to whether they knew me or not. And with the J45, regular string-breaking seemed to be a thing of the past.

Steve was focused and nearly a decade sober, and after gigs the bus felt like a calm retreat. I thought there couldn't be a better place on earth than Steve Earle's tour bus rolling along through the mountains, not far from where I grew up, with a film or TV series on the entertainment system. Steve was partial to a new western called *Deadwood*, but I think my favorite moment was riding along beneath the moonlight in a hushed bus, everyone enthralled by a biopic called *Plath*, starring Gwyneth Paltrow as the doomed writer. Not the tour bus mayhem I'd envisioned.

Charles was far away. I worried he'd insist on following along behind us in his car. But he was an admirer of Steve's music, and even though he fretted about me ending up in Steve's stateroom on the bus—as he felt suspicious of every man I came in contact with between the ages of nineteen and ninety—even he knew where to draw the line.

After the last show, when we pulled back into the parking lot outside

Nashville at three AM, there was only the moon for illumination while I unloaded my guitar and bag from the hold underneath the bus and transferred everything to the back seat of my car. As I left the protective barrier of touring and pulled out onto the road, my phone lit up like I was being watched.

Chapter Twenty-Two

"Stop being so PERKY!" shouted Hazel, as we dragged our rolling suit-cases up the hill from London's Tufnell Park tube station. I carried my new Gibson acoustic guitar on my back in a black gig bag, and my duffel bag on my shoulder, packed to bursting with clothes and shoes. Hazel carried a snare drum in a soft case on her back. Her suitcase held clothes, mine was full of merchandise: CDs in those nasty plastic jewel boxes that were the only option in the early 2000s. At least my merch case felt light-er than when we set off—everything else seemed to have grown in weight and girth over the last two weeks of touring.

There were days I believed I led a charmed life: the thrill of travel and playing for people. Other times, I thought I must be insane to be do-ing this—the physical and mental toll. Life as a touring artist was usually a combination of those two things.

The distance from Nashville reminded me things weren't exactly sane and reasonable back home. I may have been winded climbing the streets of London, but I was breathing easier than I had in months.

Hazel had been working hard to learn to play drums, guitar, and bass. Brad Jones gifted her with a cool Danelectro longhorn bass, and I think we'd been housing one of Hazel's dad's spare drum kits. Not sure where she'd stay in Nashville during this early summer tour of a few weeks, it occurred to me she might enjoy coming along on the road and I'd asked if she'd like to join me for a few songs each night. I hoped it would give her something to look forward to at gigs rather than just dragging around with me, and would benefit me too because a) she was a cute kid who could play and sing and b) who couldn't use a guest star like that every night —especially one who didn't expect to be paid?

Hazel chose the songs. First was the Cramps version of Roy Orbison's

"Domino," with Hazel ripping the guitar solo perfectly every time. We sang X's "I Must Not Think Bad Thoughts" in unison, Hazel on the snare drum, the song finally resonating with me through Hazel's passionate reading of the anti-war sentiments—another instance I'd experience more and more over the years, where I thought I knew music but realized I didn't know all that much compared to my daughter.

Last, we covered "Mannequin" by Wire, a still relevant British band of the punk era. Starting together and breaking off into harmony brought me back to the days of the Shams—a vocal blend that felt so much more comfortable than standing out there all alone. Being mother and daughter, our voices genetically fit together to sound like one voice, double-tracked.

We'd prepped for the tour performing with my brother Michael's band, Susquehanna Industrial Tool & Die Co., at Otto's Shrunken Head lounge on East 14th Street in Manhattan, just a block from our old apartment between Avenues B and C. Will and I unloaded the apartment when the building went co-op in the late '80s for a buyout of three thousand dollars, approximately one month's rent in this neighborhood in 2003. Oh, to be young, poor and stupid again! Wait—forget poor and stupid.

Michael still lived in the apartment he'd had for years. He kept a monthly stand at Otto's, conveniently located just around the corner. The back room filled up with old friends who stopped by regularly to hear Michael's original songs that sounded like lost country classics, along with his ribald and often scathing comments about his band, the audience, but mostly himself. The night we joined him, everyone remembered back to when Hazel was a tiny girl in a grimy petticoat, and it filled me with pride to see her so cool and confident onstage. At the same time, I couldn't help but feel aware I was hanging out in a bar with my teenage daughter, and would be doing so for the next few weeks. Men were talking to her, and there was lots of alcohol around.

Then I remembered I'd been doing the same thing when I wasn't much older than she was now, without the safety of the stage to lift me above it all. My mother had no idea where I was back then, or what I was up to. I knew that would happen for Hazel, but for now we were together.

We'd begun the tour in Ireland, arriving in Dublin on a bright June day. I got the nagging feeling as we lugged all our bags and instruments on and off shuttle buses and down sidewalks that I was too old to be touring like this. Maybe it was the presence of my daughter, a constant witness to the continually trying circumstances I put myself through in order to play a gig. Up and down stairs, standing in long lines, moving constantly in and out of the wrong doors. No tour manager to smooth the way. It was the rugged life of a forty-five-year-old troubadour.

We checked into an almost-nice Dublin hotel on what turned out to be the first day of the city's new light rail system: there were balloons and free train rides, so we jumped aboard and rode as far as a pub, where we ate chips and I drank a pint of beer. A taxi driver taking us back to the hotel called the new line "a fookin' train to nowhere." The poetry of the Irish.

It was hard to stay awake that first day after an overnight transatlantic flight. We turned in early, but not before I checked in with Charles. This set a precedent for the entire trip: no matter how inconvenient, exhausting, or even downright unsafe it felt to stand at a phone box in the middle of a city or the edge of nowhere, he expected to hear from me at least once a day.

I'd told him I'd move in with him at the end of the summer. A few weeks earlier, Will had asked me to meet up at Wild Oats, the healthy supermarket next to the Green Hills mall. When we'd sat down with our smoothies, he told me he was getting married and moving to Northeast Ohio—to Cleveland.

I found myself saying, "That's funny. I'm getting married too. Hazel and I are moving to Alabama."

God bless Will, he took it in his stride. A part of my soul called out for the man I'd married and had a child with, who'd made me Beach Boys tapes and taken me to my first Bob Dylan concert; who'd wept with me when my mother was in a coma. The part of me who'd loved and looked up to him, that would forever live inside me, wished he'd shake me by the shoulders and say, "NO! DON'T DO IT!"

But he'd simply drawled, "Well, if you're sure, I guess, um—congratulations?"

And... what about Hazel? When faced with the option of living in Alabama where she knew no one except a man she mistrusted deeply, or moving in with her father and his new bride, my daughter felt which way the wind was blowing and chose... Cleveland.

So, this tour felt a little like our last hurrah.

I rented a car in Dublin, and it was harrowing leaving town. Trying to find the route, pre-GPS, adjusting to driving on the other side of the road—it was hard to appear as much of an authority figure to my kid while I kept bursting into panicked sobs for the few hours it took to drive across the country. But Hazel cheered me on supportively.

In the charming city of Cork, I managed to park outside our bed & breakfast without hitting the other cars and we carried the equipment and merch across town on foot. The gig wasn't very well-attended, but our duo bit especially was a hit with the people who'd come out. Afterwards, starving for a snack, we tried waiting in the queue at Kennedy Fried Chicken but felt so conspicuously female next to the boozed-up male contingent waiting for their chicken and chips that we gave up and climbed the hill back to our lodging, making do with the biscuits and long-shelf-life milk in our room. Nothing like touring to remind a woman it was still very much a man's world out there.

The hardships of the road bound us together like we'd been until Charles entered the picture. I tried not to think about the future—me with him; her with her father and his wife. Ireland was lovely and the locals were colorful, especially in Sligo. It was one more place to add to my list of possible places to escape to. I pictured myself ambling into the town shops dressed in a poncho and turban where I'd buy whiskey and biscuits. "There goes that American lady," the townspeople would say. "The one from New York by way of Nashville…"

They loved us at Barry's Pub in the small village of Grange near Sligo, repeatedly toasting us during and after the gig and practically carrying us out on their shoulders at the end of the night. But our Irish idyll was disturbed when thieves broke the window of our rental car outside a hotel near Limerick ("the armpit of Ireland," the locals called it). They stole Hazel's snare drum and my suitcase of merchandise out of the trunk. I sobbed into the arms of a soft-spoken garda who shook his head and said, "Who knows? Perhaps this'll be the start of great things for you here in Ireland. Look on the bright side—this may be the best distribution your CDs get!"

And Hazel, being herself at least a quarter Irish, chimed in, "And we've got less luggage to carry now…"

The police recovered the snare drum and the CDs, which felt like some kind of judgment.

It was a cold night in Hull. In my experience it was always a cold night in Hull, even in the middle of July. This port city in the Northeast, where the River Hull meets the Humber Estuary meets the North Sea, kept calling me back. The robbery and dealing with the police and the rental car company made for good stage banter in London: "We had a shit time in Ireland." It never failed to get a London audience on your side, trashing the last place you played before hitting the Smoke. But up in Hull, I had a crisis of faith. What was I doing here, yet again? The B&B with themed rooms ("Egypt," "Mexico"), a shared bathroom and huge TV in the parlor blaring a lurid Guns N' Roses video was a step down from the Beverley Road one from previous trips, if that was possible. The walk to the venue took forever and both Hazel and I cursed my penny-pinching ways. I would've hailed a cab if only I could've found one.

"Does it ever get any better than this?" I shouted at the grey sky as it spit freezing rain. I'd taken some kind of absurd pride in playing this town again and again. Having my daughter along as witness made it feel more like an exercise in futility.

I told her how I met Wreckless Eric a few visits back, playing at the Bull Hotel. She loved his record, "Take the K.A.S.H." "He went to art college here in Hull," I said. Hazel was thinking of applying to art school herself.

This time I was back at the Adelphi, a rock club I first played with Sid Griffin in 2000. Amy Allison and Neil Cleary and I did our triple bill show here back in November 2003. The venues in the U.K. were all freezing during soundcheck as the landlords kept the heat off till the punters came in. The familiar smell of disinfectant mingled with the odor of beer was comforting and anxiety-inducing; would anyone show up? Hazel laughed when the club owner Paul asked if we fancied a curry, exactly as I'd predicted he would. We felt oddly at home.

There was an appreciative audience. We survived our night in Egypt and the shared bathroom. Newcastle. Wellingborough. Back to London for a set at Come Down and Meet The Folks, a long-running Sunday afternoon gig. Hazel was resplendent in a mod yellow coat, and my Nashville pal, Dave Jacques, played bass on a few songs. People kept putting fresh beers on the stage. I remembered how much I loved London—a love hard-won back in 1980-81 when I spent a year there as a penniless art student, outside the cocoon of downtown no wave New York. I'd learned survival skills then, and no small measure of humility. But there was never enough of that for an artist, certainly not in Nashville, or out in the world as a touring musician.

"I hear Wreckless Eric might drop by this afternoon," said Big Steve the promoter. Someone said Eric had a book coming out soon, an autobiography. I wanted to read that book.

Brighton, Leicester. I left my guitar on the train taking us from Leicester to... somewhere else, where we'd need to change trains again.

My litany, throughout the tour—"Do we have everything?" repeated in a shrill, frantic tone until it was almost a joke—had become so automatic I didn't even notice why I felt lighter than usual, without that weight on my back, until we were on another train to Sheffield. I screamed, I sobbed, but the conductor radioed ahead to the first train, they removed my guitar at the next station, and another conductor met me on the platform, holding the Gibson aloft in its familiar black case. I cried with relief and drank a small bottle of wine from the snack cart. Hazel pretended not to know me.

Glasgow, Edinburgh, and Aberdeen. Trains and help from friends. I rented a car in Aberdeen to drive to Cumbria for one last gig. The scenery was stunning, billowing clouds and sheep; tall hedges and tumbling hills. It was a very long way to go for a gig in a tiny village pub. The soundman was deaf, everyone drank heavily—the only reason I was there was the barmaid was the mother of the woman who booked the tour. Hazel and I tried to sleep in one of the rooms above after the gig, needing to wake and leave at three AM to drive back up to Edinburgh to catch a flight home.

"Dah-ling, you're not lea-ving!?" croaked the '50s-ish leather-clad barmaid when she saw us trying to tiptoe to our car past the drunken revelers. Then she tumbled headfirst into a beat-up van to the strains of Neil Diamond. I thought comfortingly that there were all kinds of moms in the world, and I was just one of them. Certainly not the best, but probably not the worst.

Hazel shouted at me to slow down as I careened around rabbits on tiny roads before reaching the motorway. The sun was just coming up. We listened to the Velvet Underground and ate caramel logs and bacon rolls from the motorway services and it felt like we were the only car in the whole world.

"I know you probably think it wasn't worth it to play that gig, and right now I totally agree with you," I told my daughter. "But years from now you'll remember this moment."

She probably doesn't. But I hold onto the image of her in that yellow coat; her effortless shredding on guitar and the blur of our voices singing together; the exasperated way she said "Mom."

I put it out of my mind, that we were leaving each other and Nashville—me for Birmingham, her to Cleveland. If I didn't think about it, maybe it wasn't really happening.

Chapter Twenty-Three

I was dressed in a form-fitting charcoal pin-striped dress—something a lawyer might wear, or a real estate agent. My hair was subtly colored a bit redder than natural, and I'd attempted to smooth it into waves that brushed my shoulders. I wore a lavender cardigan with a spiky lavender flower pinned over the breast. I had never worn lavender, or any color in the purple family, in my life. My mother hated purple.

Was it ironic that I was wearing purple this day of all days? I'd come to Pittsburgh to watch my father get married. It had been less than a year since my mother passed away, but my brothers and I accepted how our dad did an honorable, impossible thing looking after her for years, and he deserved some joy.

On my arm, or slightly behind me in a sharp business suit, was Charles.

I'd kept Charles as far away from my family as I could. He was prone to saying embarrassing things about my talent and his money, and how those two things made him better than everyone else. I'd never known anyone so full of themselves. What made it worse was the thrill I occasionally got from being with an asshole.

The entire population of the senior living facility came to pay their respects to my dad and his bride, Lois, like they were the king and queen of the place. Their love story gave hope to the other residents—many also in their mid-seventies and beyond—that romance might find them again too. I was happy to see my father happy, even though Lois—widowed, childless, retired schoolteacher; Episcopalian (i.e. Catholicism lite)—added a generic quality to our family we might never recover from, like when the Who tried replacing drummer Keith Moon with Kenny Jones. As much as Lois was a fine woman who went out of her way to fit into our band, she was no Keith Moon—our unique and irreplaceable mother.

I was trying to give Birmingham a chance, thinking it might even be refreshing to not be in Nashville, with its constant reminders of whatever I felt was lacking in my career. Even with a new record out, kind support from local writers and other musicians in town, a publishing deal—in Nashville I couldn't help but weigh myself against anyone I encountered in a social setting. If they said, "I'm recording," I'd think, "When will *I* make another record?" If the other person had holds on a few songs, I'd conclude that no one would ever record one of *mine*. If someone said they'd been writing with so and so, I'd think, "Why won't you write with *me*?" but felt embarrassed asking them to write with me. If they wanted to, wouldn't they ask me first? I hated this part of myself in Nashville—the needy, never-satisfied part.

Charles didn't have a particular affinity for the city he lived in, or the south in general. He was a Midwesterner who relocated for a job. His neighborhood, way up in the hills away from downtown, felt isolated, the impressive homes safely insulated from the rest of the world by massive yards, fences, giant trees, and ravines. Maybe I held some fantasy of being lady of the house, a throwback to my suburban '60s youth, where I'd get to redecorate the place, my design choices eradicating every trace of Charles' previous wife. I'd continue writing and recording, making more and better progress as an artist without constantly worrying about money. No way would I spend my time stockpiling groceries from Costco and working out in the finished basement.

So, what was I doing running on the treadmill in the basement, watching *Good Morning America* while James the cat prowled around Charles' kids' abandoned sports equipment, yearbooks, and volumes of the Encyclopedia Britannica?

Poor James the cat. Charles had relegated him to the basement. A spacious, clean, climate-controlled room, at least. It was carpeted, and there was always fresh food and water and a clean litter box for him, but he was alone. It felt wrong to sequester a cat like that. How could I have agreed to this? I'd been ambivalent about keeping a pet, but loved Hazel's love for James.

James circled me on the treadmill and cried to be let out so he could explore the rest of the house. "What are we gonna do, buddy?" I asked him.

Hazel had moved north in time to start eleventh grade at Shaker

Heights High School. A decent school. That was an improvement, but it all felt wrong. I hoped she would soon be accepted to a college she loved and then maybe all of this would make sense. I'd rented out the main part of our house in Nashville and kept the attic for those days when I needed to be in town to co-write, or as an escape hatch.

After the cake and champagne toasts and goodbyes to my father and Lois, their happiness a shield against the obvious question, "Why the fuck is Amy living in Alabama?" Hazel joined Charles and me in his BMW to drive her back to Cleveland, where she was performing that night at the Grog Shop, just down the road from her dad and stepmother's house in Shaker Heights. It was exciting that she'd join our friends, Yo La Tengo, to sing an X song in front of a sold-out crowd to benefit John Kerry's presidential campaign.

We were walking along a street in Cleveland Heights to soundcheck when my phone rang. It was a New Orleans number which felt strange. Who would be calling me from New Orleans on a Saturday night?

It was a friend of my friend Kelly, calling to let me know that Kelly had been found dead that morning. A fatal mix of drink and drugs. I crumpled to the sidewalk. Kelly was the most fun, alive person I knew—she couldn't be dead. She loved music above all else, had hosted me and my bands in New Orleans and then Boston for years, lived with Hazel and me in Brooklyn briefly before returning to her beloved New Orleans to open the Circle Bar. Kelly dead was a crime against nature.

Getting through the night, witnessing Hazel's triumph, was only possible because I was Hazel's mother. With her imprecise chestnut bob, slight frame and cool clothes—a bit of showmanship where she pulled off a shoe and hit herself in the head—my daughter won the band's admiration and respect from the crowd. For a little while, parental pride buffered my state of shock at the news of Kelly's death. Charles was uncomfortable in the rock club, stiff and close-lipped until Hazel had gone home to her dad's and he and I checked into a hotel near downtown Cleveland. Then he berated me all night. What kind of person was I, with friends who died from DRUGS? What kind of life was I leading my brilliant daughter towards? On and on until we both finally fell asleep exhausted. I decided, for the twentieth time, I must leave him.

But I'd moved my books, my clothes, my music stuff into his house. My daughter was residing in another state. Back in Birmingham, I got in the car—the one he gave me—without discussion and drove to New Orleans, to stay with my old boyfriend Robert Mache and his wife Candace.

They made me feel loved and supported. They were musicians, artists—friends of Kelly's too. They understood what had been lost.

At the funeral, there was food and music and the vivid green of Eunice, the Cajun town I knew all about from Kelly's stories. I bought a crawfish pie from the place she'd buy them when she lived with me and Hazel and would fly back to New York from Louisiana with a cooler full of pies on dry ice to stick in our freezer in Brooklyn until that moment when a party just had to happen.

Driving back north, I didn't know where to go. My daughter was in Cleveland, my house was in Nashville. Then my phone rang. Charles: "When are you coming back to Birmingham?"

Chapter Twenty-Four

I'd been living in Birmingham about two months when I needed to head out for a run of solo gigs up north. Charles blew leaves—forearms tensed, leaf blower brandished as if protecting his castle— while I packed up the car with my guitar and merchandise, thankful he was too busy with work to join me in my travels, as he'd frequently mentioned he planned to do whenever possible.

Heading towards my first stop in Virginia, I felt like an independent person again. I listened to music, talked on the phone with my brothers, checked into motels or stayed with friends. I was happy to be on my own.

Late one night, driving a dark country road, words came to me in couplets with a refrain, and I repeated them to stay awake. I missed this, being out on the road, feeling like myself. Even the challenging parts of touring: the long drives and lack of decent food. I relished the feeling of peace. Most days, I could barely hear myself think. It was always Charles' voice in my ear, in my head. Was it any wonder I hadn't written many songs lately? But here one came, like rainwater through a dried-up stream.

I Don't Wanna Talk About Love No More

I'm tired of emotional discussions
I'm tired of repercussions
I'm sick of the O's and the X's and the sex and the battle
And the battle of the sexes
I don't wanna talk about love no more
I don't wanna talk about love no more
I don't wanna talk about love no more

I don't wanna talk about it

I've had enough of the soulmate searches
I've had enough of the stomach lurches
I'm through with the me and the you, and the why and the who
And the one plus one equals
I don't wanna talk about love no more

I need a rest from the endless drama
I need a break from the oo-wee mama
I'm bored with the heart and the sword and the teardrop starts and
The minor chord
I don't wanna talk about love no more

Let's discuss the hybrid car, let's eulogize the mason jar
Let's analyze roofing tar and A Bridge Too Far
Chicago blues, the right to choose
A swingin' door, the Croque Monsieur, the working poor, the war
I don't wanna talk about love no more
I don't wanna talk about love no more
I don't wanna talk about love no more

Next day, somewhere in between Fredericksburg and Charlottesville, driving through an alley of trees etched in fading green and bright yellow leaves, I had a revelation: I didn't have to do this. Charles kept trying to convince me I couldn't survive without him, but as I drove to the next gig, I worked my way forward from where I was at the moment.

I decided I could live in my attic if I had to. I could get a job at McDonald's if I had to. I would write more songs and make records and play shows. I still had a family. I still had friends; at least I hoped I hadn't alienated all of them.

I pulled over at a rest area and called the therapist I'd been seeing back in Nashville. For months I'd been hoping she'd tell me this relationship was wrong. I left her a message saying I'd come to a decision and was feeling resolute and strong.

A phrase appeared in my head, and I repeated it as a mantra—"This just isn't right for me"—so when I returned to Birmingham to gather up my things and move out, I would have words that didn't leave room for argument or debate.

"But," I imagined him saying, "you have no money! What—you're going to live in an attic? Don't be ridiculous."

This just isn't right for me.

"Nobody will ever love you or appreciate you and your talent like I do!"

This just isn't right for me.

"Your friends are losers, your career is going nowhere. Stay here with me, you can pick out a whole new kitchen."

This just isn't right for me.

I remained calm back at Charles' house. It was early evening. He brought in the mail and opened a package. "Oh good, it's here." He held up a box set: the complete *Barney Miller* on VHS.

"Wow," I said. "You must really like that show."

"Best show ever made. You're watching it."

I liked the show, in principle. But nobody should dictate what TV show or movie another person has to love, ever.

Charles had a lazy-boy chair, like a dad on television. There was a chair for me too. "Sit down, we're watching," he said.

"I did a lot of thinking out on the road," I said. I heard the cat at the basement door—whining, scratching to be let out. I imagined myself in a few years becoming more and more like James, a shadow figure that used to have a personality and a name.

"I can't do this," I said. "Not just the show. The... everything."

"You're so cute when you're mad," said Charles. On the television screen, Barney Miller looked supportively frazzled.

"I've decided I need to move back to Nashville," I told Charles. Charles paused the video. I said it out loud: "This just isn't right for me."

I heard the screen door slam downstairs and watched the young woman who'd rented the ground floor of my house trip lightly down the front steps of the Victorian duplex, her long wavy hair flying out behind her. The mint green house that had briefly been my pride—a house I managed to buy myself, with money from a publishing deal, a loan from my dad, and owner-financing—was now a source of anguish, and not quite enough income to keep the mortgage, property tax, and insurance payments going.

My tenant unlocked her car and drove off into the soft afternoon light, to a gig or her restaurant job. I'd crept back to Nashville and was living in my attic like a boarder, cooking on a hot plate, spending most of my time at the Frothy Monkey, a new coffee shop over on 12th Avenue South, or downtown in the impressive new public library. The house —and Nashville—just didn't feel like home, because my daughter wasn't there anymore. She'd jumped ship and moved in with her father in Cleveland. I didn't blame her. I was embarrassed to see anyone I knew who might ask me how're things in Alabama. So, I hung out amongst strangers, drinking coffee and writing emails, planning to record a new album in New York.

When Hazel came for a visit, we lay side by side on the double bed in the attic, her old room downstairs now occupied by a young woman neither of us knew.

"Why did you do it?" she asked. "You changed everything."

"I'm so sorry, Haze," I said. "I screwed up, you don't deserve any of this." Hazel was quiet. I loved her so much, I would've let her hit me with a mallet if that helped her feel better. I said the only words I could think to say. "I know I'm your mom but I'm only human. Sometimes people make mistakes."

I moved my stuff out of Charles' house. Nothing too sudden or drastic. I didn't want to call too much attention to the fact that I was going.

Things I left behind in Alabama:

A copy of Larry McMurtry's novel *Moving On* I'd carried with me from East Fourteenth Street in Manhattan to Withers and then Grand Street in Brooklyn; to Nashville; to here

A pair of dark green John Fluevog Chelsea boots bought on sale at Trash & Vaudeville

A powder blue leather car coat I never liked anyway

A dark red Moschino cardigan patterned with hearts and the word "Love"

A hardcover copy of Jimmy Webb's book on songwriting, *Tunesmith*

A paperback of Tammy Wynette's autobiography, *Stand By Your Man.*

Charles bought tickets for Kris Kristofferson at the Ryman Auditorium. November 2004—Kris' first ever solo show at the hallowed venue. He was a genuine fan of everything the great songwriter had to offer. When he told me he wanted to take me to the concert, I said, "Okay—just this once," imagining remaining friends might make breaking up easier. I'd stayed on speaking terms with most of my exes over the years, hadn't I?

Kris strummed and croaked his way through the set, hit after hit. I nearly lost it during "Sunday Mornin' Comin' Down." How could one man—in denim shirt, jeans, shambling guitar playing and deeply-lived vocals— contain the whole world up there on stage?

And Charles loved him so much. There was a side to the guy that truly appreciated artists. He was no heathen. He believed in Randy Newman, Todd Snider... he believed in me. But appreciating feelings is not the same as having feelings.

I thought back to the first time I visited Nashville with Last Roundup, and we crept into this place through a side door. It was musty, dusty—in those days always a few steps ahead of the wrecking ball. I'd stood on the stage in the empty auditorium and, though I never expected I'd perform here —not false modesty, just pragmatism—I still felt like I belonged. Sitting there twenty years later in the reverent Ryman hush (it must be the church pews that offer potential for a come to Jesus moment at every concert), I felt again how there's no shortcut to self-worth. Hank Williams stood up on that stage singing about how we all had to walk the lonesome valley by ourselves.

In the lobby during intermission, I ran into Chet Flippo and Martha Hume. They'd been like guardian angels during my first year or two in Nashville. Chet, as country music editor of *Billboard*, had championed me any chance he could. Martha, talented writer and wit, had been so kind and willing to have my daughter over if I needed a babysitter. Seeing them now, I felt like I was waving through smeared plexiglass. I set down my cup of Ryman white wine to hug them and avoided introducing them to Charles. Who knew what humiliating thing he'd say? I wanted their night to remain the pure joy I saw in their faces. I didn't want them worrying about me and Hazel.

Back in the auditorium for the second set, Kris took the audience through every emotion. When he sang "The Pilgrim"—how all he'd ever gotten was older and around—I heard Charles softly singing along beside me. I had to admit, I'd loved the guy. There were moments of our time together where I'd lived in a beautiful dream, feeling appreciated and taken care of—cherished, even. He made me laugh and come; feel smart. He also harangued and insulted me, alienated my daughter, family, and friends; upended my life. He'd probably berate me later—there was no way to have a good night without it turning into a bad one in that relationship. But for the moment, in the Ryman, I tried to focus on Kris singing his songs, the way Chet and Martha rated me as an artist, and the human side of Charles.

Chapter Twenty-Five

December 2004. It felt like the whole of downtown NYC had come out for guitarist Robert Quine's memorial at CB's Gallery. Quine died at the end of May that year—I'd been holed up in a hotel room in Portland between gigs when I read the news. New York City had never felt so far away.

Now I was back on the Bowery, a place that used to feel like home: the trash and bums sharing sidewalk space with restaurant equipment stores. Lately it was feeling strangely tidy, like they were sprucing the place up. They were—the Guiliani days had given way to the Bloomberg era: construction in overdrive, stop-and-frisk, bike lanes.

It was one of those perfect, brisk days you get in Manhattan—not yet fully winter, the light between the buildings still sharp. Lenny Kaye, who'd been like the pied piper of what became punk—anthologizing the psychedelic era with the *Nuggets* compilations and accompanying Patti Smith from the beginning—had asked my old band, the Shams, to participate in the tribute. Lenny loved the Shams and produced our first and only album. We'd come along to the scene of our underwhelming CMJ Halloween appearance over a decade past. Back then, each of us had dressed as a male character we admired or aspired to be: Sue, Purple Rain-era Prince; Amanda, a cross between Joey Ramone and Willy DeVille; I'd been a country rock-era Neil Young or less charismatic JD Souther. Now, we dressed as ourselves, feeling—like everyone else at the event—that time really was moving faster and faster. Quine had been an "older" musician, in his mid-thirties back when he'd played in Richard Hell's Voidoids, before anointing albums by Lou Reed, Matthew Sweet, and Tom Waits with his lovingly vitriolic playing. He died at sixty-one.

The walls of CB's Gallery were stark white, a contrast to the graffiti-covered original CBGB that would hang on for another two years next door, but the spirit of the original club was alive in the Gallery that afternoon. It didn't feel right to see so many denizens of the night—everyone wearing black— in broad daylight, but people looked good in a way I wouldn't, until years later, understand still held the bloom of youth. Even those who'd lived hard seemed dewy in retrospect. Maybe those were even the folks who aged especially well, as years of abuse tended to halt time.

I felt sad I never took Quine up on his offer to record with me—"No offense, but some of your chord changes are a little, um, stock, and I think I could take them away from that," he'd said when I'd run into him at St. Marks Guitars before my move to Nashville. I'd been flattered—flabbergasted—that he'd listened to any song of mine beyond the ones he'd played guitar on when the Shams made our album in 1991. Quine in the studio back then had been like a visit from an elegant poltergeist. Now, in 2004, it was beginning to sink in that our heroes' and friends' tenure on earth wasn't guaranteed. Kirsty MacColl, Joe Strummer, and Joey Ramone—I could still count on one hand the influential people gone from my life before I had a chance to fully register what they'd meant.

And the biggest name of all—for me, anyway: Olympia Ann Costanzo McMahon. My mother, deceased almost a year to the day of the Quine memorial. Mourning her had been drawn out over the course of the fifteen years she'd lived with a brain injury, and will continue till I'm gone too. But I preferred not to dwell on the loss. In my mid-forties, I didn't want to think about mortality. I still just wanted to make my mark. And help my daughter get where she needed to be.

Along with the Shams' appearance at the Quine memorial—singing Richard Hell's "Time" to the crowd who all knew the song and felt it deeply in this sad new context—we were performing a whole set together for the first time in ten years at one of Yo La Tengo's Hanukkah shows. Ira Kaplan, Georgia Hubley, and James McNew had begun their tradition of playing each of the eight nights of Hanukkah at the Hoboken club, Maxwell's, a few years back. The shows were full of surprise guests, band reunions, and star turns. This year, Ira had tracked down a special guest to perform the same night as the Shams: Wreckless Eric.

Scott Schinder, who'd burned me that Greatest Stiffs album some years back, had managed to find a copy of Eric's new autobiography, *A Dysfunctional Success*, and mailed it to me in Nashville. It unlocked a little of the mystery of the guy I met briefly in Hull, who kept threatening to come see me play when I was over in the U.K. but never showed up. The book was charming and funny, full of detail about growing up on the south coast of England, art school in Hull, and his musician beginnings through his time on, and then off of, the Stiff label. But it left out some of the other things I wanted to know, like what kind of girls he liked, and how exactly did you become his girlfriend? It felt like serendipity that we'd be playing in Hoboken on the same night—we'd connected in that room above a pub in Hull, nearly five years ago. Maybe it was his green guitar, or the magic of playing his song together and the way he told me I was doing it wrong. It just seemed we were meant to be friends. Or more? I heard he was involved with somebody, and I was just extricating myself from a difficult relationship.

I'd lost count of how many nights I'd spent at Maxwell's either as an audience member or performer. The place had always been a steamy beacon in what used to feel like a far-flung corner of the hinterlands—i.e. not New York City—but Hoboken was becoming more and more developed: condos, gyms, coffee shops. Outside on that Friday afternoon, the weather had turned: a snowstorm was blowing in. The cozy front restaurant/bar started filling up with diners and drinkers. Past the kitchen and restroom vestibule, then around a corner, the Shams unpacked our stuff on the floor in front of the stage, I kept one eye towards the door, wondering when Eric would appear. Would I recognize him?

He arrived brushing snow off himself, just like the first time we met. There was an atmosphere around him that was hard to pin down, an Oliver Twist boyishness and poignancy. I told him I had his book, that I was amazed to know a person who'd written an autobiography—I saw it as a terrifying act of bravery. I hoped he'd tell me how he did it. I'd been writing an online diary but still had hopes of writing a book myself. I'd made a few attempts at getting started but in my current situation, any kind of writing felt too risky. The necessary elements of honesty were constrained when another person was measuring your every word.

Eric asked if the Shams had worked on our back-up vocals for his cover of Neil Diamond's "The Boat That I Row." We had, and rehearsed it onstage with him and the band. He was impressed by our chops, especially when Sue busted out the organ solo note for note.

"You're all so professional!" he told us, probably the first time that word had ever been spoken in the Shams' direction. This band had been so important in my development as a songwriter and musician. I would always feel like a carefree girl when Sue and Amanda and I were together, remembering the hours spent hanging out and rehearsing: blending our voices, aiming for ideas and notes we couldn't reach. Watching Oprah, passing around paperbacks by Anne Tyler and Tony Robbins; recipes for cornbread—then sitting at the kitchen table with my daughter in a baby seat in the middle while we laughed and argued about the best way to get somewhere, anywhere, with our harmonies, thrift shop aesthetic, free-wheeling covers, and the faith the other girls put in my songs.

After dinner in the front bar that transformed into a rambunctious episode of *This Is Your Life*, with friends appearing from across the years—the Parsons art school/punk days; early band and married life and parenthood era; temp years and solo artist genesis—I felt a chill that had nothing to do with the winter air and wet snow outside. Charles had arrived. It was his right to be here, he said.

I reminded myself that my actual friends way outnumbered Charles, that there was life ahead of me, and here was Wreckless Eric, looking at me like he wished we could go off together.

It turned out he had a girlfriend who cast her own heavy shadow. But once the show began, none of that mattered. The Shams goofily shuffled on and harmonized our way through forty minutes: we sang "Only A Dream," "Down At The Texaco," and "File Clerk Blues," our wistful chemistry creating a timeless atmosphere that dispelled messy midlife concerns.

Down At The Texaco

He makes my motor run, he makes my wheels spin
Round and around and around
He cleans the windshield, fills me up when
I am down down down
He's got a greasy rag in his pocket
He wears a nametag over his heart
And I know that I should stop it
But whenever we're apart
I think about his hands when he's holding the pump
Think about his smile when I tell him "fill er up"
Think about his hair falling down in his eyes
Think about the way that he never even tries
I fell in love down at the Texaco

I need a tuneup, I need some bodywork
He's the one I go to see
I could go elsewhere, but he won't be there

He's the only brand for me
He doesn't work on Fridays or Sundays
Those days I don't even get in my car
Located right off the interstate highway
Under the big red star
I think about his hands when he's holding the pump

When Eric took the stage with Yo La Tengo, I was convinced he was one of the best performers I'd ever seen. He sang Paul Simon's "America" so heart-wrenchingly, the whole room stood riveted. I thought of Reg Presley in the Troggs, or Davy Jones singing "Daydream Believer." I even forgot Charles was there, looking out of place in a tweed suit jacket and crisp shirt, the very combination I'd found erotic back when we started up.

At the end of the show when everyone was packing up, I said good-bye to Eric as he put on his parka. Our souls reached towards each other like two people on a dark train platform, one boarding an express going into that tunnel, the other taking the local in the opposite direction.

Then I went back to a Manhattan hotel with Charles and the same old litany started up again: "Your friends are losers, without me you're nothing, stop this nonsense and stay with me..." Why didn't I grab my clothes and take my guitar and head for my brother Michael's apartment only twenty or so blocks away? I could ring the buzzer and sleep on his ancient dark red vinyl sofa that always felt like home. Had I become addicted to defending my life? Charles and I had sex—along with music, my only power over him—and I finally fell asleep, thinking, "I will get away from you. I have my songs and my friends and my family, and you can take back all the gifts you insisted I accept from you, but *you can't have those.*"

A few nights later, I went alone to my old East Village neighborhood to see Eric play a gig at the Lakeside Lounge. The place was packed. Eric solo commanded the crowd easily, his humor and honesty and brutally loud guitar goosing people to laugh and cheer. I saw the woman I'd noticed at Maxwell's hanging around him looking cool—New York superior and very proprietary. Through the big plate glass window next to the stage, I could see people on the icy sidewalk in front of the club watching Eric as he hunched over his amplifier, creating squalls with the Microfret. It was like those photos of Jackson Pollock throwing paint on a canvas. When he finished, I gave him a wave goodbye and stepped out of the steamy bar onto Avenue B. "That's an artist," I thought.

Chapter Twenty-Six

I'd started wondering if I should move back to New York. Over and over, I listened to Bob Dylan's "Mississippi," from *Love & Theft*, where he sang about how you can always come back but not all the way...I feared that may be true. I'd left the city, and I needed to follow the thread that took me away from the place. Instead of moving back, I decided to make my next record there.

Maybe I felt too ashamed to face my friends in Nashville. Maybe I craved the comfort of old neighborhoods, haunts, and players—the way the city can fill in the missing or broken parts of yourself if you let it. It might be like resetting the clock, to a time before I made such a mess of my life. Almost like living there again. Like coming home, without the challenge of real estate.

Jon Graboff and I met in the one-bedroom apartment he shared with his wife Carissa at London Terrace, a stately 1920s apartment complex in Chelsea. Jon was one of my few NYC friends who lived in my Manhattan dream of an elevator building. Most people I knew were tenement rats.

We sat down with our guitars and sketched out arrangements for twelve songs. Then we convened with drummer Dennis Diken of the Smithereens, bass player John Conte, and pianist Joe McGinty, who'd rented my old Brooklyn apartment when Hazel and I moved south. Tracking took place over two days at Andy Taub's Brooklyn Recording studio out in...Brooklyn. It felt so urban—raw and exciting—taking the subway and walking the many blocks to the studio; then all of us playing the songs together, as I tried to nail as many live vocals as possible. Two days to record an entire album save for overdubs—how hard could it be?

I had a good new set of songs, and perhaps above all, New York, the dear old friend I could lean on in my moment of crisis. Whatever happened, I thought, I could always come back here, even if only in the artistic sense. The city had for sure seen way worse than my sad fuck-up.

"Girls Got It Bad," "Year of the Fling," "I Don't Wanna Talk About Love No More," "Dancing With Joey Ramone;" Lenny Kaye's song, "The Things You Leave Behind," that he'd moved everyone with at Robert Quine's memorial. I played electric or acoustic guitar and sang in an isolation booth where I could see all the players. There was even a moment where Jon and I both played electric sitars: one red, one purple. What a sound! Nothing could feel better for me at that moment than hanging out with four guys. I grew up with four brothers and we'd been a noisy gang. Same with Dennis, Jon, Joe and John. We egged each other on and created our own little world for a while.

It reminded me of when my parents had hired that cranky old babysitter, Mrs. Starrett, to watch over my brothers and me while they went away on a business trip. We'd rioted in the game room, building an unstable fort out of patio furniture, taking turns riding a Flexible Flyer down the stairs, and playing "The Lonely Bull" over and over at 78 rpm. It's possible that ability to go wild as a unit is what drew me to playing rock music in the first place—the way reason and individual judgment can recede and a unified insanity take hold; one of the best kinds of communion, not those crappy wafers at Catholic Mass.

I left New York with rough mixes of twelve songs, and flew to Cleveland to hang out with Hazel for a few days around Christmas. Her dad and his wife were traveling for the holidays. I appreciated the opportunity to see what my daughter's life in this unfamiliar place was like. Will still played drums in Steve Earle's band and his wife had a job in Northeast Ohio. They'd bought a house in Shaker Heights, the neighborhood an odd combination of huge mansions, Tudor-style apartment buildings, and humble foursquares, rich and poor, black and white.

The house was a grown-up kind of place, with original built-in cabinetry and hardwood floors. In the well-appointed kitchen, Hazel and I were mom and daughter again, preparing quesadillas or pasta for dinner.

"Such a nice house," I said to Hazel, looking around admiringly. "And Shaker Heights is a good school—famous for its excellence, even!"

"I guess," she said. "I miss our old life." Hazel was a lot like her father, not prone to emoting or revealing too much. She took the Crate and Barrel neutral-toned plates from the dishwasher and stacked them in the sleek kitchen cabinet. "I miss when nothing matched." Fiestaware, Blue Ridge, Homer Laughlin—our old jumble of flea market and thrift shop finds. I knew what she meant. They languished back in Nashville, in a box in the attic.

I'd only wanted to make life nicer for her; easier. Buy new clothes, drive a better car that didn't break down. Have the wherewithal for college. Make her proud. She was telling me that none of that mattered. The ramshackle life we made up as we went along had always been good enough for her. It was me who worried it wasn't enough.

In that second, I knew what I had to do.

I gave Charles back the BMW and replaced it with an Astrovan I'd noticed festooned with FOR SALE signs, parked around the corner from his house. The house he'd let me redecorate, the place I'd tried to think of as mine for a minute.

"You still love me, right?" Charles asked, as he wrote out a check for the minivan. I nodded and crossed my fingers behind my back.

"Sure I do," I said, feeling like the worst grifter. I'm a lot of things, but I've never been a liar. Just this once, I told myself. I'd come into this relationship with a crappy minivan and, by God, that's how I needed to go out.

Then I rented a U-Haul trailer to attach to the Astrovan, packed James in a cat carrier, and moved to Cleveland.

But first I gave in and agreed to let Charles help me.

What, you thought breaking away was going to be easy?

Chapter Twenty-Seven

"Are you sure about this?" said my friend Mike DeCapite, when I told him I was moving to Cleveland. It was January 2005. "I mean, have you ever been to Cleveland in the middle of winter?"

Mike knew Cleveland. Mike was Cleveland. He'd written a novel based on his experiences driving a taxi there. He had great stories about the place, stories that filled me with fear and admiration for the city and the people who called it home.

Mike had been my neighbor in Williamsburg, living in the apartment building across the street, along with Tony Maimone, the bass player from the Northeast Ohio band Pere Ubu. These days, Tony ran a recording studio next to the G train on Union Avenue, one of the few studios in the neighborhood back then. Mike was living and working in San Francisco while he worked on another book. They were tough, these Cleveland folk. Once they got out of that town, there was nothing they couldn't do.

Except leave it behind. Cleveland was as much a part of them as Pittsburgh made up a significant degree of who I was. Everyone is a product of the place they come from, but rust belt cities have a way of baking the base elements into a person, like a mill smelts ore to make steel.

As someone born in Pittsburgh, I was naturally predisposed to distrusting and even detesting Cleveland. The rivalry between the two cities was legendary, back in the '70s especially, mostly fueled by football— the mighty Steelers vs. the brutish Browns—as well as a long-running, no-real-winners competition for most derided, downtrodden city east of Detroit.

But I loved Mike and Tony and pretty much anyone I'd ever met from Cleveland. They had this Lake Erie twang that sounded like my mother's family (who were near that same lake but to the east, in Pennsylvania) with a similar bluntness and good humor born of necessity.

"It is what it is." I don't think I'd ever heard that phrase—or maybe had but never truly understood it—until I did time in Cleveland. Maybe they said it in Pittsburgh when I was growing up, but I'd been too young and idealistic to think any statement so resigned could apply to me. I had dreams when I left Pittsburgh for New York. I had dreams when I moved from New York to Nashville. When I left Nashville for Cleveland—well, let's just say the dreams were on hold, or at least on ice. It was, after all, January in Northeast Ohio.

I told myself I wasn't really moving to the place, just going there to be with my daughter. I'd be living in self-imposed exile, hoping to put enough geographical distance between myself and Alabama that the relationship with Charles would gradually recede. If only breaking up were that easy.

I'd sat in a coffee shop in a Cleveland Heights strip mall a few weeks earlier, with the sky darkening at 11 AM and snowflakes coming down faster and larger than I'd ever thought possible. After admiring all the cute-looking 1920s apartment buildings, the impressive public fitness center, a multi-million dollar library under construction, and picking up the fine college radio station to the left of my radio dial, I'd thought, "Hey, it's not so bad here." My daughter was in a decent school for the first time since leaving New York five years ago, and I was embarrassed to show my face in Nashville anymore. Moving made sense. Maybe Cleveland—"City of Light, City of Magic" in the words of Randy Newman—could be my Paris, the way Paris had been there for the Russian exiles after the Czar and his wife and children were assassinated? It felt like I'd decimated my life, and this was as good a place as any to hide out until I could hold my head up again.

I had a few things in place to keep me going: I had a licensing deal with Signature Sounds, who'd put out *Til The Wheels Fall Off*—they planned to release my next album when I finished it. I was swerving gently back towards New York from Nashville, envisioning my new record as a return to my solo beginnings. I was leaning on New York, which still felt like home. And it was a shorter drive from Cleveland, right over there, only eight hours east across I-80. This new album would be my city stake, like a person with no backyard seeks out an allotment where they can make something grow.

My old bandmates and my brothers Michael and Riley all held their own in a rapidly changing New York City, where money was suddenly king. I willed them all to hang in there, being the creative types who were once the lifeblood of the city. As long as they stuck it out, I felt like I still belonged in the place somehow. My brothers followed me there to begin with, and as long as they stayed, wasn't I owed a lifetime pass?

Back in Ohio, I signed a lease for an apartment on Mayfield Road, across from beautiful Lakewood Cemetery. See, that was Cleveland—a cemetery as feature. I rented out our entire house in Nashville, no more hiding in the attic. Moving furniture up two flights of icy fire escape steps, I thought, "I don't know how many more times I can do this..." But for six hundred dollars a month, Hazel and I each had our own bedrooms; all our flea market and thrift shop finds from over the years looked perfect in this place with hardwood floors and cute period features like the classic black and white tile bathroom, and an ironing board that swung down from a kitchen cupboard.

Back in the attic in Nashville, I left boxes of journals and papers and tapes and CDs, clothes I no longer wore, and my daughter's old toys I couldn't bring myself to part with. I didn't know where home was anymore, or where it would be when Hazel went off to college, but for the moment the apartment in Cleveland Heights looked like us.

With my next album unfinished—there were still vocals, overdubs and mixing to do somewhere, somehow—I needed to earn money. I made an appointment at an employment agency where they gave me typing and spelling tests, not exactly what I thought I'd still be doing in my mid-forties. But in only a matter of days I had a position: a temporary job in a frozen office park to the east of Cleveland Heights. It was one of those type of places I'd pass via the interstate, driving from one gig to another. If the tour was going well—press, radio, people showing up for the shows—I'd think, "God, I pity those poor losers who have to go in and work there every day." If things were going badly, I'd look longingly and say, "That wouldn't be so bad, having to work there, I mean—it looks clean, and I bet they've got plenty of parking."

The temp work—proofreading testimony for a lawsuit against a pharmaceutical company where the plaintiffs all described in excruciating detail how their bodies had broken down—was a mix of horror and tedium. I'd leave the apartment in darkness, dropping Hazel off at a snowy bus stop, and return home in the dark. I spent several hundred dollars fixing the too soft brakes of the Astrovan, a necessity in what I'd decided was the tailgating capital of the country. On the ground, Clevelanders survived winter with grim resignation. Behind the wheel, all their latent aggression came out, particularly in icy conditions where they'd ride your ass, oblivious to or maybe hoping for pleading looks in the rearview mirror. I guess they had to find pleasure somehow. I soon found myself tailgating with the best of them.

I'd noticed a difference between this part of the world and Pittsburgh, just two hours southeast—Pittsburghers always seemed slightly ashamed and apologetic about their bad air, potholed roads, and second-class citizen status. Cleveland folk appeared to revel in the decay—they took pride in the rusted hulking shells of former industrial glory; a river so toxic it once caught fire. The genial self-effacement of Pittsburghers would barely survive one cold, hard Ohio winter, where a thicker, spinier shell was practically a legal requirement. I hoped some of that toughness would rub off on me.

After work, I'd pick my daughter up at school, or her dad's or a friend's house, and we'd swoop down diagonal roads where the mansions of Shaker Heights sat, their glorious leaded windows alight. I couldn't figure out who lived in these places—the streets sat ghostly quiet in the snow, not another person or even vehicle in sight as our headlights illuminated huge snowflakes through the darkness that had taken hold by five in the afternoon. Some days it felt like the sun barely came up at all.

In the evenings, Hazel and I traipsed up Mayfield to Coventry to rent DVDs. Coventry was the hip street in Cleveland Heights, where the Grog Shop rock club was located. It had a record store, a bookstore, various cheap ethnic eateries, bars, and a coffee place. There was always a line out the door of Tommy's, a local dining institution, waiting for one of their rustic wooden booths and milkshakes. Anything that survived even a few years in that town was considered an institution and revered. Respect was earned.

Down the hill, through Cleveland's old school Little Italy neighborhood, Case Western University presented art films in the Cinematheque, and a mile in the other direction the Cedar Lee theatre showed quality first-run films. In a lot of ways, the town was ideal. If it weren't for the snow that came down daily, the heavy grey sky they called the Lake Effect, and frequent flashes of poverty and decades of civic neglect in certain parts of town, it could have almost been the perfect place to live. I was there, but did I really live there? I didn't even try making friends.

Back in the frozen office park, the weeks went by. I spoke to no one, and no one spoke to me. One afternoon in the lunchroom, I sat alone at a table, eavesdropping on a cheery foursome talking about the Royal Family. They were hearty and strapping in that Ohio way, not quite dressed for success but presentable enough—they didn't seem to be having too bad a time. I felt like a tourist, leaning in to soak up the mundane ambiance that felt almost exotic.

I'd temped in offices before, but only in New York and Nashville, with their adjacence to show biz or glamour; some whiff of possibility out there beyond the office walls to soften the tedium. But there in Cleveland, I felt a touch of envy for people who'd found their place in life and were fine with it. They probably had nice yards they were proud of, kids who played sports, and enjoyed doing fun family stuff on weekends. I wished that were enough for me.

One of the lunchroom quartet was holding forth: "You know, he was the one that gave it all up for the woman he loved? What was his name again?" Pre-Google, they were stumped. Everyone shook their heads. The guy continued: "He was supposed to be the king, but she was divorced and—come on, don't you guys know anything? He abdicated the throne for the woman he loved?"

I couldn't stand it any longer, I had to speak. "Edward, Duke of Windsor," I said quietly. They all turned and looked over towards where the sound came from. "We could be office friends!" I wanted to shout, but felt embarrassed and looked away. They went back to eating and talking.

I took my stir fry out of the microwave and ate as quickly as possible.

Charles kept reappearing in my life. Each time, he threatened to ruin me by calling my father to tell him what an unfit mother I was. My dad was so wrapped up in the excitement of his new romance with my stepmother, Lois, he probably wouldn't have registered anything.

Or else Charles said he'd expose me in the press: "NEWSFLASH! ARTIST FUCKS UP!" Who would even be interested?

I played one last show in Birmingham. I was trying to ease my way out of there when I wished I could burn it all down. I felt like an idiot and probably even joked about my shame from the stage. Charles and his family and work associates attended—hey, no hard feelings. The day after, the classy singer/songwriter who'd opened the show emailed, asking did I know much about this guy Charles? After the gig he'd raved to her about her talent and passed her his phone number. "Should I go out with him?" she asked. Part of me wanted to scream STOP, to tell her she should stay as far away from him as possible.

Another part of me wanted her to fall, like I'd fallen. The temptation was there to go low, make him her problem, not mine.

"Lose that number," I said.

The worst was when he'd threaten to take back the laptop he'd given me. That computer was my lifeline to the world outside of Cleveland. He'd let it drop if I accepted another offering: tickets to see Bruce Springsteen play solo at Cleveland State University, where the hushed audience felt like a buffer against reality. I'm safe in this crowd, I thought. Music was a mantle, a protective barrier. He couldn't get to me in there.

Bruce started a familiar-sounding drone on a keyboard, and I realized it was "Dream Baby Dream," the Suicide song I'd pulsed along to with the crowd at CBGB and Max's back in the late '70s. How could I have thought Charles and I would speak the same language? Yet here I was sitting next to him again, wishing I could get away. But then I probably wouldn't have been able to afford a ticket to this concert —I'd gotten used to having the kind of things I'd done without before. And Stockholm syndrome is real—you can question your very identity, live isolated from friends and family, your whole world turned upside down, but still feel unable to let go of the person who brought it all on. Because you'd let it happen, so in banishing them you risk losing yourself, again.

Bruce incantated. I liked him solo, without the bluster of the band. It felt like he was talking right to me. I let the three chords rise and fall and reach inside me like strengthening tonic, thinking, "I will end this. I WILL."

It was 8:15 AM in Shaker Heights. I'd just dropped Hazel off at high school. Snow fell all around, coming at me from every direction. It almost felt like it was snowing inside the Astrovan. The sense of melancholy was so vivid it felt almost like joy. There was nothing. There was no one. Only me, my daughter, the snowy streets of Cleveland.

And this song on the college radio station, WRUW. It had a harpsichord that might be a sample from a '60s pop record, and a faltering guitar figure that reminded me a little of the Raincoats, my beloved female group from the punk era. A far-off drum thudded. A young man sang in English, but you could tell it wasn't his first language: he sounded Dutch or Swedish. The lyrics told of heading home late at night in a taxi while I drove to my temp job in the eastern suburbs of Cleveland, across flat, endless streets that run parallel to Lake Erie. For a few minutes, we thudded and cascaded in misery together.

I waited in the parking lot to hear the DJ back announce and tell who it was: Jens Lekman. "Black Cab" was the name of the track. Music can still do this, I thought—make me feel like I'm not alone. Whatever fuck-ups in my life, somebody somewhere has done as bad. Or worse.

And then I was driving up Euclid Avenue through one of the most broken, decimated parts of Cleveland, when I heard a call-in radio show. Women talked about partners who berated them, cut them off from their friends, told them they were worthless. Every time they resolved to get away, the partner begged forgiveness, became all sweet and tender, showered them with compliments and gifts, and convinced them that no one else could ever provide the love they so deserved. Again and again. These men controlled their finances, how they dressed, every aspect of their lives with the recurring message that it was all for their own good.

I had to pull over and park along the side of the road. A person walked by, hunched against the snow in a hooded parka—I couldn't tell if they were a man or a woman. I sat and listened to the radio show, engine running while the heat blasted. The callers each described variations of what I'd been going through. I always thought domestic violence was physical. But the past months—two years almost—were as real as a fist. I was displaced and disoriented. I hadn't written a song for months, wondered if I would ever write a song again.

When I got back to the apartment on Mayfield Road, I packed the laptop in a FedEx box and sent it to Charles.

Chapter Twenty-Eight

I walked through frigid darkness to the permit parking lot a block and a half from the apartment. Got to warm up the Astrovan and drive Hazel to her school bus stop at the corner of Mayfield and Lee, then head up to Beachwood for work. The wind blew snow in from Lake Erie—not the soft fluffy kind but icy pellets that hurt when they hit my cheeks. Wait. I'm sure I parked the van here last night. My parking spot was empty.

Someone had stolen the Astrovan.

How to get to work? How to bring Hazel at least partway to school? I realized there wasn't anyone I could call on for help.

Astrovan

We only had each other for a little while
And you were never known for your grace or your style
But I miss you so
You're so hard to replace

We were together through the rain and snow
Down in Birmingham, up in Ohio
And I miss you so
You're so hard to replace

Astrovan - you took me far away
Astrovan - you worked so I could play
Astrovan - I'd turn your radio up and go
Astrovan - they left you across town
Astrovan - I cried the day you were found

Astrovan - yeah, you were better than they know

Some guy from Geico called and broke my heart
Said you were worth more now as a source for parts
And I wanted to scream
But I took the check

Last night I dreamed that we were riding again
And it felt so good to be with you my friend
I think I'll walk for a while
Cause I spent the check

Astrovan - life through a cracked windshield
Astrovan - new brakes and gasket seals
Astrovan - yeah, you were more than just a ride
Astrovan - they left you across town
Astrovan - I cried the day you were found
Astrovan - I'll see you on the other side

So I found myself getting together with men all over the outskirts of Cleveland—in Parma, Mentor and Willoughby. I knew these guys only by their first names: Mo, Nick, Sam. We met in parking lots and BP stations, after work and on Sunday mornings. They were for the most part attractive. They were also married, but I saw that as a plus.

They'd come to sell me their minivans.

When responding to my text or email, every guy who'd placed an ad for a used van on Craigslist made a point of mentioning his wife.

"This is a great van, my wife loves it but we need something bigger."

"Last kid just went off to college, so buying my wife a smaller car."

"My wife." There was an unspoken promise in those two words. The mention of a spouse bestowed a sheen of respectability. How could a man with a woman dedicated to putting up with him be shifty, a liar, a scoundrel?

Anyone who's ever loved a man knows the answer to that question may vary.

Still, I couldn't help it—"my wife" made me feel more secure.

The men and I sat side by side as a couple while I test drove their vans. They were emotionless, their neutrality the best way to keep them from blurting out helpful tidbits like, "The timing belt needs to be replaced immediately!" or "If you get another hundred miles out of this transmission, you'll be lucky." The conversation, all initiated by me, was superficial: the weather ("Think spring's coming anytime soon?"), sports ("What about those Browns/Cavs/Indians?"), the sorry state of the roads. I was like a Tourette's sufferer, spewing banal chatter instead of obscenities, the briefest silence too intimate to bear. If we were really a couple, I wouldn't need to say a thing.

One man brought along his small son, who beamed at me from the back seat. We met at a BP station out in the western suburbs. The man said he was a doctor and that his wife was too. He came from Pakistan: dark-skinned, handsome; late thirties. He stared straight ahead as I put the van through its paces. At a stoplight, I wondered what the people in the car next to us saw through the windows of the Plymouth Voyager—just your average American minivan family with an older wife whose husband preferred to let her drive? I thought how interesting and multicultural we must look. Maybe they imagined I was a doctor too, a brilliant, heroic pediatric surgeon. My husband and I met in a war zone, in between saving lives...

I paused the movie in my head, remembering I needed to look for clues as to the health of this vehicle. I noticed the radio tuned to NPR and wondered if that made the doctor more trustworthy, or maybe the opposite —lax in the maintenance department, spending too much time in his head. Maybe he relied on *Car Talk* as his sole source of automotive knowledge?

And maybe the child was an actor, hired to create the illusion of a decent family vehicle.

The doctor tapped his fingers on the passenger door. He probably had patients to see, maybe a wife waiting for him at home. I pulled out onto the highway, accelerated for a few minutes, hit cruise control, slowed down, exited and looped back around over the interstate. I parked in the space next to my rental car and told the guy I'd think about it. Then I got out and waved goodbye. As my temporary husband and little boy drove off, I tried to remember anything specific about the van—anything at all.

I finally settled on a Mercury Villager from a guy in Cleveland Heights. He reminded me of my dad: organized, obsessively clean. Also, scrupulous and caring. Hazel would be driving this vehicle too—she'd just got her learner's permit. The guy encouraged me to take the vehicle to my mechanic. When we'd done the deal and I drove off in the Villager, I was happy to own a car again, but had to admit I was going to miss the men.

I returned to New York City in early spring '05 to put overdubs on the basic tracks I'd recorded at Brooklyn Recording a few months earlier. I needed to keep momentum going or the album would just fall by the wayside. There was no manager, agent, or publisher pushing me to forge ahead, but I did have Signature Sounds to work with and was looking forward to a new release to tour behind. A new album was a clean slate, a new story to tell, a fresh start. I could really use one of those.

I roped my daughter into singing on one track; Sue and Amanda from the Shams on another. Jon Graboff, Joe McGinty, and I overdubbed keyboards and guitars and even horns here and there. Joe's basement studio on the Italian side of Williamsburg was a cheap, cozy spot to work for a few days, and the familiarity of the neighborhood was comforting: old school pizza at San Marco on Lorimer and the constant low hum of the Brooklyn Queens Expressway. I wondered if maybe I could come back and live there one day?

But Williamsburg, maybe even more than the rest of the city, was changing at warp speed. Five years earlier, my old downstairs neighbor, photographer Ted Barron, had called to let me know our landlord was selling the building on Grand Street. The news hadn't reached him way out in Queens that this was the hot new place to live—he was asking $399,000 for the three units. "Any chance you could raise some money to go in together and we buy it from him?" Ted had asked. But I'd only just cast my lot with Nashville, and the publishing deal that might allow me to buy anything was still a year off. Now, in 2005, the average dump in Williamsburg fetched a million at least. New York was a fast-moving train, and I wasn't sure I had it in me anymore to jump back on board.

Back on the West Side of Cleveland, Hazel and I trawled the racks of Sweet Lorain vintage store. Sixties music bubbled out of the speakers placed up high. I couldn't tell if people working at the place had any ironic distance from the kitschy treasures they sold—if they were even aware it was 2005, or did they think it was 1985? There was a feeling that if you came back in ten years they'd still be there, with a little less hair but relatively unchanged. It was comforting in contrast to New York's manic pace, and the way everything in my life felt like it was shifting.

I found a pristine white twill maxi coat with notched and rounded collar and huge white buttons. It fit perfectly and made me feel like Julie Christie in *Darling*, even though I was in the throes of perimenopause. Maybe that was why it was essential that I buy it.

It was Hazel's last year of high school. At times, I felt like I'd come to

Cleveland to live with my daughter so I could say goodbye to life with my daughter. I'd look back on this period of college search and admission process like Napoleon might have looked back on the taking of Moscow, if only he hadn't been trying to save his ass in Leipzig: strategic but underpowered. Calculating distances and possible outcomes consumed me way more than it crossed Hazel's mind as she juggled friends, schoolwork, a boyfriend.

I was just doing what I thought a parent was supposed to do. Aspire to the heights for my only child as I was on the wane. My hormone levels were dropping, my vagina was tired. Why had I wasted so much of it on Charles?

There were bills to pay, so I looked at Craigslist and the Cleveland. com classifieds—I started to wonder if Hazel had a better chance of finding gainful employment than I did. All those administrative assistant skills I developed over years of temping were less and less in demand as everyone knew how to use a computer now. I searched the Case Western University site and was sent for an interview at the teaching hospital with an older surgeon who was described to me as a wounded soldier— he'd been demoted and was taking it out on the support staff. He asked personal questions and then demanded that I sing him a song. Instead of walking out, I sang for him, blushing and sweating so much he pushed a box of tissues across the desk. Would I always be a doormat?

I tried out as fit model for a catalog company near Cleveland Hopkins Airport. The garments were so outdated that the interviewer apologized before asking me to try an outfit on. The purple and white gingham polyester pantsuit fit me perfectly. But I didn't get the job.

Then I signed up for a catering company. The job found me riding in a van to the Football Hall of Fame in Canton with a few other middle-aged women. The women seemed to have known each other since birth and sounded like my mom's family from Northwest Pennsylvania, the ring of feisty Italian immigrants twice removed. A harried catering manager warned us the Hall of Fame crowd could be rough—Miami Dolphins fans had a reputation—but they weren't so bad. I heard two of the ladies gossiping that the catering company was going out of business and today was their last job. It occurred to me I should grab a beer and start drinking heavily, but I worried I'd start having a good time and be left behind in Canton, Ohio wearing an extra-large polo shirt.

My Brooklyn neighbor Mike was visiting family in Cleveland and took me to Sokolowski's University Inn on the West Side for lunch. Hazel and

I lived on the East Side, with its museums and universities, a diverse and sometimes transient population. West Side felt more settled, the part of town we came to shop the thrift stores. Maybe it was the real Cleveland there? Mike and I stood in line with our trays in the cafeteria-style dining room, waiting to order kielbasa.

"Amy Rigby!" the tough guy behind the counter shouted. "I'm your biggest fan." He excitedly showed me my Mod Housewife-era head shot framed on the wall: my hair streaked with blonde, western shirt, smiling perkily over an electric guitar. My photo fit right in with all the pictures of every celebrity known to man and some known only on the West Side.

"C'mon, Mike, you paid him to say that," I laughed, but Mike insisted he had nothing to do with it.

In the Cleveland airport a week later, I ran into members of the Dayton band Cobra Verde, who also played in Guided by Voices. "So cool you live here now," they said. At the Rock & Roll Hall of Fame and Museum, the guy at admissions waved me in for free. "I saw you open for Warren Zevon," he said. I wondered if maybe I'd just end up staying here for good? The place was working its rough magic on me. Just keep your head down and do what needs to be done— maybe that was how life worked?

I finally paid myself a little out of what remained of my recording budget and made a plan to mix the new album with Don Dixon, who it turned out lived in Canton with his wife, singer Marti Jones. I'd met Dixon years before through my ex-husband, who'd grown up in Winston-Salem a fan of Don's Chapel Hill-based band Arrogance. They ruled the Carolina rock circuit in the '70s, playing original music in clubs before punk. He had serious bass chops and a deep, powerful voice, but was mostly known for producing—REM's first two albums, the Smithereens, and Marshall Crenshaw—along with polishing the pop gems Marti unearthed for her albums on A&M. Marti was Northeast Ohio-born and bred: humble, humorous, lacking in pretense, just like Don. It was a balm hanging out with them. They knew the pop music game but didn't base their self-worth on the ever-changing outcome where sometimes you won but usually you owed the house.

Snow swirled around the Mercury Villager as I headed east on I-90, approaching a town sign that read, "Painesville, Ohio." I laughed grimly—Painesville was about right. It was early May and still snowing.

The studio in Painesville was a throwback to '70s glory days. Even the walls were covered in shag carpet in nostalgic shades of burgundy and pink. This was the place where Wild Cherry crafted their smash single, "Play That Funky Music"—the equipment still seemed to be lightly dusted with cocaine. We spent two days transferring the Brooklyn tracks from Pro Tools to the ADAT format Dixon preferred to work in, and then moved our mixing operation to his basement studio in a Canton neighborhood populated by delightful Tudor, French, and Greek revival-style houses. For one brief moment in my childhood, my father had spoken of moving our family to this part of Ohio and the idea terrified us all—I liked to think if I'd been Marti's neighbor, living in one of these quaint houses, everything would've been fine.

As Dixon and I worked through the tracks, I remembered my sense of purpose, outside of being a mom and running from my bad decisions: making music. Like Ohio in late spring, I felt myself thawing and coming back to life. There were worse places to be than Northeast Ohio in late spring when the lake effect lifted and the sky turned blue. Trees and shrubs brutalized by winter cold and snow burst into the brightest greens and lushest lilacs I'd ever seen.

Chapter Twenty-Nine

"Why can't you believe in me?" I shrieked at my father. He and I faced off on the porch of a rustic bed and breakfast. "Believe in meeeeee!" echoed back from the valley across the road.

My four brothers stood around the porch and driveway of the B&B, busying themselves with barbecue grills and six packs of beer. My sixteen-year-old daughter, equal parts humiliation and curiosity, hung back by the screen door to the kitchen. It was early summer, humid and hazy in the Pennsylvania mountains.

"What about your daughter?" my dad said. "How will you pay for her college? When are you going to face reality and GET A REAL JOB?" *Get a real job!* echoed back from the valley, or maybe it was only repeating in my mind. My father and I had been here before. Both our decades-old argument about the way I lived my life, and the bed and breakfast.

When we'd stayed at the Glades Pike Inn a few years previously, I'd had a nice boyfriend, Paul. True, he was a drummer like my ex-husband. But he was such a good-natured, caring soul who also happened to be pursuing a doctorate at Vanderbilt, that my father had even relaxed his "no room-sharing between unmarried couples" rule and let Paul and I sleep together on his tab. Or maybe my dad had just been getting tired. I'd been forty-three, for God's sake—Dad past seventy. Together we'd played the same old tune we'd been knocking out since I was a teenager. The grooves were getting a little worn.

When Paul and I traveled there with Hazel a few years earlier, my van conked out in West Virginia. We'd coasted from the top of a mountainous road to a service station in a tiny town at the bottom, left the van for a repair, and driven to Pennsylvania in a rental car, reaching the B&B just in time for dinner. The inn owner had been all charm and domesticity; my mother still alive back then. She looked bewildered—who was this Paul exactly?

Mom was gone this time at Glades Pike Inn, Dad remarried, and I was single. Hazel and I lived in Cleveland—just temporarily, I emphasized to anyone who was the least bit curious. The bed and breakfast had fallen into disrepair. Empty cereal boxes and sticky, sad-looking jam jars spilled out of the kitchen shelves along with a big supply of nearly empty liquor bottles and quite a few more cats than the last time. You really can't go home again, or recreate past family get-togethers.

As my dad and I screamed at each other across the porch and parking lot, I wished I could all the way believe the things I heard myself yelling: I know what I'm doing! I'm a critically-acclaimed artist and my new record is going to be more popular than all the others! I'm sure my daughter will qualify for a scholarship to whatever college she's interested in—she's that smart and talented!

"Don't rise to the bait, Amy," one of my brothers said quietly. I couldn't help it. Convincing my dad that I'd done something of value with my life— that my sacrifices and therefore his sacrifices were worthwhile—was a quest I'd only tire of when I managed to convince myself too.

I threatened to grab my daughter, drive off, and never speak to my father again.

Then a voice piped up from the other side of the porch. It was my stepmother, Lois. I didn't really know her well enough to call her a stepmother—she and my dad had been married less than a year—so mostly I called her my dad's wife. In the short time these two had been married, I'd broken up with Charles (who my Dad distrusted and refused to engage with—he had canny instincts about some things), rented out my house in Nashville, and moved to an apartment in Cleveland. Maybe my Dad was right and I WAS off the rails?

"Amy's a good mother and a talented artist," Lois said. "She'll figure it out."

I liked this Lois character. Not only was she willing to love my dad, but she seemed to think I was okay too. I'm not sure what information she based her opinion on. Had that assessment about me being talented actually come from my dad? Maybe, like parents do, he was simply worried about me. If I were him, I'd have been worried about me too.

Things simmered down on the porch and parking lot of the Glades Pike Inn and my dad and I called a truce. We hugged, and my family breathed a sigh of relief. The B&B hostess came out to ask what we'd like for breakfast the next morning.

Back in Cleveland, Hazel and I sweated. Amazing how a place that brings new meaning to the word "winter" could turn so ghastly hot and humid. May's glorious blues and greens had withered. By early July, we were dying. Hazel accompanied me to the Walmart to buy an air conditioner. I picked out the cheapest model and stood in line with all the other unfortunates wearing as little clothing as legally possible.

"We can do this!" I said to Hazel as we dragged the large box up the apartment building stairs. After careful consultation with the manual and a close call where the front-heavy appliance nearly fell to the sidewalk two floors below, we managed to plug in the thick cable and turn the air conditioner on. Hazel and I knelt in front of the vents as if in prayer, eyes shut, letting the air cool the sweat on our faces, chests, and shoulders.

The kitchen light flickered; the stream of air sputtered and stopped.

"What the fuck, man!" shouted a downstairs neighbor.

"Shit!" cried out another. Guess we'd blown the whole building's power. Maybe we'd finally meet the people living above and below us?

In a matter of minutes, someone reset the building's breaker switch and the air conditioner roared back to life. It was probably for the best I hadn't come face to face with any neighbors—if they acknowledged my existence, that might mean I was really living there.

But as we basked in the cool stream of air, Hazel and I laughed until we cried. I felt a pure happiness I hadn't known for over two years. Charles was a thousand miles away and out of my life. My daughter and I were together. I had a new album coming out the next month.

I decided to call my new album *Little Fugitive*, partly inspired by the 1953 film by photographer Ruth Orkin and her husband Morris Engel, about a little boy who runs away to Coney Island because he thinks he committed a crime. I related to the DIY aspect of the project, and also to the plot. Photographer Stephanie Chernikowski and I took the subway out to that retro Brooklyn beach with its famous boardwalk, one of the few places in the city that repelled the kind of development running rampant everywhere else. I posed near the Parachute Jump, a towering landmark visible for miles, sitting unused—a monument to art and pointless dreams. Stephanie had lived for decades in an artist space on the Bowery; her landlord was Andy Warhol. She took iconic photos of Blondie, Alex Chilton, and the Cramps. I grabbed hold of her sharp eye that captured artists' auras like I used to clutch the bar on the Cyclone rollercoaster in Coney Island's Luna Park: let me still be just a little bit cool.

"*Little Fugitive* finds Rigby as sharp as ever, even as many of the songs evince the fuzz of dislocation..." —*Nashville Scene*

When *Little Fugitive* came out, I was finally busy the way I'd wanted to be busy, with shows and interviews lined up. My financial situation had hardly improved with the cost of touring—gas prices, hotel rooms, plane tickets, vehicle maintenance, not to mention paying musicians—keeping my earnings somewhere around the equivalent of working a fast food job fulltime. Not much had really changed since I started playing music in the early '80s: I did it for love and hoped the money would follow. Sometimes it did, enough that the concept didn't seem completely delusional.

My record release show, at the Lakeside Lounge in Manhattan, reminded me of East Village days of old: my brother Michael helped me prepare hot dogs in his apartment around the corner, and we carried them in foil trays down Avenue B to hand out before the show, in keeping with the Coney Island theme from the film. We remembered back to August 1987, when Last Roundup threw a record release party in the backyard of Michael's building, sweating the details of food and drink a good distraction from worrying about how the album would be received and would anyone even care? I'd done the same in 1996 for my first solo album release, making a big bowl of ambrosia and baking pigs in a blanket, then remembering, "Oh yeah, I need to play some songs too." Maybe it was just honoring the spirit of our mother who loved to create and entertain above all else. It kept showtime nerves at bay, having to slit weiners and slice buns.

One of my first dates was the Rockrgl music festival in Seattle. It was a gathering of female artists—panels, performing, and networking—as if the '90s and Lilith Fair were still with us. Patti Smith gave a keynote speech. The room filled with women of every musical persuasion: tattooed, carefully made-up, disheveled; average age about forty. Patti was her charming, inspiring self—a good ten or fifteen years older than most of us, she was someone to look up to. Poet, rocker, wife, and mother; hitmaker and renegade. We all leaned in as she offered us her secret to sustaining life as an artist.

"Take care of your teeth—brush, floss, and go to the dentist."

That was it. She said some other things, but those words especially rang with honesty. You've got to take care of your teeth. I nodded know-ingly— I'd spent thousands on gum surgery in Nashville trying to repair the damage of years of haphazard oral care. You needed to take care of yourself, physically, and mentally. Why didn't anyone ever say these things to artists?

The other wisdom she shared with us, a statement I vowed to re-member forever but would no doubt forget the next time I was out of money and needed to find work: "There is no shame in a day job." Patti really was the mother we all needed.

My gig that weekend felt like a non-event: a short set in the corner of a noisy café where I did my best to engage. I remembered my previous time at this festival where I'd been on a bigger stage with the weight of a record label push and national TV appearance behind me. Ronnie Spec-tor had been the keynote speaker that year, 2000. My show had gone well but the truly memorable moment was sitting in a rental car with Ronnie's husband and manager, Jonathan Greenfield. We were parked in the underground garage of the hotel, the delicious new car smell add-ing to the sense of occasion when Jonathan played the rough mix of Ron-nie's version of my song, "All I Want," through the rental car speakers. I'd written the words and melody with Ronnie's voice in my head as if I was taking dictation, and had live-pitched the song from the Bottom Line stage when I was opening for her—a rare act of blatant self-promotion on my part. She'd come right back to the dressing room after my set and said, "I like that song—I wanna record it!"

And she had. "That's Keith Richards playing guitar," Jonathan said. He sounded pretty good, but the biggest thrill was Ronnie's grit, trill, and classic whoa-oh, oh-oh on the outro. She had lived the song herself and sang it with that belief. I tried not to sob. The sedan could barely contain my pride. This was the kind of moment it was easy to forget when you were wishing the espresso machine wouldn't hiss so loud in the middle of your most heartfelt song; when you wondered why you travelled two thousand miles for a wristband and a few hugs from fellow warriors.

On a panel called "Life After Birth: Can You be a Mom and a Mu-sician Too?" I sat next to Wanda Jackson, the Rockabilly Queen who'd been making records and touring since the '50s. Now she was in her mid-sixties, with jet black hair, gleaming smile, and a hint of mischief in those siren eyes that made even Elvis say, "Uncle!" She had a husband who was devoted to her career by her side, and evangelical faith to help keep her looking up when the world fell short. During our conversation, it sounded like the secret to her longevity had been family, and faith.

I tried to give encouragement to the younger women in the audience who asked if it was possible to be a touring musician and raise a kid at the same time. I wondered what my daughter would say. I'd dragged her from New York to Nashville, and somehow we'd ended up in Cleveland. The next place she went would be her choice. I wish I'd offered her more stability.

I didn't know how to tell an audience of young women, "Never fuck up." If you really put yourself out there, mistakes were bound to happen.

Chapter Thirty

"108.4 inches—The greatest cumulative snow fall for Cleveland, Ohio. This occurred during the year that ended December 31st, 2005."
– SnowPlowNews.com

"My friend, my friend!" The old guy who collected shopping carts at the Cleveland Heights Giant Eagle on Cedar Boulevard greeted me in the parking lot. Hazel had been at her dad's the last few days and I'd barely spoken to a soul. I said hi back and gave him a big smile. I had to restrain myself from hugging him in gratitude.

I was alone but feeling stronger, busying myself practicing and booking dates in the U.K. I felt excited for Hazel, who had a gig playing bass with a band at Pat's In The Flats that Thursday— Thanksgiving.

Thanksgiving night was so cold I couldn't get the cap off to gas up the minivan. I prayed there was enough fuel in the vehicle to reach the venue and drive it back to Mayfield Road. I set out across deserted streets, headed for the flats.

The Flats, the mostly-derelict area along Cleveland's Cuyahoga River, looked a little like a WPA artist's rendition of hell: eerily stark and nearly beautiful with its hulking skeletons of old steel mills silhouetted against overlapping interstate highways, with downtown buildings rising up, out near the edge of Lake Erie to the north. Without meaning to, I was developing an affection for this city.

Inside Pat's bar, complete with smoking (the ban wouldn't go into effect for another year, if it ever did at all in this place), dollar beers, and Pat herself perched on the same barstool she'd probably occupied since her dad ran the joint, I kept to myself so as not to crowd my daughter onstage. I felt pride seeing her up there, rocking out on a holiday most families spend nestled together at home in comfort. The stage was our hearth.

The next night, I was finally filling up the van at a gas station on a desolate stretch of Euclid Avenue when my phone rang. I couldn't see what harm it could cause to answer a cellphone at the pump on a night like this, the air so cold it hurt to breathe. Surely no spark could possibly gain traction?

An unlisted number. My stomach tightened. Was it Charles, trying to trick me into answering?

"Hell-o!" It was Wreckless Eric. I felt like I was listening to a record—his voice so distinctive and *him*. "I hear you're coming over to play in the U.K.," he said. He told me to let him know if I needed any help when I was over: a guitar or amp or even just a cup of tea.

The snow on the roof of the gas station, the railway bridge overhead, the corner of East 55th and Euclid Avenue glowed like a hand-painted cell of a Disney film.

"Hazel!" I said when I got back to the apartment. She was working on her college applications at the living room desk where we kept our computer, the internet on dial-up. "Wreckless Eric called me!" I said.

Hazel's eyes widened. She knew her punk history and had a special fondness for the mavericks and renegades. Suddenly we were dancing around the room, giddy with laughter. He called, he called, he CALLED!

"He probably just wants to be friends," I said. It didn't matter. I pictured him onstage at Maxwell's in Hoboken, singing "America" —how it had moved me so unexpectedly. The look we'd shared through the crowd at the Lakeside Lounge. Wasn't it too soon to go getting involved again?

If life made any sense, maybe we songwriters would be out of a job.

I landed in Heathrow, the early morning arrival always a shock to the system. I'd barely slept on my overnight flight, anxious about being allowed through immigration with my guitar, even though I'd jumped through all the required hoops to arrange a work permit. I hoped my suitcase of merchandise arrived okay. Dehydrated, disheveled, I wheeled into the ladies' room where a girl had stripped off most of her clothes and was practically bathing in one of the sinks. I wished I could be that shameless in getting myself together. Instead, I washed my hands, tried not to look too closely at my tired face in the mirror, brushed my teeth, and spritzed myself with a little tester vial of perfume from the duty-free makeup counter: Clinique's *Happy*.

I lugged my guitar and suitcase down to the train station, traveled

to Paddington and transferred to Kensington, a more frenetic, less familiar part of London than my usual Bayswater or Notting Hill tube exit.
And even the old familiar places in old familiar London were changing.
Where once there'd been an occasional cafe, alternating with pubs and
greengrocers, now there seemed to be nothing but cafes: Costa, Star-
bucks, Pret A Manger; Aux Delices d'Europe. I wedged myself into a
phone box to call Tony Thewlis, the guitarist who'd offered me a place to
stay for the night after we rehearsed and before we set off for Scotland
the next morning. I pulled out my calling card and dialed the toll-free
number, then the fifteen-digit passcode, then Tony's London number.
I examined the business cards for escort services and Dial A Cab tacked
inside the box as the phone rang: "Barbie Doll VERY BUSTY" and "Julia,
Russian Top Model *Too Good To be True.*"

No answer. I tried a few more times—toll-free, passcode, Tony's
number, wait—and then thought I might cry. Or fall asleep in the phone
booth. Was it possible to do both at once?

I'm too OLD for this! I thought. Where was a tour manager, or a driver? A manager... a HUSBAND?! I shuddered, remembering where that
idea got me—first to Alabama and then to self-imposed exile in Cleveland. No, husband was not the answer. Just... something better than doing everything myself all the time.

I remembered how Wreckless Eric called me a week ago as I was
filling up at that gas station on Euclid. "If you need anything when you're
over on tour—a guitar, or any help at all," he'd said in his charming voice
that sounded like it belonged in a speech bubble on a poster taped to a
teenage rebel's bedroom wall. "Just call," he'd said.

Turned out I'd gotten Tony's number wrong. A few hours later,
thanks to Eric – who knew a guy who knew Tony – I'd reached my host
and climbed the stairs up to his Kensington flat. Tony was Australian,
way more gentle and nicer than you'd expect after listening to his band,
the Scientists. He may have been the first vegan I ever met. We ate a
healthy snack, gathered up guitars and Tony's Watkins Copicat echo
unit, and caught a bus to a Shepherd's Bush rehearsal space. I felt like
the soft American, thinking how hard it was to travel to rehearsal via
public transport.

Tony, Rob Coyne the bass player, Yan Quellien the drummer, and
I ran through a set to get us started in Glasgow the next night. The rehearsal space felt vaguely familiar —I think it's where I got together with
Sid Griffin and his outfit before my first U.K. tour in 2000, five years but
what felt like a couple of lifetimes ago. I think I probably imagined back

then I'd be on a tour bus by now, like Steve Earle.

Very early the next morning I rented a right-hand drive van, met up with the guys, and somehow managed to drive out of London through rush hour traffic (shades of my first right-hand drive rental car in Dublin), hitting the motorway to head north to Scotland. An eight-hour journey and we'd done a decent job of playing for a small audience in a too-big venue when a cute guy in a parka walked up to me and said, "I fucked off right after my set so I could see you."

It was Wreckless Eric. He was just a little shorter than me or the same height if I slouched a little. He took off his black cashmere scarf and wrapped it around my neck when I told him I was cold. Then he offered to drive me to my friend Lindsay's house in Grangemouth, where my band and I were spending the night. No more Glasgow B&Bs from hell for me.

As we travelled the hour or so to Lindsay's, he told me his tips for keeping healthy out on the road: Drink water. Eat apples and Green & Black's Organic 70% Dark Chocolate.

"You have to suck it," he said. My hormones sat up. I felt myself falling. What? I asked, just so I could hear him say it again. "You have to suck it." Oh, right—the chocolate.

I had a night off before the next gig in Edinburgh, so Eric picked me up to see him open for the Damned at the Liquid Rooms. We were running a little late for his soundcheck and the club was deep within the warren of winding, cobbled roads that all lead eventually to Edinburgh Castle. Pre-GPS, Eric seemed to sort of know where he was going, but we ended up at the top of a street where we could see the Liquid Rooms, but the one-way system was against us. "Fuck it," said Eric, and drove his Ford Mondeo down what felt like a flight of granite stairs while terrified students and tourists waved their arms and shouted, "You're going the wrong way!" Somehow, we reached the club without hurting anyone.

It was a different experience watching Eric play in the U.K. I'd only seen him in New York and New Jersey. I remembered the ferocity of the British punk audience when my brother and I saw the Cramps at London Dingwalls back in the late '70s. We'd made the mistake of standing right in front of the stage, and when the band came on the crowd's fervor pinned us face down at Lux Interior's feet. It occurred to me in that moment that for all their cool, New York audiences were kind of reserved. In Edinburgh, the Damned's audience was tough—downright surly—and Eric was sharper, harder, and funnier than he'd been with Yo La Tengo at Maxwell's or on his own in front of an adoring crowd at the Lakeside in

Manhattan. I felt proud to stand beside him in the audience afterwards when the Damned came on.

After a little while we headed out to an Italian restaurant down the street. Eric said he was treating.

"Oh... could I have a steak?" I asked. Eric told me he felt relieved I wasn't one of those American princesses who only drink herbal (pronounced with the long "h") tea before playing so they won't mess up their voices. He said he'd read an interview with Eric Burdon of the Animals where he'd admitted he never worried about protecting his voice before performing: "I just groove with whatever comes out." I thought of all the talented Erics—Idle, Clapton, Ravilious, and my one-time illustration instructor at St. Martin's, Eric Stemp—and how there must be a religion based on their teachings.

The next night, after my gig in Edinburgh, this Eric accompanied me and my band to a pub. Two frightening types loomed up over us as we made our way to a table. They looked like they had it in for Eric.

"Y-eeeeeuw," they said. "Y-eeeeeuw!" We wondered if we should find a different pub. Then they were practically hyperventilating, trying to express themselves. "Fuckin' great, man—fuckin' GREAT." Turned out they'd seen Eric open for the Damned the night before. He nodded thanks and ordered a glass of water.

"Scottish tap water, the best," he said. He told me he hadn't drunk alcohol in many years. "You would NOT like me drunk," he said. I liked him very much.

After the pub he offered to take me for a deep-fried Mars bar, a Scottish delicacy. My band exchanged looks with each other, then reminded me we needed to leave early in the morning for a long drive to Cardiff. So Eric went his way and we went ours.

What a character, the guys said. "Scottish tap water, I'll have a bit o' that, please!" Somebody tried to imitate Eric's accent, but it came out Dick Van Dyke as a cockney. We all laughed and shook our heads: me in enchantment, the guys a little trepidatious, like they hoped I knew what I was doing.

Historically, no. But I called him the next night from Wales. And the night after that. It was so nice to have someone to talk to, someone who understood how there are gigs you can't win, and it feels like the world is against you. But how there's always tomorrow.

And how other times it all lines up perfectly. But then there's still... tomorrow.

Chapter Thirty-One

"Hello, you're listening to BBC Radio Leicester! We're speaking today with singer/songwriter (consults sheet of paper) *Amy Rig-sby*). Amy will be performing at The Musician tonight. Now tell me Amy, how long have you been doing this?" The female host of a certain age peered over her glasses at me.

"Oh, you know—twenty years, maybe?" I said.

Pause. "And how old were you, exactly, when you started?"

All I could think was: *Do they have a word for "bitch" over here in England? Or is it just... "bitch"?* But I answered that I'd been playing in bands for years, and didn't put out my first solo album until I was thirty-seven.

"That's a bit late, isn't it?"

I'd been feeling guilty about silently calling her a bitch but decided it was absolutely the appropriate word. "I mean," she continued, "isn't that something young people do when they're unsettled?"

Her words stung. The tour was kind of a shambles. The fees weren't enough to justify paying, transporting, and lodging three other musicians—another instance where magical thinking had me convinced it'd all work out for the best, with no supporting factors except it felt pretty special when I rocked out with a band, so surely I'd make a bigger splash over in the U.K. if that's how I presented myself? In reality, the songs I played solo were often the ones that connected most—the lines of communication were clearer. Me and the band were under-rehearsed and our equipment worked against us some nights: amps gave out, guitars refused to stay in tune. The guys were supportive, though, and good company. Some nights we clicked.

Cardiff, Winchester, Nottingham. A house concert in Liverpool. Afterwards, I tried to sleep in an upstairs bedroom of the narrow, terraced house but there was a party raging below. I smelled cigarettes and beer. I finally gave up and went down to the kitchen.

Earlier that night, we'd played to a friendly audience who'd filled the front room. Our stage was a portion of the floor in front of the bay window, shared with a Christmas tree and large-screen TV. I'd done a good job of convincing the Liverpudlians I was a hard-rocking chick, but as I drank milk and ate a mince pie in my pajamas next to the boozing stragglers, they could see me for what I really was: the uncool kid at a slumber party who just wished everyone would shut up and go to sleep.

Except they were too drunk to notice. I went back upstairs to close my eyes for a little while. The guys in my band were sacked out in various locations throughout the house. We needed to leave in a few hours to drive back to London, where I'd return the rental van. My head and heart were racing. Once the van was gone and the band returned home to their flats, I was taking a train from London up to Norwich to visit Wreckless Eric. It was four in the morning, the dawn of the first day of the rest of my life.

I wasn't sure where I was headed—what exactly was Norwich? Was it a town? A city? Though I'd gained some understanding of the geography of the U.K. from several tours there, Norwich, in the eastern county of Norfolk that faced the North Sea, had never been on my itinerary. It felt like a far flung corner. I had a solo house concert in the neighboring county of Suffolk next evening that Eric was offering to drive me to, and then one last band gig in London at the 12 Bar. I had my suitcase, guitar, and what was left of my CDs. Eric had mentioned he had a spare room, and he seemed like a gentleman. But I wondered how *I'd* behave. When attracted to someone, I was inclined to fuck first and figure it out later. I didn't know what my style was anymore. A relationship like the one I'd just extricated myself from skews your image of yourself. Since puberty, I'd struggled with a shaky sense of self-worth, but at least I'd known the self I was dealing with. At forty-six, I felt like I was starting over.

I wrote in my journal, December 5th, 2005:

The most wonderful weekend of my life started on Saturday when I caught the train to Norwich.

Eric picked me up at the station. It turned out he was cooking dinner back at his place a few miles from the center of Norwich. He lived in what I think was called a garden flat, a surprisingly tidy and spacious ground floor apartment with a studio tucked into one room, amplifiers taking up space in the living room, and a pretty, private courtyard at the rear. "He just moved back from France, and he lives on a boat," I remembered hearing the first time I met him. All that remained of the boat were a pair of art deco light fixtures and a wooden stepladder he'd turned into a bookshelf. France was given a nod with a tasty lamb casserole Eric called *sauté d'agneau*. Was it possible to be both worldly and provincial, I wondered, as I watched him dishing up portions of lamb from an ancient cast iron pot.

After dinner, we sat with our guitars on our laps in the living room and played songs for hours. "What about this one?" we each said, over and over. Archies, Kris Kristofferson, "I Can Help" by Billy Swan, "Save The Last Dance For Me." We sang harmony—"Are you lower or higher?" we both asked. A few times I lost track of which voice was my own. It was that simple. When we strummed and picked guitars together, it sounded like one bigger guitar.

We kept on like this for hours. After a couple weeks of gigs, I remembered music—not the trying to get somewhere aspect but how melody, harmony, and rhythm, combined with the right lyrics, create a world of their own. Songs have been my private sanctuary, but it felt wonderful to share that world with another person, like back when I played in bands with my brother and friends, for fun.

I took a bath. Eric asked if I needed anything and I told him I'd like a glass of milk. His place just felt so cozy, like I was home. Eventually we went to bed together and stayed there until the sun was going down the next afternoon and it was time for my gig in Suffolk. I put in hair curlers and wore them in the car while Eric drove. He said, "I feel like I'm transporting Tammy Wynette." I laughed that he'd equate me with a queen of American country music, but he felt like British pop music royalty to me.

December 13th:
...he's a genius...
December 24, 2005:
Even Cleveland would be funny if he was there. I love you, I love you, I love you Eric.

The day after Christmas I waited in Newark Airport's international arrivals baggage claim. We'd come to the city for the holidays and Hazel was hanging out with friends in Brooklyn. It had only been two weeks since I'd said goodbye to Eric at Heathrow, but it felt like years. Would I recognize him? Would he still love me? Were we crazy?

Then I saw two guitar cases heaped on a baggage trolley being pushed towards me. He wore a brown velvet suit with faint chalk pin-stripes, slightly flared trousers, a silk muffler around his neck. Sunglasses, of course. I wondered if anyone had ever looked so shabbily elegant after an eight-hour transatlantic flight.

Somehow word of our love affair had reached Hoboken. Yo La Tengo invited Eric and me to be special guests at their Hanukkah show at Maxwell's. Had it only been a year since the Shams played and Eric did his thing at the annual event? The eight-night run raised money for various charities and was an unofficial celebration of Jewish songwriters. The band suggested they back us on Paul Simon's "Red Rubber Ball," a hit for The Cyrkle in 1966, along with Serge Gainsbourg's "Je T'aime ... Moi Non Plus," where Eric would sing Serge's part in French, about coming and going between my kidneys (literal translation), while I handled Jane Birkin's orgasmic coos and moans.

At my brother Riley's apartment in Greenpoint—Riley was in Ohio with his girlfriend, Natalie—Eric and I interrupted lengthy make-out sessions with attempts at learning "Red Rubber Ball," a song that had felt like one we just instinctively knew—until now. We listened to Serge and Jane a few times but decided that one would make more sense with the band behind us.

New Year's Eve. Eric and I spent the early part of the evening parked in the Mercury Villager on Washington Avenue, Hoboken, just around the corner from Maxwell's. We needed to rehearse our songs for the show but couldn't seem to stop kissing.

Then we stood in the audience, as midnight and the year 2006 approached. Yo La Tengo played "Autumn Sweater," and it was one of the most romantic things I'd ever heard. I'd known the song for years, but I finally *felt* it—whatever the details and possible pitfalls, this relationship was happening. I'd been there in the same room at Maxwell's for Ira and Georgia's wedding reception almost twenty years before—and their enduring comradeship gave me hope that it was possible to find a partner, one who understood music as an essential element, like eating and breathing. Will and I had tried, but were too young and unformed to make it work when you added real life to the mix. Maybe me and Eric...?

The audience was on a high when we took the stage. I felt like the whole room was celebrating our new love. And then—

"Red Rubber Ball" was a car crash. We decided to change the key and maybe neglected to tell the band, that suddenly included a horn player.

"I thought you told them," Eric said to me, and I to him.

What might have felt like public humiliation if we'd been on our own only bonded us together. Us against them. "I like that trick you did with the capo," Eric told me.

Then "Je T'Aime." Without the string parts that are the backbone of the record, I didn't know when to say "Je t'aime, oui je t'aime," so I just kind of grunted and panted into the mic. Eric lit a joint, then pulled an apple out of his pocket and took a bite. The audience stared in confusion. Everybody loves a lover, but we were obnoxious in our private laughter. We left the stage to awkward silence and a smattering of applause.

"That was perfect," said Ira. I think he was being sarcastic, but I've never been sure.

We couldn't wait to get back in the van and make out some more.

Do You Remember That?

It was a cold December night
I was sorting out my life
You were headed for a mess
But you didn't know it yet
As I pushed in through the crowd
You were turning your amp up loud
Then our eyes met —do you remember that?
Then eleven months go past
I'm stuck in Cleveland pumping gas
When you called me on the phone
Said you were back to living on your own
I celebrated in my head
Laughing at everything you said
Then the battery went flat —do you remember that?

Do you remember Glasgow and that pub we went to
Everyone said that I should stay away from you
But I didn't listen
You took me out for steak and we heard PP Arnold
You drove your car the wrong way down a one way street
Then we were kissing
Okay I made that last part up
It wasn't til we next met up
You had me over for some tea

And we played guitar, sang me and Bobbie McGee
Danced to Crazy Elephant
Wondering where the bad times went
You changed my life in seconds flat
Do you remember that?

Do you remember Glasgow and that pub we went to
Everyone said that I should stay away from you
But I didn't listen
You took me out for steak and we heard PP Arnold
You drove your car the wrong way down a one way street
What am I missing?

The way it all began in Hull
You wrote a song so magical
I learned it halfway around the world
And wished that I could be your girl
Yo La Tengo liked it too
But as for Je T'Aime Moi Non Plus
That New Year's Eve they backed us up
We really fucked it up
Together we were crap —do you remember that?

"Amy, I hate to tell you but—I had an email from Charles today," my brother Michael told me over the phone. It turned out he copied my entire family to let them know what a whore and unfit mother I was.

"You should nail this guy," my brother Pat said. Charles emailed him at his work address. Thankfully my father and new stepmother didn't have email. They'd tried briefly to use the computer at their senior living, but were old enough that such newfangled inventions seemed too complex and suspicious. Plus, they had each other, and their relationship was still new enough they kept the rest of the world at bay. If my father couldn't comprehend email, how would I explain the mess I'd extricated myself from.

And oh, by the way, Dad, I'd like you to meet this Englishman I've just fallen in love with.

I just wanted to put the whole awful Charles chapter behind me. I'd told Eric everything. He'd had his share of missteps too. We sat in my brother Riley's apartment in Greenpoint, holding hands and wondering how we could be together. It seemed like that would make everything right.

Eric and I collected Hazel from a grade school friend's house in Park Slope. She'd been making her way around Brooklyn like the native she was. But now it was time to head back to Ohio. One more semester of high school before she left for college: would it be a school in New York or Chicago? And where would I end up? I was glad at the easy rapport Eric and Hazel shared from the moment they met. It was as if Hazel could feel that Eric was on our side. I drove the three of us in the minivan across I-80, the snow-covered Pennsylvania hills still and shining in the moonlight. We listened to *Coles Corner* by Richard Hawley and Eminem's *Curtain Call*.

"Oh, Mom," said Hazel, about my love for Eminem, and Eric. I remembered feeling that way about my own mother at times—watching her get down to "Spinning Wheel" by Blood, Sweat & Tears or swoon to William Holden in *Picnic*—like I was the grown-up and *she* was the child.

Chapter Thirty-Two

I felt at a crossroads personally and professionally. *Little Fugitive* was as well-received as any of my albums, but touring was still a hodgepodge of opening slots for bigger artists; underattended club shows; the occasional festival or Mountain Stage slot; house concerts that were low profile but rewarding financially and emotionally. I'd imagined there was a clear trajectory where you started off small and worked your way up to bigger audiences and rooms, small theatres, a tour bus even. How? What magic combination of elements created that alchemy and which of them was I missing?

I never lacked hustle, and had been kicking around an idea for a live performance: me and a girlfriend onstage together like a coffee klatsch. For years I'd looked longingly at concepts like "Four Bitchin' Babes" and "On A Winter's Night," where a group of singer/songwriters joined forces to create a special experience combining their songs and personas, linked by a theme. Not a co-bill but a whole evening worked out in advance, adding up to more than the sum of its parts.

Marti Jones felt like the perfect person—she and her husband Don Dixon were musical relatives I'd never gotten to know until I'd mixed Little Fugitive with Don.

I'd admired Marti's plainspoken persona and lush voice from afar, remembering an interview where she talked about having a zit and how it ruined a Maxwell's show for her. Right there I knew she was a kindred spirit, revealing the kind of vulnerability that was taboo even in the most DIY corners of showbiz. She'd had a serious music career, with releases on A&M and RCA Records, but remained happily living in her hometown. Spending time with Marti in her kitchen each time her husband and I took a break from mixing had felt so comfortable and fun—what if we continued our coffee talk on stage, with songs and a few scripted bits thrown in?

Marti and I sketched out ideas for the show, a nice little package promoters could get a hold of: "Why, yes, that sounds like an evening people will enjoy!" Marti rarely played live anymore, preferring painting soulful portraits and wistful film stills to the uncertainty of touring. The booking agents I'd started working with were enthusiastic about the concept.

I wrote out a list of possible names for the duo: Our Long-Haired Life (after one of Marti's album titles); The Good Girls after one of my songs; Pop Rock Carpool; Bang Theory (we both leaned pretty heavily on hair styles that included bangs); Art School Casualties. We decided on Cynical Girls after the Marshall Crenshaw song, which we would play via a 45 rpm record spinning on an old record player onstage at the start and finish of every show. Typical of our production—done on a shoestring, with no stage manager and sparse knowledge of theatrical tricks—we relied on arcane technology and literal interpretation. A cannier pair might have asked a sound person to play the track via nascent mp3 technology neither of us could quite get our heads around, or even a CD player at the sound desk, while we went through the charade of dropping the needle on a scratchy old single. But that would have been too easy, too consistent—every night Marti and I would aim for the grooves and hope the stylus didn't screech across the disc, or get stuck, or any of the possible pitfall reasons record players became almost obsolete for a while. Coming up in the post-punk, post-modern era, neither of us cared to, or were even capable of, being thoroughly professional.

Cynical Girls' stage set consisted of a table with two microphones and two chairs for the chat show part of the night. We brought along our own folksy patterned tablecloth and favorite mugs (to be filled with wine a la Kathy Lee Gifford's morning TV talk show) for the coffee klatsch part of the evening.

We began our set with Marti and me on guitars, one of them a 12-string that refused to stay in tune. We alternated Marti's songs with mine, and as Marti was more of an interpreter of other people's material, she was very generous in doing quite a few of my songs. We included covers: the Roches' "Married Men" (like many of their songs, one I wish I'd written) and our version of "Cynical Girl." With only a few rehearsals before we set off on the first dates, we didn't exactly have things down pat. But with Don Dixon's help setting up our gear and tuning the 12-string, the first show in February 2006 at Beachland Tavern in Cleveland went well. It attracted the biggest crowd I've ever played to at the Tavern, before or since.

And then there was a wild card: his name was Wreckless Eric. Even though he and I lived on two separate continents, we were determined to make a go of our relationship. Maybe the Cynical Girls could use a special guest?

Eric hadn't done a huge amount of U.S. touring since his days on Stiff Records in the late '70s/early '80s. A New York City show here, a South by Southwest appearance there. There was definitely interest from promoters and the public to add him as a special guest. We worked it out that Eric would play an opening set: songs from all facets of his catalog with a reading or two from his autobiography, *A Dysfunctional Success*. Then he'd join Marti and me in our set. We decided to introduce him with what, in our minds, was a brilliant piece of stagecraft. Every night, Marti and I sat and chatted at our homey little table. When it seemed like the talk show portion of the show had gone on long enough, a doorbell would ring. We were proud of ourselves for stopping at a Home Depot for a real digital doorbell. The only mistake was leaving the job of pressing it to Eric. The first night, we waited for the ring—nothing. So we filled the dead air by asking the audience for questions. After a few nights we realized it made more sense for Marti and me to ring the buzzer when we were ready for Eric to make his entrance... with no theatre background between us, none of this stuff was exactly obvious.

When the doorbell finally rang, we were off and running.

"Who could that be?" said Marti. "Were you expecting anyone?"

"No," I answered. "Maybe we'd better go see who's—"

And then Eric burst onto the stage. Wearing a bathrobe.

"I'm the next-door neighbor and I want to know who's making all this bloody noise!" he said. The robe was awful—white terry cloth covered in slippery beige polyester, stolen from the laundry cart of a nice hotel we'd stayed in. The robe came off. Next thing, the three of us stood at microphones center stage, Eric in his underwear playing his big green Microfret guitar, Marti and I with acoustic guitars on either side. We played Eric's hit, "Take The K.A.S.H."

"You're Gonna Screw My Head Off," one of Eric's songs he'd recorded with the Len Bright Combo was next, and then "Whole Wide World," to the audience's delight and confusion. Then Marti and I played a few more songs and finished up with "Cynical Girl."

The audience at the shows was divided. There were Marti People and Amy People, but they aligned somewhat in terms of taste and sensibility. But then there were Eric People. Now Eric People could become Amy

People and vice versa. There were instances for sure with open-minded fans who were Marti, Amy, AND Eric People. But several nights were like the theater piece, *Tony n Tina's Wedding*, with the older punk contingent (Eric's People) doing battle with the older folk contingent (Marti's People), while my outliers filled the seats in between. There were shouts like "Let Marti play one!" or "GET HIM OFF THE STAGE" from fervent Marti-ites. One night, in Chapel Hill, an audience member poured a pitcher of beer over another's head and the police were called.

At Rams Head in Annapolis, an enraged Marti acolyte in an expensive brown leather jacket stood up, his face red, mouth twisted, arms waving, and screamed for Eric to leave the stage. The soundman was working his first job ever and kept raising the level of a microphone on stage, which led to screeching feedback during Eric's set. A security man and the house manager came onstage to escort Eric off and into my arms backstage. It was awful, yet we couldn't stop laughing. I hadn't known show biz could still be outrageous like back in the '70s, but with Eric that was built in.

At the Birchmere in Alexandria, Virginia, things went well. All our factions aligned, and nobody shouted at the stage. We ended the show on a high. Then my older brother John came backstage. He'd traveled up from Fredericksburg, further south, as he did when I opened for Warren Zevon there six years ago. Warren had thrown a fit about an overcooked hamburger but was really sweet to my brother and that meant a lot to John, who was a huge Zevon fan and always showed up to support me.

"Umm, I need to tell you something," John said. I immediately worried, is the family okay? Ever since my mother was in an accident, I try to head off bad news so I'm never caught off-guard. John continued, "You'll never guess who was sitting next to me."

Charles had traveled eight hundred miles to be there. It dawned on me that he could find and follow me anywhere. I post my whereabouts online any time I have a gig.

And then he appeared at the merch table, carrying a bag of things I'd left behind at his house. Some papers, a book or two. He said something insulting about Eric while I kept the table between us and a fake smile on my face. I wanted to push the table over. I wanted someone to get him away from me. "Take care," I said, like I'd never seen him before in my life. "Thanks for coming."

When he was gone, I told Eric, "That was him."

"Why didn't you tell me?" Eric said. "I would have kicked him in the nuts!"

The next day when I looked at my email, there was an awful message from Charles: threats, nastiness. I contacted a lawyer friend from my CBS temping days and asked him to send a cease-and-desist letter. I kind of wished I'd seen Eric's threatened nuts-kicking in action.

Out on the west coast, Cynical Girls played well-attended shows at Mc-Cabe's Guitar Shop in Santa Monica and the Lobero Theatre in Santa Barbara, with our friend Kelley Ryan joining for the mid-set coffee talk. Kelley's husband, Dan, founded Bug Publishing with his brother Fred, and though I'd left the fold for Welk during my publishing deal years, they'd been supportive through my last decade of songwriting. Kelley was a talented writer and pop musician and added to the camaraderie, but I missed the edginess Eric's presence naturally heightened.

When he joined Marti and me for a performance in San Francisco, a last-minute Phil Lesh late show pushed our set time an hour early. A member of the Grateful Dead playing in the Bay Area naturally meant a line around the block before our gig even began. It was the kind of thing you just had to laugh about and not take too much to heart. As Eric, Marti, and I huddled in the dimly lit dressing room, someone mentioned a Stiff Records tribute happening down the street, and how the club was packed to the rafters. Their capacity crowd was treated to a bogus Wreck-less Eric singing "Whole Wide World," while just around the corner the real thing performed to thirty-five people.

Before we went on, the promoter bounded up the stairs, shouting, "Good news! Good news! Phil Lesh is *on his way!*"

Eric snorted. "The only good news we want to hear is that you've got a lightbulb." The promoter stared open-mouthed for a second, then went back to hyperventilating about Phil Lesh.

No one had ever taught me to stand up for myself before. Or talked to me about my equipment. I'd tended to do my best with whatever I had.

"When was the last time you changed those guitar strings," Eric said. "And please tell me you've got your own vocal mic." I'd never had a roadie or a sound engineer of my own. When I hired musicians to back me, they wouldn't dare criticize the shambolic way I went about things: guitar cables in a shopping bag; broken strings; pedals that crapped out mid-set. The dates I played with Steve Earle or Billy Bragg were the only opportunity I had to see a guitar tech at work, during and after a show: tuning, changing strings; executing small repairs that are a daily neces-sity for a touring musician. I saw in Eric a teacher—the musician mentor I'd never had. He began touring in the '70s with a crew, those British roadies of lore who'd mark out their territory—call it "MY STAGE"—and take a pride. They taught him. When the wilderness years happened, when he fell off the map, he did their jobs himself: driving the vehicle, fixing the equipment, wrangling the sound.

I'd always expected that someday someone would step in and take care of all that for me, but surprise, I was nearing fifty years old. I didn't feel it, maybe on a good day didn't look it. But this might be as far up as I was going to climb. Maybe it was time to face facts and learn a few things.

"When the student is ready, the teacher will appear," said Lao-Tzu, the early Chinese philosopher. Eric was the kind of artist I hoped I could be. He had lived in the margins for much of his career, though he wouldn't even think of calling the decades he spent playing guitar, writing songs, making records, and touring a career. "Careering through life," I'd heard him call it.

There was this magic about Eric that protected him, even when things looked bleak. What was that spark? Maybe it was madness, certainly it was genius. Mostly it was faith, a belief in what mattered: doing your work, whether anyone else cared or not.

Chapter Thirty-Three

When Hazel received her acceptance letter from School of the Art Institute of Chicago—with a generous scholarship— I felt relieved we could leave Cleveland. But somehow, in the time we'd spent in a place I never imagined myself living, I'd grown fond of it. Like a boxcar some hapless hobo happened to climb into, it took me from a place I couldn't stay and dropped me somewhere I hadn't planned to go. I'd forever feel a pang when I saw the names of those local roads that go on and on for miles: Mayfield, Euclid, Cedar...Chagrin Boulevard. *Chagrin—a feeling of disappointment or regret as a result of one's own failure.* The rough neighborhoods and the fancy ones, side by side, the factories still hulking up out of the flats, Lake Erie above it all.

With so much coming and going in the apartment on Mayfield Road, James the cat had gotten in the habit of knocking things over in the kitchen: pots and pans, bowls, cereal boxes. When Eric stayed for a few nights, James would perk up, placing a large proprietary paw on Eric's thigh and narrowing his eyes at me as if to say, "He's mine."

Wouldn't it be simpler to just stay in Cleveland? Surely more than a few life paths have been chosen due to exhaustion and proximity to not one but two decent cinemas, cheap airport parking, and a great Thai restaurant?

I walked around the Tremont neighborhood on the west side of Cleveland. Cheaper and more artsy than the Cleveland Heights neighborhood we'd been living in. A cold wind blew in off Lake Erie as I stood alone in a little park ringed by churches and dilapidated buildings.

My phone rang. It was Eric, back home in his groovy garden flat on the outskirts of Norwich. I pictured him recording a guitar track while a casserole simmered in the cast iron pot on the stove. I wished we were together. "Have you ever been to Nashville?" I asked him. Sometimes I forgot I owned a house there.

"What a dump," said Eric, sounding not at all like Bette Davis. It was his first visit to Nashville, and I admit he wasn't seeing the best side of town. It was springtime, the humidity already descending; you could see it fizzing around streetlights on the outskirts of town, Hillsboro Road to West End Avenue near Green Hills Mall. High-end chain stores and traffic. The majority of vehicles seemed to be SUVs, their drivers to a man—or more often, a blonde-haired woman—talking on cellphones. They all had a way of taking their sweet time, and served as helpful reminders of how on edge I often felt living in that town.

We were on our way to the Bluebird Cafe, where I was participating in a round to celebrate the release of a Peter Case tribute album to benefit the Hungry For Music charity. Eric and I had driven from Atlanta that afternoon and were ourselves badly in need of something to eat. We weren't looking for a cultural experience—no meat and three, or Nashville hot chicken—nothing that required a wait. And I wanted to avoid any spot that might involve introductions or explanations to friends or acquaintances, of where I'd been, who I was with, and what was going on. There weren't many places in town where that kind of encounter wouldn't happen, so we settled on Chipotle.

The air in the West End Chipotle felt blessedly cool, and I didn't recognize any of the high school students working behind the counter, though there was a good chance one of them went to school with my daughter. We devoured our fajita salads and headed to the Bluebird. Eric took a seat in the audience, and I greeted my friends in the center of the room, where microphones were set up in a circle facing each other. Everyone was plugging in and preparing for the show: Will Kimbrough, Kim Richey, Peter Case himself, and Susan Cowsill in the round. I'd played gigs with all of them. Toured the south with Will in my Aerostar van, sharing a band, and had him play on the two albums I'd recorded in Nashville.

Peter Case had hosted me at a songwriters' night at a rebooted revered folk club, the Ash Grove on the Santa Monica pier. We'd swapped songs with actress Mare Winningham and Stew of The Negro Problem, and it felt like heady company. Peter started in '70s Los Angeles as a rocker and had never stopped creating and touring.

Kim Richey and I shared a bill at the old train station in downtown Nashville, back when I was making plans to move to town. It felt like starting at the top, playing a rocking Friday evening set for a big crowd. I loved Kim's album, *Bittersweet*, and her song "I'm Alright" inspired me to write... a song called "Balls." (I'd wanted to write an uplifting, positive song like hers, but as sometimes happens, things went in a different direction between my opening chords and the first line.)

Susan Cowsill, one of my childhood idols with her brothers and mom in the Cowsills, had been married to Peter Holsapple, from my ex-husband Will's band, the dB's, and their band, the Continental Drifters, backed me up occasionally. I'd stayed with them in New Orleans and had loved being part of the big dysfunctional family of that band that also included Vicki Peterson of the Bangles and my old boyfriend, Robert Mache. Our music world back then was a small one with lots of recurring characters, like a community theatre production with the same townsfolk playing multiple roles, or Frank Morgan in *The Wizard of Oz*: one minute a doorman, then a ticket seller, a horseman, or the Wizard himself.

This evening at the Bluebird, we settled in and went around a few times playing our songs. Then, bursting with excitement and pride, I told my fellow performers and the audience I had a special guest.

"He wrote this classic song you might recognize," I said. I noticed Eric sitting at a table, looking around the room, wondering what marvelous Nashville star I was calling up to sit next to me. "Let's hear it for Wreckless Eric!"

Then Eric was stumbling over people's feet to reach the center of the room. He picked up my guitar and pulsated the opening E chord so you just knew something momentous was coming. When he sang the first line, Peter and Will grinned. Susan and Kim beamed at me because I was beaming, so in love. By the chorus, everyone was singing along. I thought back to playing the song in the Dairy Dip parking lot six years ago, and smiled—that's music, the closest thing to magic there is. It brought us together.

Back by the restroom after the show, I saw my old headshot up on the wall. I looked perky in a western shirt, circa 1996, when *Mod Housewife* was released. I'd worried I was over the hill then, at thirty-seven, but was only just getting started as a songwriter and playing solo. I'd taken a leap of faith coming to Nashville around then, starting with the Monday open mic and finding my way into songwriter rounds again and again. There'd been plenty of good will for me in this town, even though I'd lost touch with it; neglected the friendships I'd made.

And now I was throwing my lot in with Eric. Would I just fade away from this place? Had it ever really felt like home? I wasn't sure, but it felt sad to say goodbye. I was thinking I needed to put my house up for sale. I knew it would sell quickly—great house, good neighborhood; everyone wanted to live in Nashville now. Once the house sold, would I have any reason to come back here?

Eric and I said goodbyes to everyone and drove north to Ohio, where Eric had a gig the next night at a punk club in Akron, the Lime Spider. The contrast to the respectful if slightly staid atmosphere of the Bluebird in Nashville was marked: chaos reigned. Sound difficulties, the stench of beer, rabid fans expecting Eric to revisit his hits circa 1978. But there was also freedom— to fuck up, play loud, and transgress. I came up onstage to play a few after feedback nearly ended the show prematurely. Eric commanded the audience. Was he the same modest guy I introduced at the Bluebird? The air was rank; we sweated and cursed. When Eric invited me to play "Dancing With Joey Ramone," I dug in while Eric worked his green Microfret guitar next to me. I remembered a group of guys backing me up onstage, or singing harmony with the Shams, or the honky tonk stomp of Last Roundup. Even trying to hold it together behind a drum kit in the short-lived No Wave outfit, the Stare Kits. We'd all been friends, even family. But me and Eric playing together felt like *being a band*, even if it was just the two of us. It was synergy and standing up for each other—a gang of two.

Afterwards, we loaded out, fending off lovable loonies and locals. Someone handed us a sculpture that was bound to end up broken before we got back to—wherever home was.

Chapter Thirty-Four

The plan was to move Hazel and her stuff to Chicago. But first I had a tour of the Netherlands to do. *Little Fugitive* had been released in that tiny country and there was actually some interest. The European label put me together with artist Tracy Bonham, who'd had a big moment in the '90s with her visceral Grammy-nominated song, "Mother Mother," and the video had been everywhere. She continued to do well when she went out to play. I'd never met Tracy, but she wore her dark hair in bangs and had that good girl with an edge vibe, so I felt sure we were kindred spirits.

The label had booked us a proper tour through an agent: decent-sized places with a road manager to do the driving and accommodation arranged in every city. Ah, so this is how other people do this, I thought. All I had to do was show up with my guitar, ready to play. It was a dream of life as a touring musician. Big crowds in every town, packed from the front of the stage to the rear of the hall. Stage lights, pro sound. Dressing rooms with riders of sandwiches, fruit, nuts, and chocolate waiting for us upon arrival for soundcheck.

Back in those days, before European countries lost a lot of their arts funding, most touring musicians were aware of the wonderful way certain countries treated artists, but you needed a label or promoter—or teaming up with another artist—to gain access. Our road manager drank a little too much, but Tracy was lovely, inviting me to join her onstage for a fun cover of Beyoncé's "Crazy In Love." Classically trained on violin, a stellar vocalist, Tracy was almost intimidatingly talented, but we had fun playing and hanging out after the shows in Nijmegen, Rotterdam, Groningen, and other towns that all seemed forty-five minutes from each other but worlds apart with their subtle cultural differences.

Eric joined me for the last show in Amsterdam. We said goodbye to Tracy and the slightly more sober road manager who'd replaced the first one. Eric and I headed south in his right-hand drive car for my first and only solo gig in Paris. We laughed the entire way through Belgium and an afternoon traffic jam, on into the northeast corner of France ("It's fucking freezing here, even in summer," said Eric.)

The Paris show took place in a charming basement bar in the Latin Quarter, La Pomme d'Eve. Low stone arches and a folky, dark atmosphere, it offered everything you'd want from a Paris nightclub, except maybe an audience. I asked Eric to come up and sing "Whole Wide World" during my set—I felt so proud, I couldn't believe this song I loved had brought us together and here we were in Paris.

After all the turmoil of the last couple years, I felt like my life had suddenly turned miraculous. The gig ended early enough that it was still light out, and Eric and I checked into a hotel the venue had arranged, the Studia on Boulevard Saint Germain. Then we wandered out into the Latin Quarter to find something to eat.

And in the way that being in love turns Paris into the perfect backdrop for romantic dreams, the cafe we entered was honest, with red and white checkered paper cloths and good steak frites and delicious wine that didn't cost much. Even the upstairs toilet, lined with old theater posters, was perfect.

Of course it was perfect. It was May, and we were newly in love, fucking half a dozen times a day. Paris bowed down in front of us. Every person we talked to immediately turned from slightly chilly to ebullient. Eric spoke French fluently and, chatting with a bartender, revealed he'd wanted to move back since he left the country seven years ago. He'd lived nearly a decade two hours west of Paris and had always thought maybe the simple country life he'd been seeking was further to the south. Would I consider moving there with him? he asked.

My high school French teacher, with his wide bow tie and Elton John glasses, who called himself "Le Plus Beau." Belmondo and Seberg in Breathless, *Bardot and Piccoli in* Contempt. *Dewaere, Depardieu and Miou Miou in* Going Places. *Fashion photos in* Marie Claire *and* Elle, *the real French '70s magazines I pored over in the library at Parsons.* Cousin Cousine, *Beatrice Dalle in* Betty Blue; *Lizzy Mercier Descloux. The dress I found in a flea market on my only other trip to Paris, 1981, and the way the colors of the floral print—violet, green and blue—were more vivid than any other item of clothing I owned. Watching Jacques Tati's* Mon Oncle *while in labor. Escargots at Cafe Loup on West Fourteenth*

Street and crayons and paper tablecloths at Cafe Un Deux Trois—this was the sum total of my experience with France and things French.

It was enough.

"Why—sure!" I said. I'd always thought I'd live in Europe at some point in my life, imagining that it would probably be Italy. But sex in Paris and steak in Paris felt dirtier and juicier than they'd ever felt anywhere else. He asked, and I said yes.

Of course, I said yes.

"I know this real estate agent about four hours south of here," said Eric.

Chapter Thirty-Five

Hazel popped a mix tape into the Mercury Villager's cassette player. She, Eric, and I all sang along to a varied assortment of hits of the '60s and '70s: "Run Joey Run," "In The Year 2525," and "Sugar Sugar." We were on our way from Cleveland to that year's family gathering, after Hazel's high school graduation.

We all took turns driving. Hazel at seventeen proved herself a decent highway pilot. I felt alternately relieved and terrified that she loved to drive as much as I did. Eric at the wheel managed to evade the state troopers who lurked behind bushes and highway signs. In England and France, they use cameras to catch speeders, so the concept of cops lying in wait was a little novel to him.

Our destination was a bed and breakfast in the quaint mountain town of Cumberland, Maryland. My family had stayed here once before, a year or two before my mother passed away—the rare get-together where I didn't have a man in tow. This would be Eric's first chance to meet my father, though he'd encountered most of the other members of my family at various tour stops, just as I'd met Eric's mother and his daughter, Luci, when he and I played a gig in Brighton. I'd even become friends with his former girlfriend, Karen, in Norwich.

It was a perk of being a touring musician: encounter friends and family in the course of playing shows and avoid the pressure and awkwardness of arranged first meetings.

At the last summer's meet-up I'd been full of uncertainty and angst, facing off against my dad's fears on the porch of a rundown Pennsylvania B&B. This year felt almost celebratory, as Eric ran the gauntlet of meeting the remaining members of my family. My dad sidled up to him after the more formal introductions, itching to tell him a bit of vital information. Eric looked pale—it wasn't like I was some dewy-eyed virgin bride. I was a forty-seven year old divorcee who'd been through a lot the last few years. What warning could my dad possibly issue? What piece of advice did he have to share?

"Eric, do you know why the English are so fucking miserable?" my dad asked.

"Why, no, Phil, I don't," Eric said, trying to be polite, but drawing the line at calling my dad "sir," thank God. "But I expect you're going to tell me. Why are the English so ah—um... miserable?"

"Because they only shit once a week!" my father said, and thumped Eric on the back.

It looked like my new boyfriend had made the cut.

Later in the evening, my brother Pat and his wife Karen busted out their karaoke machine. Pat and Karen had good jobs, a popular, pretty daughter, and a beautifully-maintained home in the suburbs north of Pittsburgh. But when the backing track kicked in, I saw in Pat's eyes the performing madness so deeply instilled in all of us through our mother's love for anything related to show biz. Pat and Karen went all out for "You're The One That I Want" from the *Grease* soundtrack—back to back, shoulder shimmies, the entire film choreography sequence. Their routine brought the B&B living room down. I thought that was a good kind of couple to be— on each other's side.

Not to be outdone, Eric grabbed the mic and unleashed an "I Will Survive" that married the rawness of Cake's '90s version with Gloria Gaynor's original class and authority. I could only look on in awe and adoration.

I took James to a cat-sitting place south of Cleveland. I'd found the animal hotel online, completely random but I didn't know who to ask for recommendations, so I was just hoping the care was decent. I stopped at Bruster's Real Ice Cream a few miles before I reached the cat-sitting spot, to bolster myself with a treat. Sitting alone at a picnic table off an Ohio state road populated with strip malls, I wondered what I was doing scattering my little family all over the Midwest. Hazel was off to Chicago, her dad and his wife were in Cleveland for now, I'd rented a storage space in Cleveland Heights. I was keeping a stake there: a mailbox near Case University; the Mercury Villager minivan in a massive parking warehouse in Bratenahl. I was selling the house in Nashville.

Dropping James off with strangers in a strange place was wrenching, but the people seemed nice, and the animals looked happy. When I came back to pick him up, the owners told me what a joy he'd been, how sociable. It made me sad to think the life we'd given him had gone against his true nature. He'd done his best to tell us just how isolated he felt by wreaking havoc and pushing stuff over in every place we'd lived since he joined us in Brooklyn almost ten years before.

Or maybe he was just a troublemaker.

My old Williamsburg neighbor, Kit the painter, told me she would take him. She had two other cats, and they'd all get along together. Hazel would be living in a dorm, and where exactly was home for me?

The future felt so hard to imagine, me and Hazel both going off into the unknown. I was glad my daughter would attend her first choice of schools in a city she was excited about. But I didn't know Chicago except as a tour stop. I felt comforted that at least one of the family was headed for familiar territory; going home.

James was moving back to Brooklyn.

And then I was looking at France on the internet from Mayfield Road in Cleveland. Farm buildings, small village houses—all under 80,000 euros; fairly rustic. Eric had flown back to England and was looking at houses online too; sending me links to the ones he found interesting. Then he traveled to the Limousin, where he knew an estate agent, and looked at a few possibilities. It was an agricultural region, more cows than champagne. We didn't really know what we were getting into, but without really debating or weighing the pros and cons too much, we'd made the decision to move in together.

In rural France.

Eric's garden flat outside of Norwich sold the day he put it on the market, snapped up by the daughter of the architect who designed the complex back in the early '70s. She wanted one that had been left with all the original features intact, a perfect brief for Eric, who had a deep appreciation of old linoleum, amplifiers, fabric, even paring knives. I think I knew we were meant to be together when I saw his colorful mismatched plates and chairs, ancient skillet, and Le Creuset casserole.

I returned to the U.S. and a voice message from L.A. Sam: "Hey girl! What's up? Sounds like you and this Eric guy are for real? Give me a call sometime."

I thought of the years I'd kept a small flame burning for this guy who could take or leave me. It used to feel safe to have an unavailable fallback person to fantasize about. I'd outgrown that idea at last.

We are for real, Sam. Goodbye.

My house in Nashville sold. I felt a necessary detachment—the place worked as a home for me and my daughter, when I had a publishing deal and wrote songs believing something might happen for me in that town. Had I blown my chances of professional songwriting success by getting together with Charles and derailing that Nashville dream, or had I gotten together with Charles when that dream revealed itself to be not the right one, or too far out of reach? As I signed all the closing documents, I mostly felt relief I wouldn't have to deal with the heat and humidity anymore.

Hazel was getting ready for college in Chicago. She'd gotten her own band together in Cleveland, playing bass and singing. The first time I stopped by a rehearsal and witnessed The Box, I turned into my own mother for a few seconds, clapping along as they kicked into a song, my hands held high, mouth involuntarily open and smiling. Hazel rolled her eyes a little but laughed and looked pleased by my enthusiastic response. When The Box opened for Eric at the Beachland Tavern, playing mostly covers, Eric referred to the trio as "Every Man's Dream"—not meaning it in a pervy way, just in awe of their youthful energy and effortless attention to detail. I almost dissolved with pride when they backed him for a song, their arrangement of "Take The K.A.S.H." almost identical to the original record. Hazel was bursting with excitement about moving to Chicago. I thought she'd be just fine there—France didn't seem that far away.

As I began imagining life without the combination of worry and pride at being Hazel's mom, I also started saying goodbye to my solo touring life. This wasn't just a reaction to Charles' ambushing me at the Birchmere. I think I'd been building up to it for a while, missing the shared sense of purpose that comes from being part of a combo. And maybe I'd said all I could say as a solo artist—or the risks were too great, exposing myself up there like that. Joining forces had been what I was looking for, leading to the duo show with Marti, and it's what Eric and I hoped to work up to—from the safety and calm of the French countryside. It was an idea.

Whoever said life's a marathon, not a sprint, had to have been talking about life as a musician. How do you keep putting yourself out there, through all the challenges life throws at you? Sometimes the road seems long and dark, the way forward unclear, and you just can't go it alone anymore.

Back in New York City, I received a slip through the mailbox of Amanda's Ridgewood apartment where I was spending a few nights—UPS had a box of merchandise for me, at some far-flung location on the border of Queens and Brooklyn. I drove over in the heat, thankful I'd forked out a few hundred dollars to fix the Villager's A/C.

I waited in line at the UPS warehouse, glad I no longer had to deal with these kind of daily urban experiences, surliness all around. When I advanced to the window and handed over the delivery slip, the woman wanted to see ID. I showed her my Tennessee driver's license.

"Hmmm. That's not this address. And your license says Amelia McMahon Rigby. The box is for an Amy Rigby."

"Yep, that's me—I'm the same person."

We argued for a little while. Maybe she was just bored and wanted some drama to get through the afternoon. I told her "Look, it's my CD in the box, I wrote the songs, my picture is all over the cover!" I offered to get one out and show her.

She grunted. "Okay." I held up a copy of *Little Fugitive*, photo IDs past to present.

"Well, I don't see it. Which one is you?"

"I wish I knew, lady," I thought. "I'm still trying to figure that out."

It was the end of one thing, and the beginning of something else. I'd moved away from New York City seven years before, but those seven years had felt like a series of tentative goodbyes—like checking your makeup in the mirror again and again before leaving the house. Maybe I'd been hoping a hand would reach out from my reflection and pull me back into my old hallway in Brooklyn, the one with the big wide full-length mirror, where I'd look at myself as if nothing had changed and think: you belong here.

But if I'd never left, I'd never have written all these songs, scored a publishing deal, bought a house. Who knows in what other ways I might've screwed up, but I might never have met Eric either. I likely would have never gotten a gig playing at South Street Seaport on a Friday evening in August—a prime booking that said I'd made a name for myself out there in the world.

It felt poetic coming down to perform in the same Manhattan shopping and dining complex where many years ago I'd worked behind the counter of a fancy stationery store, when the Seaport wasn't all the way finished being built. I'd been there as the place faltered to its feet like a colt trying to stand up and walk—there'd even been straw all over the

ground as construction lurched along, bucking public opinion; the idea
of what this area of town meant—fish and finance—and how outrageous
an idea a mall downtown had seemed. New York wasn't like other places
in the '70s, '80s, and '90s. We'd all come here to get away from malls,
and the sameness of everywhere else. Now, Manhattan was transforming
as it became more and more like everywhere else.

My band and I set up in the steamy afternoon as the sun went down
between fingers of skyscrapers densely packed around lower Manhattan,
like stalagmites in an underwater cave, with water all around: East River
right there, harbor below, the Hudson only a few blocks to the west.

As I often did when I was nervous about playing a gig, I set off on an
errand: hairspray. Must find hairspray. The CVS on Water Street put me
right in the thick of the neighborhood, the other shoppers a mix of workers set free for the weekend and day trippers buying snacks and bottles
of water. Standing in the makeup aisle, I felt like I belonged again, like
I'd just gotten off a week-long temp assignment at the New York Stock
Exchange or Standard and Poor's on Broadway. I thought of my time at
Deloitte Haskins way up in the World Trade Center, gone five years now.
It was 1988 and I was five-, then six-months pregnant, heaving myself up
out of the subway and riding an elevator one hundred stories above the
city. How I'd wished I could be anywhere else.

For a second in CVS, I felt envious of the office workers, even wished
I was still one of them: the routine, the Au Bon Pain coffee and bagel,
the extra shoes under my desk. It was easy to impress people with your
talent when no one expected anything of you. Now I caught sight of myself in the mirror above a Revlon display, my hair frizzy and skin shiny
with sweat. I remembered so well wanting to have it all together, running
home from a temp job and back out to a gig. Hadn't my dreams come
true at least a little bit?

Robbie Fulks played his set and then my band and I were onstage. I
felt like I was floating above it all: nothing could touch me, nothing could
go wrong. There was a great crowd out there and the buildings served
as concrete baffles to lift the sound and carry it up and back to me. We
roared and churned through the set and the disparate Friday evening
collection of people, pausing for a moment in their busy New York City
lives, melded into a happy mass of listeners.

I felt satisfaction knowing I'd been writing and recording steadily
since I'd left the city. I had three more albums' worth of songs to choose
from for the set list: "Like Rasputin" and "Dancing With Joey Ramone"
hadn't existed three years ago. But I'd hardly written a song since leav-

ing Nashville in August 2005. I was afraid of making myself vulnerable again.

For a second, I wondered if Charles was out there in the crowd. I couldn't decide which was worse: the idea of him presenting himself to me after the gig like he'd done at the Birchmere, or the thought of him watching anonymously.

I shook the idea away and dug into another song. Playing the electric guitar especially made me feel powerful. I wanted to hold onto this moment forever.

And then—lightning struck. Thunder cracked. The heavens opened and rain fell in sheets, in torrents.

The audience ran. They headed for the edges of the buildings, for the subway, for a restaurant. The intrepid remained. A fan who'd emailed a birthday request climbed up on stage to sing "All I Want" with me. I finished the set feeling like everything had come together in spite of the deluge.

"Amy Rigby, one of the best in the world at 47, playing South Street Seaport for free in intermittent rain to 150 people," wrote Robert Christgau in *The Village Voice.*

I felt it as a triumph. As far as I was concerned, I was going out on a high.

Chapter Thirty-Six

It looked like Eric and I had settled on the Limousin in our search for somewhere to move. I didn't know anything about this (or any) region of France, except that it was the beginning of the Southwest part of the country. Sparsely populated, rural, mainly agricultural, the Limousin region produced very large cows, and its main city, Limoges, was where the fine porcelain that bears its name originated.

Also, it was cheap.

I couldn't move to a place I'd never even visited. I flew to England and Eric and I drove south to catch the early morning car ferry to France. First, Eric showed me the house where he was born, just near the docks of Newhaven, and the Parker Pen Company where his father worked as a draftsman. I remembered being moved by the story he told at the beginning of his autobiography, how on that day in 1954, his father stood at the front gate of the family's rented terraced house, holding Eric's older sister in his arms as fellow Parker employees walked past on their way to the railway station, while Eric's dad announced over and over, "It's a boy." Fifty-two years later I doubted much in the street had changed—the modest two-story building part of a tidy row, the net curtains in the windows, the gate. Life in postwar Britain contrasted starkly with my mid-century American suburban upbringing. There was so much to learn about each other.

We crossed the Channel to Dieppe where we ate baguettes spread with butter and filled with ham and cheese. Welcome to France. I thought of my first time there, in 1981, when Angela and I caroused through Paris as students, looking for the next thing after punk and finding it in Prince at Le Palace gay disco. *Impressionante*, I'd eventually learn to say in French. For the moment, I was silent and let Eric order our sandwiches, and then expertly pilot his right-hand drive vehicle on the opposite side of the road to the autoroute. We passed through Rouen, with its famous cathedral painted so often by Monet, and skirted around Paris via Dreux in the Eure-et Loir, the area where Eric had lived through most of the '90s. We traversed Chartres, with its asymmetrical cathedral.

"The workmen took so long for lunch every day, by the time they built the second tower, it was a different era," Eric said. I was so in love I didn't question it.

Around Orleans, the landscape softened into the dreamy greens and gentle dips and rises you'd see in a faded French film, so that I almost forgot what century we were in; what was real and what was my imagination. I couldn't believe we were really doing this. The route took us through one village where there was a medieval feast going on, and villagers in antique costumes walked by the car as if we were invisible—the Volvo a time machine. Horses' nostrils, women with tobacco-stained teeth, men in scratchy-looking brown tunics, a fountain in the village center making me thirsty, and then we were on another autoroute near Chateauroux, with tantalizing glimpses of fairy tale castles tucked in between the hills.

We made our way through Limoges, a city that managed to look simultaneously characterful and drab, and followed the river Vienne past factories and mills, through quaint, empty towns and villages until we rolled up to Nick the estate agent's house in a sleepy village. Nick was English and his wife Francoise French; they showed and sold houses together and also drove three-wheeler Lotus sports cars. Their house was a work in progress: ancient stones outside, modern tiled floor inside, with advertising art, a female mannequin in evening dress, and brightly patterned cushions and rugs. Our hosts were in the midst of a dinner party with French and English friends, and we joined them at the table. I felt overwhelmed—where the hell was I? I called my daughter from a phone booth in the village square as a big iron church bell chimed and immense rust-colored cows gathered in an adjacent field.

"Mom, where are you?" Hazel asked. I explained I was in a tiny village in southwest France, and we were looking for a place to live there. "I guess you know what you're doing..." she said, having every reason to believe the opposite. Look how my previous decision upended our lives, derailed things, left us marking time in Cleveland, of all places.

I'd probably spent more energy choosing a blouse off the clearance rack at TJ Maxx than I had making the biggest life decisions: get married, have a baby; plan to marry one unsuitable guy; move in with the right one, in another country. But things have a way of working out when they're meant to—and falling apart when they're not. My big wish, that Hazel go to a college she felt excited about, was coming true. France seemed like a benign way for me to step aside and let her go, for now. I imagined her coming to visit regularly, maybe even ending up at L'Ecole de Beaux-Arts in Paris. There's always some degree of magical thinking in an artist's life—a belief in fate and alchemy. How else to explain the creation of a piece of work—a song, a story, a painting or performance —where there was nothing before?

I'm not saying a musician can't be practical. We spend half our time dealing with logistics—distances between gigs, timings, scheduling, cost of hotels, transport. But there has to be a part of the brain that shuts out careful consideration, to let intuition or a higher power take over. To walk into the unknown every day—a blank page, a new workplace. You operate on blind trust most of the time. Results may vary, of course.

Back at Nick and Francoise's, our guest room had old fashioned wooden shutters we kept closed while we made love in the morning, afternoon, and night, in between looking at properties.

With our small budget, the house selection was... interesting. In one offering, a toilet sat square in the middle of the bedroom. Another house required climbing up one set of steps, down another, through a dirt-floored barn and into a tiny added-on room to reach the bathroom.

There were weird land configurations where the patch of grass directly in front of the house belonged to someone else. Others came with a garden, but you needed to cross the road to reach it. Every farmhouse came with at least one or two bread ovens in rough stone outbuildings; many had massive, attached barns housing rustic carts we were assured came included with the property. Burgundy-tiled bathrooms, bedrooms dense with wallpaper; a house adjacent to a duck farm redolent with the strong odor of duck manure.

One house was situated in a tiny hamlet—to reach it we drove by an open doorway where a family sat around a kitchen table in an unlit room, the floor bare earth. The vision of France I'd conjured as an American didn't extend beyond the Paris city limits—chic, tall windows; luxe fabrics. Eric reminded me that two world wars decimated the French economy. In the countryside, even here in the twenty-first century, a forty-watt bulb might be considered extravagant.

In the midst of house hunting, we visited the medieval town of Chalus, known for its twelfth century castle that played an important part in the story of Richard the Lionheart. This was the spot where, after achieving glory in the Crusades, the King of England died of gangrene, said the plaque at the base of a tall stone tower. Eric and I picnicked on strawberries and goat cheese in a patch of grass between the tower and yet another house with its sign, "A Vendre." We poked around outside the empty, shuttered House For Sale, thinking how cool it would be to have Richard Coeur de Lion as your neighbor. But the place looked like it needed a lot of work, and the town felt eerily deserted. It was two or three in the afternoon on a Friday, so the weekly market had packed up and everyone had headed inside to do whatever it was French people did in their houses all day—I think it involves cleaning in near darkness.

"It will be nice to see the place when there are people here," I said. I had a lot to learn about rural France.

We walked around through the stillness of the afternoon, enjoying examples of early to mid-twentieth century architecture and signage represented in the shop fronts: "Elle et Lui" proclaimed one *moderne* shop window—was it from the '30s or '50s? Featureless male and female mannequins posed in timeless clothing, impossible to date because the fabrics were faded of all color and pattern from so many seasons of exposure to sunlight. The Boucherie/Charcuterie looked straight out of a Claude Chabrol film, its letters a red I'd only ever seen on an art deco Bakelite bracelet from the '30s. Tous les Tissus was devoid of merchandise, but the racy black and gold font made me think "Grand Prix," and the windows served as a regal display for someone's sports trophies.

The Laurence d'Arabie bar, situated on the ground floor of an ancient building on the town square, with a non-working fountain, appeared to be open. We were hot and thirsty and decided to see if we could get a cold drink inside.

The hip-looking guy behind the bar said a quiet "Bonjour." He was rangy, with dark brows, a wispy goatee, and dark shaggy hair. He busied himself drying glasses, then raised the volume of the sound system. Eric and I looked at each other hopefully—was he playing the Velvet Underground?

Eric began conversing with the bartender, and if I listened very carefully I could make out about a third of what they were saying. This gave me hope I'd pick up the language, not overnight but easier than if it was Spanish, Italian, German, or Dutch. All that time spent at the cinema with Godard, Rohmer, and Truffaut had to be some help.

It turned out the guy behind the bar was the proprietor of the place, that there was a kitchen and rooms above; that it was once a hotel that accommodated Lawrence of Arabia when he was a student biking through

France. I estimated the owner was in his thirties—I'd learn younger people were a rarity in sparsely-populated parts of France, where they shipped the teenagers off to larger towns for high school. After, they'd go to the city, any city, for university or to find work, and were rarely seen again except on holidays until they reached the age of retirement, when they'd return to sell the houses of their elderly or deceased parents.

Eric and I asked the owner if there was any chance we could play a gig in his bar? Nico, who'd introduced himself in exchange for our names, disappeared behind a large desktop computer for a minute. When he came back around to the bar, he said he'd be proud to have us play there. We all shook hands.

Outside the bar, we blinked in the sunlight and laughed. "This is gonna be easy!" we said, amazed that we'd found a place to play, just like that. We imagined ourselves setting up gigs all over the French countryside, playing covers and our own songs. I liked the romance of it; the purity of music for its own sake, after years of striving to get someplace. It didn't hurt that I was so in love I would follow Eric down into a coal mine if he told me it was a good idea—that's how much I believed in him.

And the next day, we saw a place right on the main road, Rue de Limoges, that ran through a small workaday village. The house was clean and attractive, cool in the summer heat. The entrance hall felt almost elegant, with soft light coming in through glass panes in the dark wooden door that opened out onto the road. The front room would make a perfect studio. The kitchen was large with tall windows and actual French doors that led out into a charming stone courtyard with an old water pump and wisteria branches. Kitchen might be an ambitious word for it—there was a patterned linoleum floor and a sink in one corner, that's it. A small bathroom with a half bath (for dunking half a granny, Eric said) and up a winding staircase of dark wood sat three bedrooms with varying patterns of wallpaper on walls, doors—even light switches. But bright and spotless. After some of the horrors we'd seen, it looked like heaven. We could move right in without having to do anything, except buy a stove. Nick and Francoise drew up the paperwork.

"Let's walk back over to the house," I said the next day, ever the New Yorker eager to hoof it. It was beautifully warm and sunny outside. I wore a red shirtdress and Keds, feeling like the heroine in every Godard film I'd ever seen, my rogue boyfriend in jeans and a striped jersey.

The walk was fun for about half an hour. Soon the sun was beating down, our throats dry. There's wasn't a shop—anything at all—between

Nick and Francoise's village of Champagnac and our soon to be village of Cussac. Only cows. This was deepest countryside. On either side of the road were fields and fields of the massive Limousin cows, alternating with swathes of bright yellow plants Eric informed me were called colza or rapeseed.

We decided to cut across one of the fields, thinking it might help shorten the trip a little. The field was muddy and the cows loomed at us from all directions. They lowed, they snorted.

"There aren't any... bulls around here, are there?" I asked Eric. In the heat of July midday, I didn't *think* the cows were going to start chasing us. They barely seemed energetic enough to lurch to the stone water trough under a tree. "Maybe walking wasn't such a great idea." Like so many times in my life, I rush headfirst into a situation having absolutely no idea what I'm getting into.

But I do it anyway.

At last, we reached the village, where a statue of Christ writhing in agony on a cross greeted all visitors. We climbed the gentle slope of the road and unlocked the door of the house. We gulped water from the kitchen faucet and climbed the stairs to the bedroom we knew without discussion would be ours, the one with the prettiest view. I saw roses climbing up the stone wall just outside the window. We took off enough of our clothes to pretend the floor was a bed and laid down and held each other there.

"This carpet is spotless," I said.

"Guess we found a house," said Eric.

Chapter Thirty-Seven

November 2006. Back in England, Eric and I waited to hear when the funds would come through so we could move into the house in France. We hosted our first house concert, called "You Come To Us," thirty or so hardcore fans paying twenty pounds each to receive entree into Eric's living room, where we played songs for over two hours.

We aimed to provide food for everyone—I remember guests mashing up avocados to help restock the guacamole supply. The audience also stocked the kitchen with more alcohol than I'd ever seen in my life. It began to dawn on me what lightweights we Americans were. After years of touring and visiting the U.K. as a U.S. artist, I was finally getting an insider's view. The night ended with two superfans nestled in each other's arms, sleeping it off on the pavement outside Eric's front door. Better that than drive to their B&B. Everyone declared the night a success, and nobody stole anything. In fact, we ended up with enough wine and beer to last for weeks. All mine—Eric gave up drinking decades ago. "You would not like me drunk," he reminded me, and I believed him, though I think I would still love him. I admired his self-discipline in getting and staying sober.

There was still so much to learn about my new boyfriend. Some people do things gradually, get to know each other through dinner and a movie; weekend outings. I move to France with a person.

Eric threw open the door to his garage, a structure I'd never noticed before at the back of his row of garden flats. The garage space was piled floor to ceiling with tape machines, interesting-looking ephemera, guitar cases.

"What's all this stuff?" I asked, trying to contain my hysteria. "Where are we going to put it?" I remembered his drill sergeant-like rigor talking me and Hazel through the decamping of our belongings from the apartment on Mayfield Road in Cleveland into a nearby storage space: *Dump that! Box those! Fold these. Tell me you're not keeping this?*

"I assumed you knew what you were doing, planning this move?" I said.

"Oh, never assume that," he said

Yes, there was so much to learn. The week before our house concert outside of Norwich, there'd been Canterbury, one of our first gigs together as a duo act. Without any big plan, we'd been working things out to be a band. Just the two of us: the Eric & Amy Show; Wreckless Eric & Amy Rigby. At first, we played almost as a co-bill: I played my songs, Eric played his, then we did a few together. It had worked beautifully at a bar in Norwich, at the Half Moon in Putney. In Canterbury, it didn't quite go as planned.

There'd been a nice crowd at the Orange Street Arts Centre. I started with some funny songs and a few rockers. Then Eric took the stage on his own for a little while, building intensity. Everything was going fine until a drugged-out local started making a racket, shouting unintelligibly up at Eric, who invited him to come up and make his thoughts known to the public. The local lunged towards the stage and Eric parried with his green Microfret guitar. The local was subdued by a bouncer.

Then things began to get louder onstage. The promoter, who looked about twenty and had talked and laughed with his mates for most of the set, started asking Eric to turn down his amp. The promoter climbed onstage and actually turned the amp down himself. The soundman cut off the P.A. Eric threw a mic stand sideways across the stage, and Eric and the promoter began brawling onstage. A large man held Eric back while another called for the police on a walkie talkie.

"Let him go! Let him go!" I cried, pulling on the bouncer's arm while the audience sat open-mouthed before us. Eventually the promoter ran out of steam, or the cocaine wore off, or the alcohol took its toll. He loped off into the night, while Eric and I loaded out and went back to a friend's house to open an email from the promoter demanding money for damages to the equipment.

It was the type of drama I'd never experienced. I'd allowed soundmen to insist I use their inappropriate mics or place my amplifier wherever it was most convenient for them or another band on the bill. It had never occurred to me I was allowed to decide how the stage should be set up for my show.

I never saw Eric act outrageous or unkind to a soundman out of ego or on a whim. But he demanded respect. After Canterbury, we played a house concert in a family home in Kent and there was a feeling of working together, even in a living room setting, that made for fine production values and a good time for everyone; the host became a dear friend. This was the start of our performing partnership, and the lessons I was eager to learn from an artist I admired. I knew from the time the punches flew in Canterbury that things wouldn't always be easy. But I decided then and there I would be on Eric's side. He'd worked too hard for too long to be mistreated. From that point on, we've been for each other—a gang of two.

In the HMV in Norwich, I found a copy of Ronnie Spector's new album, *The Last Of The Rock Stars*. In the prime track number three spot was "All I Want," the song I wrote with Ronnie's voice in my head. I paid for the CD and when I opened the package it turned out Keith Richards played guitar on my song too. Maybe I knew that already, but it had taken some years since Jonathan, Ronnie's husband, first played the track for me in his rental car at the Rockrgl conference in Seattle. Nothing feels the same as an actual credit on an album you buy in a store. Hearing that trademark "Whoa-oh-oh" over my chords and melody is one of the biggest thrills of my life as a songwriter. Eric was thrilled for me too, though he thought maybe they should've shortened Keith's solo a little.

Since *Little Fugitive* came out, people have asked me to play "The Trouble With Jeanie" in my set. It's something good that came out of my relationship with Charles. Songs are my main currency, my assets.

Based on real-life, but like all my songs a fictionalized version, the song describes the kind of friendship I don't think anyone envisions when they're falling in love: the experience of becoming close with the ex of your partner. When Eric and I first met in Hull back in 2000, he was seeing a woman named Karen. Because I felt an immediate spark with Eric, I thought of Karen as a threat, an obstacle. And Eric says Karen sensed the same thing about me: "I always had a feeling about that Amy," she said.

They broke up shortly after that night in Hull—nothing to do with me—but Karen was a creative partner to Eric as well, and has remained his dear friend. She and her boyfriend (now husband) Peter have become like family to us. I think it speaks well of a person, that they can remain so important in the life of a former love—it proves there was a connection beyond lust and ego, that each of you really do want the best for the other.

As we packed up and vacated Eric's house outside of Norwich, Karen and Peter took us in, fed us, gave us a room to sleep in, a warm fire to sit in front of while we watched *Strictly Come Dancing* and *The Apprentice*, all the British tv shows. Karen is a brilliant artist and photographer; Peter is half-American so understands and appreciates my need for a decent sandwich. Charles and his ex-wife were well out of my life, but the song still rings true, and Eric's Karen is my Jeanie.

The Trouble With Jeanie

Jeanie is my new husband's ex-wife
It looks like she's gonna be a part of my life
Cause there's a couple of kids and twenty some years they share
So I guess Jeanie isn't going anywhere
I even tried to hate her like I thought I should
But since we met she's been nothing but good

And the trouble with Jeanie is she's alright
And the trouble with Jeanie is she's so nice
Could somebody explain to me this modern life?

How can I pick up where she never left off?
We're like a club of two who've seen him with his clothes off
And there's nowhere to hide because it's all out in the light
Can I help if I'm a little bit uptight
I must admit I don't know how I'm supposed to act
She's hugging me instead of stabbing my back

And the trouble with Jeanie is she's alright
And the trouble with Jeanie is she's so nice
Could somebody explain to me this modern life?
The trouble with Jeanie is
The trouble with Jeanie is

I've heard of divorces, where bitterness forces
Extreme mortal combat, and I wouldn't want that
But I hadn't planned on something quite so hands on
Instead of a blessing, it seems to be messing with my mind

Word arrived that the small mortgage Eric applied for through a tiny bank branch in Rochechouart, the nearest town to Cussac big enough to have a bank, had come through. We loaded up Eric's Volvo wagon, an automatic I hoped to drive when I worked up the nerve, and set off to catch the ferry from Dover. We left behind a storage space full of the rest of Eric's belongings, while MY storage space moped by itself in Cleveland.

The drive from Norwich to Dover and the ferry crossing to Calais were unmomentous, the only inconvenience being a dish drainer that kept coming unmoored from the back of the car and making its way into the front seat. I wore hair curlers, as a photo taken by Karen attests. We're in an old car stuffed with mattress, refrigerator, table, and chairs; guitars, bedding, curtains, suitcases, and boxes of books and records—all the essentials—and we may have looked like the Beverly Hillbillies but as far as I was concerned this was the most glamorous thing I'd ever done in my life: I was moving to France.

Eric and I spent the night in a hotel in Saint-Omer, a somber-looking town not far from Calais. We were up early the next morning, and after a hotel breakfast of coffee and croissants we set off full of high spirits and anticipation. After about forty minutes on the autoroute, we noticed smoke pouring out of the Volvo and had no choice but to pull over and find a garage in a place called Roye. It's a part of France called the Somme, where a famously bloody World War One battle was fought, killing 20,000 British troops on the first day alone. There was a dark desolation to the place that didn't bode well for the Volvo. The garage mechanics tolled a death knell for the car —either the repairs were too extensive, or they simply couldn't be bothered—and Eric and I stood along the side of a country road trying to hitch a ride to a car rental place in Amiens, the next town over. I'd put on a skirt and tall boots a few hours earlier; fixed my hair and put on makeup for our big adventure. Now I was standing in the grass with my thumb out. "I'm hitchhiking," I thought. "In France."

A tiny red car pulled up and a gruff farmer shooed his dog out of the front seat, making room for us. He deposited us at the car rental place but the sign on the door said they were closed for lunch. Bienvenue en France. They finally reopened and rented us a car, and I followed behind Eric with the Volvo, the engine smoking and sputtering, to a rest area parking lot where we moved the bed, chairs, and table, etc.. into the new, smaller vehicle while other motorists gave us scornful looks. One very flustered older couple pulled up beside us, rolled down their window and berated us for causing a spectacle. "It's not done, this that you're doing here!" they shouted, according to Eric's translation.

We left the offending dish drainer and a rogue broom and dustpan behind in the rest area when we simply couldn't fit another thing into the rental car. I followed Eric again in the Volvo, this time to a Carrefour supermarket, where we left the smoking car at the corner of the large parking lot, not even bothering to remove the license plates. "Maybe we'll come back for it?" Eric said. I kind of had the feeling we never would.

Finally, we were back on the road, bypassing Paris, traveling deeper into France, the landscape growing more magical, the city names (Poitiers; Aubusson) more lyrical. We listened to a new Who album, *Endless Wire*, and the latest Yo La Tengo disc, and it was reassuring to hear the familiar voices of Roger and Pete; Georgia, Ira and James, as if they were along with us on the ride, offering a blessing and probably also shaking their heads a little: "What the *hell* are you two doing?"

When we arrived at our new village, there was still the technicality of the house sale funds being transferred into the seller's account, but they took pity on us and gave us the keys to the place anyway.

It was cold and wet outside, late November deep in the French countryside. We wondered how long it would take to warm the house up. Not long at all – it had sat empty for twenty years but the owners, a pair of brothers, kept the heating system—cast iron radiators fueled by an oil burner in the massive, attached barn—running the whole time out of respect for their childhood home and their dear departed parents.

I chose my spot to work on the first floor at the front of the house (what Americans call the second floor—just one of the many cultural differences I'd never all the way absorb). The room was wallpapered from floor to ceiling in a once-tasteful beige, pink, and pale blue flocked pattern. Even the back of the door and light switch panels had been wallpapered. Light flooded in from two large windows when the wooden shutters were thrown back. Eric showed me how to set the windows he said were called *espagnolette*—traditional French locking style that allowed the air in even with the shutters closed. There was so much I would have to learn about living in France, and I'd need to rely on Eric for most of it.

But somehow, even after my previous relationship, where another man orchestrated my dependence, I trusted Eric. Trusted him enough to throw fate to the wind and come to a place where I knew no one and would spend my days, weeks, months, and eventually years living and learning another language and culture. But Eric had recently gotten free of a disastrous relationship of his own, and he needed and trusted me too.

Looking out the window onto the countryside that stretched for many miles, all the way to the Atlantic coast at Royan two hours west, it struck me how little contact I'd had with nature and the countryside. In a field just across the road, next to the electrician's house, there were nothing but cows until the next village, and then the one after that. I thought of my first New York City view, the spire of Grace Church on Broadway pointing my way towards the tenements and bohemians in the East Village, or the little sliver of Manhattan I'd glimpsed and longed for through the laundry lines and water towers of Brooklyn. For so many years I'd based my identity on being New York, even when I'd moved to Nashville. It's what I measured everything against. But I thought of my Grantland Avenue neighbor running alongside his old car, trying to start the engine in the morning, or coffee at Bongo Java and working on songs at my old art deco table and hadn't I felt at home for a little while in Nashville? The grand cemetery across from me and Hazel's apartment on Mayfield Road in Cleveland, a quiet place I walked alone, trying to make peace with where life had taken me. I'd ended up in the rust belt just down the road from Pittsburgh without meaning to, each move adding one more layer between what I thought I was, that city girl, and this —wasn't it time I started calling myself a woman? My own mother was gone, my daughter was in college, my hormones were dwindling.

I wondered what life held for me in France. Down in the kitchen, Eric made a racket with guitar and amplifier—the very first things he'd unpacked. My Gibson sat in its case. It was pretty much all I'd brought with me from Cleveland, along with a large suitcase of clothes, a few of my favorite old linens, mod tea towels, Vera scarves, some melamine plates, and a couple of paperbacks: Raymond Carver; Annie Dillard and F. Scott Fitzgerald —Americans to remind me who I was and where I came from.

I smelled the woodsmoke from the neighbors' house on the other side of our barn and wondered who they were. What would they think of us? I hoped we'd get along. I'd better learn to speak some French fast, if I wanted to say anything besides hello.

Back in September, I'd toured for the tenth anniversary of *Mod Housewife*. I thought one decade since my solo debut was worth marking (and what in my life hadn't changed since 1996?). I also needed to make some money. I pressed up an expanded version of the CD to sell at gigs.

The first show—Schuba's in Chicago—went well. It was the fourth time I'd played to a good-sized crowd in the club; I was glad Hazel had chosen this brisk city for college, and imagined the entire audience as honorary aunts and uncles—not that my daughter would ever ask any of these strangers for help. But knowing I had some kind of community there felt like a comfort when I thought of how far away I'd be.

In August we'd driven together for the start of her first year—just the two of us in the minivan, the same way we'd done so many journeys. The dorm had been underwhelming, her roommate not a fit, but oh the beauty of the lake and the Art Institute and Chicago parks and buildings, at their best on a perfect summer day. I'd imagined us standing together at the parents' reception in amongst the antiquities, clocking who was interesting or potentially obnoxious, but I sensed pretty quickly she didn't need me hanging around as she met up with friends of friends or friends from Facebook—colored hair, thrift store clothes; the cool kids set free from high school. I threw down a glass of wine and went back to my Hotwire hotel, feeling like she'd be just fine without me, and I needed to figure out how to do the same. I'd enlisted Hazel as my accomplice, imagining my every move and adventure that spelled possibility providing the same for her, when what she'd probably wanted and needed was some consistency and stability. I wished I could go back and do better.

Oh well. She was going to love France. We'd already made plans for her to fly over at Christmas. Meanwhile, every day at three PM I still felt like I should be picking her up from school—it would take me years to not feel like I'd lost the most important job in the world: being a mom.

Downstairs, the kettle was boiling. We didn't have a stove yet, just a British electric kettle fitted with a French plug adaptor. We needed to figure out how we were going to get by in this place. As of the previous morning, we were without a car. We walked up the hill to buy milk, bread, and cheese. *Du lait. Du pain. Fromage.* In any language, it all cost money. Better book a few shows to earn some euros. I remembered Nico and his offer of a gig at the Laurence d'Arabie bar in Chalus just down the road.

Eric shouted up to ask if I wanted a cup of tea. I had a partner. We didn't have a car, or a stove. But we had a house, and guitars. I hoped I'd be able to write songs again. In the meanwhile, there were always covers. We had Crazy Elephant and the Archies.

"Yes, please!" I yelled down the stairs. We took our tea out into the courtyard. It was cold, late November. Eric and I stood in a patch of sunlight streaming through the branches of an old pear tree. We laughed at nothing, at everything—and clinked our mugs together.

Epilogue

Years later, I flip through the formative places of my life like postcards in one of those five-packs you used to buy in a tourist shop: Pittsburgh, New York, Nashville; yes, even Cleveland. In the fifth spot I put the village of Cussac, France, where I moved in 2006 to start a new life with Eric.

The postcards keep changing, time-lapse, sped-up video style. My brothers John and Patrick stayed true to our hometown of Pittsburgh, which became a much groovier place than a Steel City kid of the '60s and '70s could ever imagine: top chefs, craft breweries, Google, a thriving literary scene. We moved my father to New York City, a place he barely tolerated, after he lost his wife to Covid in 2020. He died in New Jersey at the memory care unit of the Actors Fund Home in 2023. I feel proud my life as a musician—a path he never understood but tried in his way to support me through—qualified him to be taken care of there.

Who can keep up with New York? The edgy Williamsburg of the early 2000s has hardly seen a hipster since 2011, when the first J. Crew store opened on Wythe Avenue. Rough Trade came and went, and now there's a Chanel boutique; loads of luxury hotels and condos. Our old building on Grand Street sold recently for just shy of $4,000,000. I look at the stylish listing photos and want to cry—not because I regret leaving, just remembering the still-young (though I didn't feel it at the time) song-writer and her daughter who once lived there, with beer bottles piled up in the hall, The Simpsons on VHS, and a note saying "MOVE CAR" stuck to the enamel-topped kitchen table.

Time moves on, especially if you're not there to keep tabs on things. Music venues are mostly big business in the city now, and occasionally I manage to score a gig somewhere in Manhattan or Brooklyn and work my ass off to fill a small room. My brother Michael is still in the East Village, in the railroad apartment where Last Roundup rehearsed every

Tuesday, Friday and Sunday through the `80s. He's the oldest guy in the building now, his neighbors twenty-something finance bros and doctors paying five times the rent he does for their granite countertops. Michael treasures his original linoleum. He still plays around the corner with his band the last Thursday of most months. Riley and his family live up the road in Rhode Island. My daughter eventually returned to put in her own time in NYC, and is now happy in Los Angeles.

With my habit of impeccably good or bad timing, I sold the Nashville house at what felt like the top of the market but was closer to the bottom that came two years later in the crisis of 2008. Jack White moved to town the year I left, and the city's changed to a happening place young people who've never hoisted a guitar flock to for marketing and tech jobs, partying, chic restaurants, and exquisite cocktails. Duane Jarvis died in 2010, Greg Trooper is gone; so are Chet Flippo, Martha Hume, Jim Ridley, Linda Allen, David Olney, John Prine, Dave Roe, and Peter Cooper. Some of my old songwriting buddies remain there: Bill Lloyd, Bill DeMain, Steve Allen. Paul got out and is on a beach in California. Sherry Rich returned to Oz. Joy White left, but I think she might be moving back. When I pass through town to play a gig I sneak up on the pain of how I left, circle around it, and leave feeling grateful I was part of the place for a little while.

In 2018, I received a Facebook message from Bob Kirsch, who signed me to a song publishing deal at Welk Music in Nashville. "Hey, have you heard the good news?" the message said, and something about money coming to me from Publisher's Clearing House.

"Bob!" I wrote back. "How are you?"

He asked again if I'd heard the good news, and I wondered if he meant I'd be getting my catalog back from Welk. Or maybe they'd finally found someone to cover one of my songs?

It took me a minute to realize Bob's Facebook had been hacked. I found out he'd died earlier that year, at the age of seventy-two. I felt sad I'd fallen out of touch with him. He'd really believed in my songs and done the best he could for me. He made my big dream come true: a publishing deal in Nashville. Maybe that "life-changing amount of money" hadn't really changed my life—the changes happened gradually, and didn't have a whole lot to do with publishing.

A year after Eric and I moved to France, I heard from a former colleague of Charles' that his life had been derailed, like mine, when Charles turned his attention towards the colleague's wife. Coercive control is now considered a crime in the U.K., Ireland, and Australia. In the U.S., they have expanded the definition of domestic violence to include non-physical abuse used to gain control over another person through manipulation, intimidation, and humiliation. Charles' colleague and his wife stayed together, and ended up moving to another state to start over. I hate that this nice couple suffered abuse they didn't deserve. But it made me feel less alone, and reminded me that I didn't deserve it either.

I emptied the storage space in Cleveland years ago, but return to the city every time I put out a new piece of work, a record or book. I play the Beachland Tavern and feel almost at home.

Eric and I threw ourselves into French country life— we made records together and toured as a two-piece band, moving to New York's beautiful Hudson Valley in 2011.

But I'll leave that story for the next book.

Acknowledgements

A quote popped into my head when I started to write this acknowledgments section: "Look for the helpers." I wondered, who said it and had to look it up. It made sense when I learned it was a Pittsburgh guy, Mr. Fred Rogers. His mother said it to him when he was a kid fretting about scary things in the news. "You will always find people who are helping." I think it extends to an artist's life too. I've begun to realize how many people have had my back over the years: fellow musician and songwriting pals, house concert hosts and promoters, the writers and radio folks who put my work out there, and all the people—many who've become friends— who come along to gigs year after year, and who read and listen to what I write—you help me keep going.

Thanks to Eric Goulden for the love story, to my daughter Hazel Rigby for your calm wisdom, and to my family—I love you.

Thanks to David Menconi and Rob Spillman, early readers, for your encouragement with this book. Respect and love to Joyce Maynard, you are a brilliant writer, teacher & friend. A huge thank you to Paul Slanksy, my editor —I feel lucky we met, it was such fun working with you.

Love and gratitude to Julia Gorton for your priceless design help and friendship. Much appreciation to ace photographer Jim Herrington for the cover photo—see you `round the grog tray.

Big thanks to Alan Coon and Kelley Drahusuk and all the gang at Spotty Dog in Hudson NY—being around all those books (and okay, the beer too) sustained me through years of writing and I miss you all.

Garden bouquets to friends Karen, Peter, and Daisy Hall, Luci Chester, Marc Valentine & Billie Gomez, Gina Birch & Mike Holdsworth; Angela Jaeger, Karen Schoemer, Dan & Liz Ferguson, Tobi & Clyde Kaplan, Norma Coates, Kate Flynn, Kevin O'Neill and Robert Vickers.

Thank you to Gunther Buskies, Sean Newsham and everyone at Tapete Records.

As I get older, the list of people who've had an impact on my life but are no longer around to thank could fill a short book. I won't go into all of them here, but I want to mention the two Scotts. One is Scott Cornish, intrepid music enthusiast who lived in upstate New York and, without a car, traveled to more shows than anyone I can think of. I *think* he took the photo on the back of this book, at the Avalon Lounge in our old town of Catskill NY. He is missed. The other is music writer Scott Schinder. Not only did he take me to see Brian Wilson a couple of times, as well as some of my other heroes like Richard Thompson, Tom Petty, and PF Sloan, it was Scott who put that Wreckless Eric CD in my hand back in the late 90s, the disc that would eventually lead me to Eric himself. I don't know if I ever thanked Scott for his friendship—I hope he knew how much it meant.

www.ingramcontent.com/pod-product-compliance
Lightning Source LLC
Chambersburg PA
CBHW021614120626
46545CB00001B/224